Fearing Together

Fearing Together

Ethics for Insecurity

AMI HARBIN

Oxford University Press is a department of the University of Oxford. It furthers
the University's objective of excellence in research, scholarship, and education
by publishing worldwide. Oxford is a registered trade mark of Oxford University
Press in the UK and certain other countries.

Published in the United States of America by Oxford University Press
198 Madison Avenue, New York, NY 10016, United States of America.

© Oxford University Press 2023

All rights reserved. No part of this publication may be reproduced, stored in
a retrieval system, or transmitted, in any form or by any means, without the
prior permission in writing of Oxford University Press, or as expressly permitted
by law, by license, or under terms agreed with the appropriate reproduction
rights organization. Inquiries concerning reproduction outside the scope of the
above should be sent to the Rights Department, Oxford University Press, at the
address above.

You must not circulate this work in any other form
and you must impose this same condition on any acquirer.

CIP data is on file at the Library of Congress

ISBN 978-0-19-753837-1

DOI: 10.1093/oso/9780197538371.001.0001

Printed by Integrated Books International, United States of America

For my children

Contents

Acknowledgments   ix

Introduction   1

1. Where Do Fears Come From?   13
   1. A Picture of Acquisition: Identity and Independence   13
   2. Perceived and Actual Threats   21
      A. Misperceptions of Threat   22
      B. Perceived Risk May Not Be Actual Risk   24
      C. Many Factors Shape How Different People Perceive Risk Differently   25
   3. Coming to Fear Things Together   28
   4. Conclusion   31

2. What Is Fearing?   33
   1. Fears, Causes, and Objects   34
   2. Fear and Embodiment   41
   3. Fearing with Others   48
   4. Conclusion   59

3. Compelling Fears   61
   1. Nonstatistical Threats   63
   2. Know Better, Fear Less   67
   3. Displacement   74
   4. Compelling Fears   81
      A. Fears of Proxy Threats Are Relationally Acquired   82
      B. Fears of Proxy Threats Are Relationally Experienced   84
      C. Fears of Proxy Threats Are Relationally Expressed and Interpreted   85
      D. New Terminology   85
   5. Conclusion   91

4. Controlling Threats   92
   1. Removal   92

2. Escape 97
3. Destruction 99
4. Assimilation 102
5. Overpowering 105
6. Damage of Control 109
   A. Controlling Strategies Are Attempts to Threaten Objects 110
   B. Perceived but Not Actual Threats May Be Controlled, but Attempts to Do So Subject These Objects to Morally Problematic, Unjustified Harms 111
   C. Controlling Actual Threats 113
   D. Some Responses 117
7. Conclusion 118

5. Fearing Better 120
   1. Developing Awareness of Our Practices and Habits of Compelling Fears 121
      A. Mindfulness 123
      B. Somatic Regulation 126
      C. Politicized Somatics 131
   2. Alternative Modes of Fearing Together 134
      A. Staying with Fearers 134
      B. Complications of These Relationships 138
         i. Relating to Others Whose Threats and Fears We Do Not Share Is Difficult 138
         ii. Relating to Others Whose Fears We Share Can Be Dangerous 139
         iii. Fears Are Dynamic 141
      C. Concerns and Caveats 144
   3. Fearing Crisis Together 152
      A. Fearing Pandemic 152
      B. Compelling Fears and Controlling Threats during COVID 153
      C. Fearing Together in Crisis 158
   4. Conclusion 161

Notes 163
References 183
Index 193

Acknowledgments

The Department of Philosophy and the Women and Gender Studies Program at Oakland University (Michigan) have been hospitable and supportive places to work. Thank you to my colleagues and to Department of Philosophy chairs Mark Navin and Mark Rigstad, to Women and Gender Studies Program Directors Jo Reger and Valerie Palmer-Mehta, to Ann Zimmerman, and to the Office of the Dean of the College of Arts and Sciences for their support of my work on this book.

Thank you to Lucy Randall, Lauralee Yeary, Hannah Doyle, and everyone at Oxford University Press. Thank you to the anonymous reviewers who offered feedback and wisdom that significantly shaped the manuscript. Thank you Suganya Elango and Patterson Lamb. Thank you, Daniel Hanneman, for your excellent and good-humored editing work. Errors are my own.

For generative responses and feedback, thank you to the participants and organizers of conferences and events where I presented earlier versions of parts of this work, including those at the Eastern Society for Women in Philosophy (2016); the Canadian Society for Women in Philosophy (2017); the Workshop on the Value of Disruptive Moments for Our Lives, University of Antwerp (2018); the Public Issues and Public Reason conference, Carleton University (2019); the Dalhousie Philosophy Department Colloquium Series (2020); New Scholarship in Bioethics Symposium (2016 and 2020); York University Philosophy Department (2020); and Michigan State University Philosophy Department (2020).

Many people work to make the profession of philosophy a welcoming and nourishing place and to create new paths for the discipline. I am fortunate to have so many such people in my life. Thanks in particular to Robyn Bluhm, Kirstin Borgerson, Elizabeth Brake, Danielle Bromwich, Ann Cahill, Megan Dean, Peggy DesAutels, Lauren Freeman, Jennifer Gammage, Michael Garnett, August

Gorman, Lisa Guenther, Joyce Havstad, Corinne Lajoie, Dan Lowe, Douglas MacKay, Norah Martin, Constantin Mehmel, Joseph Millum, Kate Norlock, Greg Scherkoske, Lisa Schwartzman, Şerife Tekin, Lisa Tessman, and Marika Warren.

I have had the extreme privilege of being surrounded by feminist mentors who model the kinds of thinking, commitments, and care I hope to bring to my work. Thank you for everything, Lorraine Code, Cressida Heyes, Christine Koggel, Jo Reger, and Phyllis Rooney. Susan Sherwin, thank you for your wisdom, humor, and for all you are still teaching me. And I will always be grateful to Sue Campbell, who continues to inform and challenge me in so many ways.

A lot happened during the years I spent writing this book. Gratitude to my friends and loved ones, for their presence, care, laughter, and honesty through all of it: Dean Adams, Adam Auch, Liat Ben-Moshe, Suze Berkhout, Danielle Bezaire, Lee Brackney, Jeff Broxmeyer, Scout Calvert, Rich Campbell, James Cheatley, Chris Cohoon, Michael DeLuca, Chris Dixon, Barrett Emerick, Rich Feldman, Janice Fialka, Shea Howell, Grayson Hunt, James and Grace Lee Boggs Center to Nurture Community Leadership, Heather Jessup, Victor Kumar, Maureen Linker, Rina Mackereth, Nora Madden, Erin Meyers, Mark Navin, Alison Powell, Ted Rutland, Karen Schaffer, Sue Sherwin, Alexis Shotwell, Jan Sutherland, Janine Webster, Matthew Webster, and Alex Zamalin. Thank you to Shira Roza, Alice MacLachlan, Jen Hoyer, and Erin Fredericks for being my closest (distanced) companions through the incredible fucking ride that was 2020–2022. Thank you, Linda Diaz, for helping me grow. Thank you to my mom, Vicki Easingwood, my mother-in-law, Susan Bryson, my sister, Alex, and my extended family for all of the ways they have shaped my life since its beginning.

This book would not have been written without the work of the childcare providers and educators who supported my family. Thank you to all the exceptional teachers at my children's schools, and to Adiva Wayne. You make so much possible.

Michael Doan, for all you continue to press me on, for being wildly smart in ways that expand and generate, for cooking our family's every meal, and for all the reality TV, thank you.

Cleo and Iris, you bring me so much joy. This book is dedicated to you.

Introduction

When I was a preteen, my friend Lisa and I rode bikes in our neighborhood. Nearby was an alley, no wider than a sidewalk, running between two residential lots. It had chain link fencing on either side, and was so overgrown with cedars that it felt like a tunnel. Lisa's family had a tandem bike. It was creaky and a bit big for us but we occasionally attempted it. Lisa was a strong rider and in general very at home in the world. I was neither and always sat in the back.

One time, Lisa wanted to take the tandem bike down the alley. I didn't want to, but I went along. As we approached the alley, she sped up. Soon, we were flying through the tunnel of trees, branches scraping our arms. My feet couldn't keep up with the pedals. I couldn't see anything beyond Lisa's back. It was too fast. I wanted, more than anything, off.

I let go of the handlebars and reached into the cedars, trying to grab onto the chain link, as though I would be able to pull myself off the bike. I couldn't grip the fence, somehow remained seated, and we sped out the other side. Lisa was thrilled and ready to go again.

This story has come to mind while I was writing, not because it is especially unique, nor because there was serious danger involved. Rather, that impulse I had in the alley—to avoid fear at all costs, to choose *actual injury* over continued fear—is a key focus of this book.

We are living in a time of great fear. Our lives are set in a context of climate catastrophe, military threat, ethnic violence, and forced migration. In North America, we are experiencing an amped-up, urgent time of political chaos, police shootings, school shootings, racist violence, queer-phobic violence, violent crackdowns on protest movements, violent crackdowns on migrants, highly publicized gender-based violence, and attacks on health care. COVID-19 has exacerbated these conditions, hitting the nerves of many of our most foundational fears: of illness; of loss; of financial, food, and housing insecurity; and of the unknown. Fear is by no means unique to our times, but it is certainly looming.

First-person accounts—memoirs, autobiographies, public interviews, published journals/diaries—give detailed senses of the diversity and extent of fearers and fears.[1] Artistic and cinematic sources, including so many postapocalyptic books, films, and television shows depicting life in the midst of social, economic, and climate collapse, further flesh out the picture of what people fear.[2] Qualitative research provides information about the fears of communities and populations.[3] Even political campaigns can be read as texts reflecting what parties and organizations have reason to believe are the greatest fears of communities, usually coupled with assurances that these fears will be addressed if the desired candidate is elected. We are all the time gathering information about what people fear by observing what they say and, perhaps most important, what they *do*. Where people carry weapons, vote for authoritarian governments who promise to protect them, excessively fund military and police, support national border protections, and conduct active shooter drills, they demonstrate their fears.

As an experience so in the forefront of our minds, fear has been written about extensively. Some theorists have urged the need to fear less. Others have pointed to the need to stop fearing some things or to start fearing different ones. Still others call out external forces, political or otherwise, that manipulate individuals into feeling more fearful. All these responses identify something wrong with such fears and provide correctives.

This book aims to change the conversation. It moves beyond suggestions about how individuals should fear differently. It instead accepts that fears exist, understands them as a central part of our ways of relating to others, and contends that even "unreasonable" fears can be informative—provided we can gain clearer understandings of the perceptions of threat underlying the fears and the too often morally destructive ways in which we cope with such fears.

In addition to the host of fears expressed in response to dramatic current events, this book reflects on the ordinary places where fears emerge. Fears of those convicted of sex-related crimes motivate the creation of a registry to ensure such offenders keep their distance. Do we fear that these specific individuals with past offenses will actually harm us or our loved ones? If we did, is our use of the registry the most effective response? Fears of harms to children translate into swift charges of parental neglect, even for such actions as leaving a child in a locked, well-ventilated car, within eyeshot for five minutes.[4] Are parents who do so putting children in danger? How might charging them with a crime serve to alleviate broader fears? Fears of toxic substances and untrustworthy health care systems lead to vaccine refusal and thus to preventable outbreaks of infectious diseases. How do these fears of toxicity and untrustworthiness reflect deeper fears about the inability to ensure safety for those we love? Fears of challenges to gender norms translate into violence against children, teens, and adults who identify with something other than the sex they were assigned at birth. How do such responses embody incapacities to cope with the unpredictable?

This book offers an account of fear in contemporary times that draws attention to what I argue is a common pattern of behavior exhibited by those facing deep-seated, uncontrollable threats, like the unpredictability of the future, or the inability to fully protect loved ones from harm: first, displace one's fear onto another, more manageable perceived threat. Then, attempt to act in some way as to control that threat. As such, the book contends that the political psychology of fear in response to great threats is often avoidant. Such avoidance can result in misdirected and harmful actions against living beings, people, communities, and environments that are not themselves the original sources of threat and often not threatening at all. This process is neither emotionally satisfying, since the deeper fears persist, nor morally acceptable, since often the objects misidentified as threats are subjected to intolerable violence.

As will become clear, the book calls into question a number of assumptions about fearing. For one, it challenges the positioning of fears as primarily the private emotional states of individuals. By contrast, it suggests that we start from a relational understanding of fears as experiences individuals have and express always in the context of interpersonal relationships, social structures, and institutions. What we fear, how we experience fearfulness, how we identify and understand our fears, and what we do to cope with them are all established in and through our relationships with other fearers, which are all situated in social structures of fearing. Central to the book is my interest in the moral complexities of these relational experiences: the ethics of fearing together.

Further, the book contests the idea that fearers are always experts on our own fears. We will see that fearers can be mistaken about what is worth fearing: perceived threats are not always actual threats. Beyond this, fearers are quite regularly wrong about what we are in fact fearing: I might think I am fearing X while in fact I am fearing Y. I might believe that if I could only neutralize the threat of X, I would no longer feel fear, when in fact, my fear would persist in the absence of X, since it is really fear of Y.

Some might think fears are beyond reproach. Not so. On my view, we are morally responsible for our fearing. By "we," I mean not only those experiencing and expressing fears but also those witnessing expressions of fears and all those involved in the social contexts that shape fearing. This book insists that practices of fearing not only *can* be contested for moral and other reasons, but in some cases, they *must* be.

My greatest concern in the book is that, when fearers are not able to cope with their fears, such fears can prompt actions that endanger nonthreatening others. My priority is reducing the harms of people acting on their fears in morally dangerous ways. We must develop strategies for coping with fears and social contexts that make such strategies accessible.

In chapter 1, I begin by asking *how we come to fear the things we do*. We might expect that in fearing, an individual observes or anticipates some object, the object is perceived as a threat and is in fact threatening, and the individual feels, understands herself to feel, and reports feeling fear about that object. In fact, the connections between these components of fearing are not always so straightforward. I turn to the risk perception literature, initially developed in the 1960s through 1980s, to understand the cognitive mechanisms and heuristics individuals use to evaluate risks, the emotional basis of risk perception, and the ways sensitivity to risk can vary among individuals. The literature makes clear that perceived threats are not always actual threats, and that actual threats are not always perceived as threatening. Chapter 1 concludes by laying the groundwork for a properly relational understanding of fearing. It acknowledges that the things we are afraid of are not ones we arrive at alone. All of the ways we ask, tell, and show each other *what we are afraid of* are part of the context that directs our fears toward particular objects and not others.

In chapter 2, I ask, *what is fearing?* I engage two significant conversations from the last half century. First, I turn to philosophers for an examination of causes and objects of emotion. In many cases, the *object* and *cause* of my fear are the same: I am fearful of a snake (object), and my fear is triggered by the sight of the snake coming toward me (cause). But in other cases, the object and cause of my fear are not the same, and fearers can be wrong about both. Cases of object/cause nonalignment are most interesting to me because fearers are not always immediately aware of the difference between the object and the cause, and this lack of awareness can have important (and troubling) consequences for how we relate to the objects of our fears. My account of the moral complexities of fearing in the coming chapters will require that we get clear on how fallible fearers can be.

Second, I turn to neuroscientists who clarify the physiological and neurological dimensions of fear and how these interact with other cognitive processes. Over the last half century, neuroscientific research has revolutionized our thinking about threat detection processes in human brains. The research shows that in humans, when a threat is perceived, the amygdala triggers bodily responses that prepare the body to protect itself. All this happens before the slower, analytical processes of reasoning kick in, which might indeed come to reason that the perceived threat is not actually or certainly a threat after all. Addressing the effects of fears will require taking seriously both the physiological aspects of threat detection, and the effects of those aspects on individuals' cognitive processes.

These philosophers and neuroscientists focus on answering the question of what fear is for individual fearers. Fear is largely positioned by them as something individuals do alone. I conclude chapter 2 by drawing on feminist philosopher Sue Campbell's account of emotional expression to challenge the individualism of these discussions. Campbell's view helps us see how the expression of fear to others can be central to the actual formation of the feeling. Further, Campbell's view makes clear how, in many cases, our capacities for fearing will depend on what expressive resources are available to us.

Having established in chapter 1 that our *perceptions of threat* are relationally shaped, here I shift us further away from thinking about fearing as an activity of individuals toward understanding fearing as relationally constituted.

Together, chapters 1 and 2 establish the point that fearers regularly come to misunderstand our own fears given tendencies to understand fearing individualistically. We tend to understand fears as the property of individuals, acquired by some combination of evolutionary process and idiosyncratic experience, to be experienced and borne alone, and best interpreted as straightforward pieces of information about actual threats. These misunderstandings make it difficult or impossible for fearers to properly relate to our fears. Chapters 1 and 2 reframe fearing relationally in order to prepare the way for the moral claims of chapters 3 and 4 about the harms of certain ways of coping with fears and the prescriptive claims of chapter 5 about how we might fear better.

Chapter 3 turns to one of the major contentions of the book: the threats individuals perceive as needing to be addressed may not be the actual sources of their feelings of fear, but substitutes or proxies.

We have already seen *that* perceived threats are not always actual threats (chapter 1), and that fearers can be wrong about the causes and objects of their fears (chapter 2). More remains to be said about *why* and *how* fearers come to fear nonstatistical threats or come to mistake the causes and objects of their fears.[5] One plausible explanation for the persistence of fears of nonstatistical threats is that fearers are manipulated by others who have an interest in sparking or stoking such fears. I survey accounts from a growing literature about the "culture of fear" that make the case for the central role of manipulation in generating fear of nonstatistical threats. While the political commitments and specifics of their accounts vary, these theorists aim to show that by coming to fear particular nonstatistical threats, populations can be manipulated by governments, political parties, and corporate agents who stand to gain from their fears. I suggest we think of these as "know better, fear less" models: they have the goal of raising awareness about manipulated fears, helping agents and communities know better, and thereby hopefully helping them fear less. While these accounts offer valuable insights, they insufficiently consider what makes fearers so prone to manipulation in the first place.

I argue that in some cases, nonstatistical threats come to serve as proxies for what individuals actually fear most: great, unmanageable threats (e.g., of suffering, loss, failure to protect loved ones, and unpredictability). The threats that become such proxies are often good alternatives because they are more *manageable* than these great threats. Drawing on psychoanalytic approaches, I note that the process of displacement is rarely done intentionally but rather happens swiftly and without the consciousness of the fearful individual. The chapter concludes with my argument for why processes of coming to fear proxy threats are more relational than psychoanalytic accounts of displacement suggest: fears of great threats are not merely ones individual agents displace on their own. Fears of proxy threats are relationally acquired, experienced, expressed, and interpreted. We would do better to understand fears of great threats as ones agents *compel*: working together, we push these fears away.

In chapter 4, I offer an account of what too often happens to the nonstatistical threats that come to serve as proxies. I contend that fearers often employ *controlling strategies* against these proxy threats. Using examples, I outline five controlling strategies: removal, escape, destruction, assimilation, and overpowering. *Removal* of a threat can involve more or less active tactics, from the creation of spaces where perceived threats are not welcome, cannot enter, or cannot stay, to active eviction or expulsion. I consider examples of hostile architecture, walls at the borders of nations, the use of spaces like pocket parks to remove sex offenders from neighborhoods, and all forms of incarceration and nonvoluntary institutionalization. When a perceived threat cannot be removed, individuals may instead attempt to *escape* from the path of the perceived threat. I consider examples of gated communities and anti-vaccination movements as escape strategies. If a perceived threat is vulnerable to *destruction*, then this may be the most thorough and permanent response. I discuss police shootings and capital punishment as clear destruction strategies. It is also possible to destroy *parts* of living things without destroying the entire organism, as in efforts to make a community's language extinct, or in practices of solitary confinement that destroy prisoners' psychic and emotional lives. In some cases, a threat is such that it cannot be readily removed, escaped, or destroyed, but it may still be controllable. I consider attempts to *assimilate* perceived threats, where I bring a perceived threat into alignment with my own values, perspectives, or actions. Conversion therapies and Indigenous residential schools are clear examples of such strategies. Many sources of threat do not make it easy or possible to remove, escape, destroy, or assimilate them. One might still attempt to *overpower* them. I offer examples of attempts to overpower the nonnormative gender performance of a child, or overpower the efforts of pro-choice reproductive rights organizations.

I then make the case for why the five kinds of controlling strategies outlined here are morally damaging when used against perceived but not actual threats. Threatening these objects involves unjustifiably harming them, and so it is morally unacceptable. Evaluating the moral status of the use of controlling strategies against actual threats is complicated. Great threats cannot be controlled, and attempts to do so regularly result in the morally unacceptable cases of controlling proxy nonstatistical threats. In cases where other actual threats can be controlled, we must employ a fine-grained analysis of whether controlling strategies are the only or morally acceptable responses.

If the claims in the first four chapters are convincing, my hope is that many of us will see the need to fear differently. Chapter 5 concludes with a consideration of practices that might help us do so. It begins with three approaches that might support fearers in gaining awareness of practices and habits of compelling fears and controlling threats: mindfulness, somatic regulation, and politicized somatics. It then charts alternative modes of fearing together, suggesting the importance of building different relationships within which fear can be received, instead of ones that contribute to the sense that fears must be acted upon, resisted, or fixed. The goal of *staying with other fearers* in their experiences and expressions of fears is neither to make the fears go away nor to endorse any and everything a fearer might express. Rather, the goal is to work toward making experiences of fearing sufficiently bearable that fearers will not be so desperate to avoid them. These relationships are not without complications, and the responsibilities that issue from them are not without caveats. But my prescriptive claims stem from a conviction that our priority should be not preventing fears themselves but preventing the (sometimes fatally) dangerous actions that can come from an inability to cope well with such fears. The chapter concludes with a consideration of the potential role for these practices of fearing better in current and future contexts of crisis.

Throughout the book, I employ a feminist relational approach to understanding individuals, their experiences, their actions, and their responsibilities. This means that I understand individual agents as *constituted by* their relationships with others—they would not have capacities for personhood if not for the caring labor of many others, and they are all the time contributing to the growth and shaping the lives of other individuals. Furthermore, individuals always have experiences while being influenced by other experiencers. As Sue Campbell writes,

> We develop and live our lives as persons within complex networks of institutional, personal, professional, interpersonal, and political relationships—both chosen and unchosen. We are shaped in and through our interactions with others in ways that are ongoing; and we develop cognitive and moral capacities and skills ... in relational contexts that not only give these capacities and skills specific content but also offer methods of evaluation and self-evaluation. (Campbell 2003, 156)

Fearing is both a cognitive and a moral skill, to be developed and evaluated in relational contexts. Following relational ethicists, I hold that individuals' actions, moral and otherwise, are made possible by, and evaluated against the background of, others' actions. We are only able to act in the ways we do because the possibilities have been opened up for us by others' having acted before us. What responsibilities we have, and whether or not we can live up to those responsibilities, depend on other people—what others are calling for us to do, and whether or how others are participating with us in trying to meet those responsibilities. My relational approach counters an individualistic understanding of fear in our moral lives: fearful individuals are never feeling or enacting fear in isolation. As much as we are fearers, we are co-fearers. Fearing is a significant part of how we do well by each other, or fail to.

Many of the fears I discuss in the coming chapters are *unwarranted* in the sense of not being reflective of actual or statistical threats. They are, in many cases, fears of things that will very likely not pose the threat we fear, nor perhaps any threat at all. There are facts of the matter about whether a threat is statistically likely, and certainly these facts should shape how we act and evaluate fear-motivated actions. The majority of the examples of morally problematic fearing I discuss involve a fearer perceiving a nonthreat as a threat, having an unwarranted fear, and pursuing a controlling strategy to cope with that fear.

One approach to morally evaluating responses to fear would be to argue that the controlling strategies I outline in chapter 4 are morally problematic in response to nonthreats (unwarranted fears), but morally acceptable in response to actual threats (warranted fears). If a threat is actual, why not remove, escape, destroy, assimilate, or overpower it?

By contrast, my approach in this book is not to prioritize the task of differentiating warranted and unwarranted fears and prescribing distinct appropriate action for each. This is because my concern is primarily practical: many of the controlling strategies fearers use to cope with fears, whether those fears are warranted or not, have harmful effects. For a number of reasons, including our persistent and predictable difficulties in accurately assessing the difference between actual and merely perceived threats in our own lives, as well as the legitimate questions of whether controlling strategies are likely to reduce or exacerbate actual threats, I argue for the moral benefit of becoming more able to bear fears without being motivated to enact controlling strategies. In other words, I argue that developing the capacities for bearing fears described in chapter 5 can be morally useful, whether in response to actual or merely perceived threats, warranted or unwarranted fears. The practice of having the fears without trying to control the perceived threats can be valuable in either case. I take this point to be both contentious and central to my project in this book.

Practically speaking, we know that fearers do not typically respond well to demands to stop fearing, even when supported by evidence of the statistical unlikelihood of certain threats. People regularly *know something is not a threat*, and still fear it. Tamar Gendler (2008a) nicely illustrates an example: the Grand Canyon Skywalk is a 70-foot-long

INTRODUCTION 11

glass walkway, allowing people to walk 4,000 feet above the floor of the Grand Canyon. Visitors to the Skywalk believe that the walkway will hold and that they will be safe to walk across it. But alongside the belief that the walkway is not dangerous, Gendler argues that they often *alieve* something else (Gendler 2008a, 635).[6] When a person steps onto the Skywalk,

> input to her visual system suggests that she is striding off the edge of a cliff. The visual input activates a set of affective response patterns (feelings of anxiety) and motor routines (muscle contractions associated with hesitation and retreat), and the visual-vestibular mismatch produces feelings of dizziness and discomfort, leading to additional activation of motor routines associated with hesitation and withdrawal. (Gendler 2008a, 640)

In the case of many unwarranted fears, fearers might believe and be prepared to defend the belief that X (e.g., the Skywalk) is nonthreatening while still behaving in ways consistent with fearing X.[7] Gendler's analysis of alief offers one way to account for how fear of X may persist even in the face of evidenced-based demands that one stop fearing.

In the chapters to come, most of my examples of unwarranted fears are morally charged. If I choose to escape rather than attempt the Skywalk, presumably no serious harm is done. But if I employ other controlling strategies in response to a person sleeping in front of a condo building or a Black man in an elevator, serious harm can be involved. And, as I will endeavor to show, others are deeply involved in our fearing. Beyond being sources of immediate information about potential threats (e.g., people showing me they can proceed safely onto the Skywalk), other fearers are now, and have been at all earlier points of our lives, intimately involved in whether, what, how, and how much we fear. If we are to grow capacities for fearing better, other fearers will be intimately involved in that, too.

Gendler notes that we do not simply throw off aliefs, though we may gradually change them over time, particularly by performing alief-averse action to create "new patterns of representational-affective-behavioral association" (Gendler 2008a, 655). As I characterize it, the goal should be to become able to bear the fears we have without needing to avoid them by controlling the things we perceive as generating them. Just as we have arrived at our current coping mechanisms by complex relational processes, so too will cultivating new ones depend on more than individual will.

The dual meaning of the book's title draws attention to fearing as a set of practices we do with others—we fear together—as well as to the fact that a significant part of what we might fear is our fundamental *togetherness*—the fact of our relationality makes us vulnerable to pain and loss that we would not face were interdependence not so foundational in our lives. Coming to embrace rather than resist these vulnerabilities has the potential to make our fears more bearable and all lives less threatened.

I wrote this book because I have become convinced, particularly in recent years, that practices of fearing form the basis for much of our moral lives. Fearing badly is a central part of many of our moral failures, and fearing better is a central part of our moral repair. The fear I had on the tandem bike was so uncomfortable that I was prepared to do anything necessary to make it stop. I reached for escape, and in doing so, I created the possibility of actual threat for both Lisa and myself. Ending my fear (by landing on concrete or getting us launched into a fence) was not going to make anyone safer. In fact, avoidance of fear can *create* the greatest threats. A key part of our growth as moral agents involves coming to grips with what kind of fearers we want to be and become.

At the heart of fearing is an encounter with central aspects of the human condition: our connection to others and our vulnerability to loss, suffering, failure, and unpredictability. What do we as individuals and communities owe ourselves and others when facing what we cannot control? How might our encounters with insecurity be the basis for responsible lives?

1
Where Do Fears Come From?

How do we come to fear the things we do? In this chapter, we begin with a picture of *where our fears come from* that I suggest often underlies our actions in response to our own fears and those of others. The picture makes it look like the fears we have are typically straightforward responses to fearers' independent interactions with threats in the world.

We begin in section 1 by identifying this picture in order to understand two key presumptions it involves and how they shape action. In section 2, we interrogate one presumption, drawing on the extensive literature on risk perception to establish why the perceptions of threat that generate fears may or may not reflect actual threats in the world. In section 3, we challenge the second, laying the foundation for a relational reorientation in understanding fear acquisition. Together, these points prepare the way for the consideration in chapter 2 of the roles of others not only in fear acquisition but also in the formation and expression of the fears we acquire. From this relational understanding of fearing, we will be prepared to think clearly about the moral hazards of some forms of fearing in chapters 3 and 4, and the potential for fearing better in chapter 5.

1. A Picture of Acquisition: Identity and Independence

Think of some everyday examples of fearing: I feared the too-fast tandem bike described in the introductory chapter, and I acted in response to it—attempting to launch myself off. More than tandem bikes, I now regularly fear computer failures that might mean the loss of my files. I make sure that I have backups of everything and save my work often. To take an example of another person's fears, think of my friend who is planning to introduce her new girlfriend to her parents and siblings, and fears they won't approve. In another case, some years ago, my partner and I were in Barcelona, and I found out how afraid he is of heights just as we were about to embark on a chair lift ride down Montjuïc.

What can we learn by looking at how we respond to our own and others fears? Does our behavior in response to our own and others' fears reflect an accurate understanding of where our fears come from?

I want to begin by outlining a *picture of fear acquisition* we see expressed in many of the ways we act in response to our own fears and those of others. The picture I will outline involves two presumptions. These presumptions are most clearly seen in how we act, and perhaps also (though not always) in what we say we believe.

First, the picture involves a *presumption of identity* in fear acquisition: a presumption that my fearing something indicates that it is an actual threat. This presumption might be understood by philosophers as a kind of naïve realism about the connection between fears and actual threats: it is a presumed *identity* of the seeming and the real. Those things I fear are presumed to be actual threats, and I come to act as though the things I fear are actual threats. As part of the picture of fear acquisition, a presumption of identity can be expressed in our actions in a number of ways.

When I fear something, I regularly act as though that thing is an actual threat. Consider how readily we might slide from fearing someone approaching behind us on the sidewalk to *acting as though they are a threat*. We clutch our bag or cross the street. Or think of cases where someone pulls a gun on someone they fear. *They act as though* their fear tells them straightforwardly that the person is a threat—and to such an extent that it makes sense to point a gun at them. When I was with Lisa in the tree-covered alley, I treated the too-fast tandem bike as an actual threat, and I acted in a way that responded to it as such (i.e., trying to escape it). I did not pause to consider whether the fear I had on the tandem bike meant that the tandem bike was *in fact* a threat. My actions (gripping the fence to pull myself off the bike) demonstrated that I was responding to the thing I feared as a threat. I presumed those things to be identical. Similarly, I treat the potential of my computer malfunctioning as a threat and act in light of it. I save and resave and make sure things are saved in the cloud and occasionally also email things to myself, just to be sure. I treat the thing I fear and the actual threat as identical and act accordingly.

When others I trust fear something, both they and I also regularly act as though their fear indicates an actual threat. When my friend fears that her family will not approve of her new girlfriend, she treats this as an actual threat. She coaches her girlfriend on safe topics of conversation, suggests things for her to wear, tells her which bottle of wine to bring to dinner, and so on. Seeing my friend's fears, and assuming that I trust my friend, I might come to act in ways showing that I too presume that her fear indicates an actual threat. Even if I do not come to have the same affective intensity in fearing, I might join in helping coach her girlfriend or perhaps offer to attend the dinner as a buffer in case anything goes sideways. When my partner fears the great height of the chair lift on Montjuïc, he acts in a way that treats this as an actual threat. He clutches the sides of the lift and holds very still as we descend. Given that I trust him, I might also come to act in ways that show that I too presume his fear indicates an actual threat. Before we get on I might look carefully at the safety harnesses and the care with which the operators seem to be treating the endeavor, and I ensure that we are both safely ensconced in the chair and make no sudden moves on the way down. I may or may not become actively fearful myself, but my actions show that I take my friend's and partner's fears to be reflective of actual threats.

Note that the requirement of trust in these relationships is important, and we will return to this point shortly: how much authority we give to others' fears, and how likely we think it is that they are reflections of actual threats, depends a great deal on whether or the degree to which we trust them. To some extent, the same holds of ourselves: how much authority we give to our own fears depends on the extent to which we trust our own perceptions, and such trust can be dramatically affected by interpersonal and social circumstances. My point is not that we always or automatically take everyone's fears to indicate actual threats. Rather, the presumption of identity between the thing we fear and actual threat is expressed for many of us, much of the time, in the ways we act toward ourselves and those we trust.

Further, when *many* others fear something, whether I know these people or not, I might also come to act as though their fears indicate an actual threat. Consider one source of information about what many people fear: *surveys*. The Chapman University Survey of American Fears is perhaps the best known of surveys attending specifically to fear.[1] The survey is completed annually by a sample of adults from across the United States, with participants balanced to match the US population by age, gender, region, education, race/ethnicity, and phone usage. In addition to demographic questions, participants are asked a variety of Likert-style or yes/no questions regarding over ninety different possible threats: felt safety helping strangers, experiences of crime, trusted news sources, illness, death, environmental issues, money/employment, emergency preparedness, modes of transport, technology, terrorism, natural and manmade disasters, animals, medical procedures, and more. In 2021, 1,035 surveys were completed and the ten fears for which the highest percentage of participants reported being "afraid" or "very afraid" were as follows:

1. Corrupt government officials (79.6 percent afraid or very afraid)
2. People I love dying (58.5 percent)
3. A loved one contracting the coronavirus (COVID-19) (58 percent)
4. People I love becoming seriously ill (57.3 percent)
5. Widespread civil unrest (56.5 percent)
6. A pandemic or major epidemic (55.8 percent)
7. Economic/financial collapse (54.8 percent)
8. Cyber-terrorism (51 percent)
9. Pollution of oceans, rivers, and lakes (50.8 percent)
10. Biological warfare (49.3 percent)[2]

When I see these results reported in the media, I might well come to, or come to more decidedly, treat corrupt politicians or cyber-terrorism as a threat. The information about what many others fear can reshape or bolster what I respond to as an actual threat. The Chapman Survey is just one of many sources of information about what many people fear, alongside media, literary, artwork, and other sources, and it can have the effect of shaping what we understand to be threats, based on the knowledge that a lot of people fear them.[3]

We would be hard-pressed to find someone who does *not* relate to a significant portion of their fears as though they indicate actual threats. This is part of why fearing is so fraught: if I feel fear, it might seem odd *not* to understand myself as threatened. Indeed, to predominantly act in this way might signal a kind of pathology or troublesome social circumstance. Would it not have been somewhat odd for me to take the time to consider whether the tandem bike was in fact such a threat while I was in the thick of the alley? If it turns out my fear might *not* be a reliable indicator of my being threatened, what else might become questionable about the links between my feelings, beliefs, motivation, and action? It might be unsettling to take seriously challenges to the presumption of identity. The ease of this presumption is partly explained by neuroscientific accounts of fear (which we will discuss at length in chapter 2). Often the path from feeling fear to acting in ways that treat things we fear as actual threats is rapid and does not wait for reflection.

In all these ways, our actions can demonstrate a *presumption of identity* in the acquisition of fears, where the things we fear are presumed to be identical with actual threats. Part of the picture of fear acquisition is an image of fears as something we gain directly, by a relatively straightforward perception of threats in the world.

The second part of the picture is a *presumption of independence* in fear acquisition: a presumption that the fears I have are ones I have acquired independently.

If I ask you where your fears came from, it may be difficult for you to say. It may seem that you have simply always had them. You may consider some of them universally shared by all humans, perhaps as a result of evolutionary history (e.g., fearing contaminated substances or dangerous animals). For more idiosyncratic fears, you might point to your own triggering childhood experiences (e.g., having seen a movie about a bigfoot living in the basement at a young age and maintaining a persistent fear of basements). Many of us relate to our own fears as ones we have because of evolutionary inheritance or ones we have acquired individually, and to the fears of others likewise.

When I fear something, I regularly act as though I have acquired that fear independently. For instance, I treat my fear of the tandem bike as something I have come to as a result of my independent experience and as a result of who I am, including parts of my evolutionary history (which I assume would partly dispose me to be cautious about riding fast things through small spaces). I do not treat my fear of the bike as the result of manipulation, or of social influence, or of something I was trained to acquire. I can tell a story of how I came to fear the tandem bike that does not refer to anything beyond my own experience, personality, and (potentially) evolutionary history. The fear feels like it is *mine* in some meaningful sense and not something that I have taken on because of the actions of others. Similarly, I might note that I came to fear computer malfunction only after I once lost a bunch of work to a frozen laptop, and henceforth I feared it happening again (and acted to prevent it). It is my own fear and I do not consider other people a relevant part of my having acquired it.

When others fear something, both they and I also regularly act as though they have acquired that fear independently. My friend who fears her family's response to her girlfriend acts as though she has come to this fear herself, because of her intimate knowledge of and experience with her family dynamics and not, for example, because anyone is trying to shape what she fears. Her family members are historically unwelcoming, she knows (and fears) this based on her experience. My partner who fears the height of the chair lift acts in such a way as to reflect the presumption that he too has come to this fear independently: he's not being duped or controlled by an irrational phobia. Heights are an actual threat, and he has come to fear them based on his own evolutionary history and personal experience.

I too act as though others I trust have come to their fears independently, perhaps most notably in the ways I *evaluate* their fears. If the fears of my friend and partner are ones that I perceive as legitimate, I credit them for reaching those fears. If the fears are ones that strike me as illegitimate or overstated, I might blame or criticize (or decide to overlook or forgive) them for having those misbegotten fears. I may ask them: *why would you fear X, Y, or Z?* Either way, I take the fears to be ones they have independently acquired and thus ones for which they are to some extent responsible—ones for which they might deserve some credit or blame.

I expect that many of us can already think of a more complex history or context for the acquisition of fears, involving more interpersonal involvement. As will be clear in section 3 of this chapter, I agree we will need to move beyond the presumption of independence. My point for now is simply to register that many of our actions, both in response to our own fears, and in response to others' fears, do not express a more complex picture. In many cases, we act as though our fears are ones we've acquired as individuals on our own.

Note that in many cases, these two presumptions go hand in hand as part of the picture of what it means to acquire fears, at least as *reliable* fearers. I act in a way that takes my fears to indicate actual threats (tandem bike, computer malfunction) and in a way that demonstrates my autonomy and independence at arriving at those fears (I acquired them by some combination of evolutionary inheritance and personal experience). My friend and my partner act in ways that take their fears to indicate actual threats (her family disapproving of her girlfriend, the height of the chair lift), and also in ways that demonstrate their autonomy and independence in the process of arriving at those fears (not by manipulation or phobia, but by their good judgment based on past experience).

Actions reflecting this picture of fear acquisition are clearly not universal. My point has been that the examples here and others like them highlight how regularly our actions express a certain underlying picture that portrays the fears we acquire as identifying actual threats and as being ones we acquire largely independently. This general picture of fearing is manifested in many of our actions, in how we act in response to both our own fears and those of others.

If asked, *do you believe that the fears you or others have reliably reflect actual threats*, hopefully many of us would be inclined to say no—I and others regularly fear things that are not actual threats. My preschooler fears a speck of dust on the floor, believing it to be a fruit fly. Neither the speck of dust nor the imagined fruit fly is an actual threat. It likely does not surprise most of us, at least in our cooler moments of not actively fearing, that those things we fear may not be threats at all. But it is necessary to get very clear on both that fact—fears do not necessarily indicate actual threats—and the habituation of the slippage from fears to actual threats as part of the foundation for my analysis in the coming chapters.

As noted above, the question of epistemic authority and the extent to which fearers take themselves or particular others to have it is of central importance. There are many things that encourage and validate a person's sense of their epistemic authority with respect to fearing. I might feel validated in my fears of corrupt politicians when I see that such a high percentage of participants in the Chapman Survey fear the same. When I surround myself with people who fear similar things to me, my sense of my own epistemic authority can be strengthened. By contrast, there are also many things that discourage and diminish a person's sense of their epistemic authority with respect to fearing. I might question even fears that seem to be justified if I do not see others acting afraid of such threats (e.g., climate change). One might come to question the reliability of one's own fears as indicators of threat for any number of reasons, including being subject to regular gaslighting or other forms of epistemic harm by others, such that one no longer trusts one's own perceptions, or by coming to recognize one's own past mistaken identifications of threat and proceeding with greater caution in the future. Further, given that we attribute authority to some people and not others, we are likely to trust only some people's fears. Which people we trust is likely to change over time, sometimes in subtle ways as we grow and other times in dramatic ways that may cause us to entirely stop trusting the fears of people we once trusted very deeply.

If asked, *do you believe that the fears you or others have are ones you have acquired independently* (including by your individual genetic or evolutionary inheritance), our answers might be more mixed. Perhaps some of us would say no, but many might say yes. Beyond acting like this picture of fear acquisition is true (a mode of action we see in the above examples), we might also be inclined to *believe* ourselves to be independently in charge of and responsible for having acquired the fears we have.

Whether all or many of us would claim to believe either of these presumptions, we see them sufficiently expressed in action to merit identification as part of a picture of fear acquisition we must consider. We regularly act in ways that treat the things we and those we trust fear as actual threats, and consider them as fears we and they have reached independently. Both these presumptions combine to form a rough picture of fearers as fairly reliable perceivers of threat who come to the fears we have largely on our own. This is not the picture of fearers we should maintain if we want to work toward fearing in morally better ways.

Having identified and described this picture, our next move is to challenge it. In section 2 we will establish why fears are not in all cases reflective of actual threats, and in section 3 we will lay the groundwork for understanding fear acquisition as a thoroughly relational process. If we want to understand how we might come to relate differently to our fears, and especially those not reflective of actual threats, we need to start with a firmly relational understanding of fear acquisition.

2. Perceived and Actual Threats

We often assume that processes of fearing operate like this: an individual observes or anticipates some object, the object is perceived as a threat and is in fact threatening, and the individual feels, understands herself to feel, and reports feeling fear about that object. For instance, I observe a wasp in my backyard. I perceive it as a threat, and it is in fact a threat. I feel fear, understand myself to be feeling fear, and report feeling fear about the wasp. So far, so straightforward.

In some cases, however, the connection points in this process do not fully align. Working our way backward from the end of this process to the beginning, as noted in our discussion of first-person reports in fear surveys, an individual may perceive an object as a threat, the object may indeed be a threat, and the individual may feel and understand herself to feel fear without *reporting* fear about that object. She may not report for any number of reasons. She might feel embarrassed, ashamed, or fearful of reporting, and/or distrustful of the context of reporting.

Working further backward, an individual may perceive an object as a threat, the object may indeed be a threat, and the individual may feel fear and yet not *understand herself to be feeling fear*. As we have discussed, it is sometimes only with the passing of time or with the involvement of sympathetic others that we come to be able to understand what we have felt as fear.

We do not always report the fears we feel. And we do not always know that what we are feeling is fear.

But we have not yet addressed the point of contact between a threat perceiver and the object perceived as a threat. As above, sometimes the connection between perception of threat and existence of actual threat is straightforward. I perceive a wasp as a threat, and the wasp may in fact be an actual threat. But as we will establish in this section, an individual may alternatively perceive an object as a threat, and feel fear, perhaps understand herself to be feeling fear, and perhaps report herself as having fear, *without the object she perceives being an actual threat*. Individuals can perceive things as threats that are not in fact likely to cause harm to them.

A. Misperceptions of Threat

In *The Culture of Fear: Why Americans Are Afraid of the Wrong Things*, Barry Glassner offers a survey of many fears of US residents which, while they are in some cases very common, are fears of things that are statistically unlikely to happen. In the 1970s, families panicked over the possibility of poisoned Halloween candy when in reality only very few children were reported to be harmed by sharp objects in trick-or-treating bags (and some of those reports were themselves hoaxes) and there were only two cases of fatalities from poison, both of which were actually instances of violence inflicted by family members (Glassner 1999, 30).[4] Many people fear road rage when in fact drunk driving kills eighty-five times as many people (Glassner 1999, 8). Many white people fear violence at the hands of Black men, when in fact Black men are much more likely to be victimized than white people are.[5] While panic about child abduction rose in the 1980s and 1990s, spurring the appearance of missing-child advertisements everywhere from billboards to milk cartons, in fact the rate of child abductions by strangers was very low (Flores 2002). Children are in fact much more likely to be injured or killed by family members than by strangers (Glassner 1999, 31, 62). Many US adults fear that having access to violent video games will make it more likely that children and teens will become violent offenders when, in fact, a much greater predictor of violent behavior is the accessibility of guns, which account for 60 percent of teen suicides, for most teen homicides, and many other fatal accidents (Glassner 1999, 44, 55).[6] In *How Risky Is It, Really? Why Our Fears Don't Always Match the Facts*, David Ropeik (2010) further considers ways in which fearing some objects too much can connect to not fearing other objects enough. For instance, fear of flying after September 11, 2001, led many to drive to distant destinations instead, yet driving is in fact a more dangerous way to travel. And people are more likely to be fearful of cancer than of heart disease, which is the cause of death for significantly more people every year. For Glassner and Ropeik, the point in surveying these and many other fears is to show that they are unfounded while other legitimate threats may go underrecognized. As Glassner (1999, xvii–xviii) writes, "I do not contend, as did President Roosevelt in 1933, that 'the only thing we have to fear is fear itself.' My point is that we often fear the wrong things."

A variety of explanations might be given for what has *motivated* individuals to fear nonthreatening things. We will consider some of these in chapter 3 in our discussion of the "culture of fear" literature, including Glassner's and others' suggestions about politically motivated and profit-oriented strategic manipulations of the fears of communities. But before we get there, we need to pause to reflect on how to explain the sometimes-significant gaps between what individuals perceive as threats and what constitute actual threats.

We can find some of the most needed explanations in the now-extensive multidisciplinary literature on *risk perception*. Starting in the mid-1960s, spurred largely by public expressions of concern about the development of nuclear technologies,[7] researchers developed analyses of how individual risk perception may involve biases and heuristics, and thus why providing individuals with *more information* might not be sufficient to change their perceptions. Amos Tversky and Daniel Kahneman (1974) detailed the cognitive mechanisms and heuristics individuals use to evaluate risks. They noted that individuals are more likely to judge an event as probable the more often they have seen or heard of that kind of event. Because we more commonly see or hear of "large risk events" (e.g., murders) than we see or hear of "small risk events" (e.g., death by common disease), we may overestimate the likelihood of the large risk event happening and underestimate the likelihood of the small risk event happening (Fischhoff and Kadvany 2011, 99). Further analyses focused on the emotional basis of perception. Johnson and Tversky (1983) established that an individual's emotional state can make a difference to their perception of risk. They found that positive emotions trigger more optimistic risk assessments and negative emotions trigger more pessimistic ones; specifically, participants who were prompted to feel negative affect consistently communicated more pessimistic estimates of frequency of bad outcomes than participants who were prompted to feel positive affect (Johnson and Tversky 1983; see also Slovic, Fischhoff, and Lichtenstein 1982).

Through the 1980s and into the 1990s, researchers continued to hone explanations of why perceptions of risk could vary widely. Mark Warr and Mark Stafford (1983) focused on how not only perceived risk but also the perceived *seriousness* of a potential threat would shape how fearful an individual is. Stafford and Omer Galle (1984) demonstrated that greater-than-average past exposure to risk could generate greater present concern, and Warr (1987) established that *sensitivity* to risk (i.e., the relation between fear of a harm and the perceived risk of that harm happening) could differ among individuals.

While this field of research is now extensive and raises many more considerations than I survey here, the following two key claims are most important for my purposes: (1) perceived risk may not be actual risk, and (2) many factors shape how different people perceive risk differently.

B. Perceived Risk May Not Be Actual Risk

An *actual threat* is an event or an object with both the capacity to cause harm and some likelihood of doing so. An actual threat *to me* is an event or object with the capacity to cause harm and some likelihood of doing so to me. Our perceptions of threat can be mistaken in both cases. I might identify something as a threat that has no capacity to cause harm. Perhaps I perceive rainbows as a threat, while (let's imagine) in fact there is no sense in which rainbows could be threatening. Here my perception of threat is not an accurate indicator of actual threat. However, because almost anything *can* cause harm in the right conditions, more commonly confounding are mistaken perceptions of the likelihood of threats. I may perceive a threat as very likely to occur (to me, or someone else) when it is in fact relatively unlikely to do so. A minimarshmallow can cause harm but, absent certain circumstances, is very unlikely to do so. For something to count as an actual threat, it must have *some* statistical likelihood to cause harm, beyond just a nonzero chance. Determining exactly how much more than a nonzero chance will qualify a threat as *likely* is complicated and can vary in light of the gravity of the threat in question, but the threshold of likeliness required for something to count as an actual threat is also not a subjective matter for each individual to decide.[8] It is clear that some perceptions of risk are not reflective of actual risk. If a perceived threat has no possibility or an exceedingly low statistical likelihood of occurring to a person, and if that person nonetheless perceives it as and claims it to be a genuine threat to her, she can be challenged.[9] To return to the discussion from the book's introduction, fears of things that will very likely not pose the threat we fear are unwarranted. Having a nonsubjective standard for determining the identities and likelihood of threats is clearly important for moral practice: in some cases, not distinguishing between one's own perceptions of threat and facts of the matter can be both an epistemic and a moral failure.

C. Many Factors Shape How Different People Perceive Risk Differently

It is not surprising that different people can perceive risk very differently. The risk-perception literature has shown how dramatically differences in past and current experience, social circumstance, and identity can shape how individuals perceive risks. We have already seen that current emotional state can make a difference to how individuals perceive frequency of bad outcomes—those with negative affect are more likely to report bad outcomes happening with greater frequency (Johnson and Tversky 1983). Others have sought to distinguish effects of different kinds of "negative affect," including distinguishing the different effects of anger and fear. Lerner and Keltner (2001) have found that individuals who are feeling fearful are more likely to perceive greater risk and to make risk-averse choices, while those feeling angry are more likely to perceive *less* risk and to make fewer risk-averse choices. Different forms of "negative affect" have different effects.

Environments also make a difference in how likely a person is to perceive risk. Having direct personal experience with particular threats has been shown to heighten perception of risk of that threat, as has having information about threats amplified by media, personal networks, scientists, and community organizations (Kasperson et al. 1988). Further, individuals have been found to perceive levels of risk differently when rating risk to themselves or to their family and to rating risk to people in general—overall, individuals are likely to judge the risk of some harm happening to oneself as *significantly lower* than the risk of the same harm happening to people in general (Sjöberg 2000, 2–3).

Features of identity like gender and age have also been demonstrated to make a difference in risk perception. Warr (1984, 1987) demonstrated early on that sensitivity to risk is highly age- and sex-dependent, with higher sensitivity to risk found among participants identifying as women and elderly individuals. Though elderly individuals have a lower risk of victimization, they have been shown to have the highest fear of crime of all age groups, with fear of crime being highest among elderly women, elderly African Americans, and poor elderly people (Joseph 1997, 699).[10]

In summary, the risk-perception literature shows that perceived risk may not be actual risk and that many factors shape how different people perceive risk differently. Individuals can perceive something to be a threat—feel, understand, and report themselves to be feeling fear—without that object being a threat. Alternatively, an individual might perceive something as a nonthreat when actually it is statistically likely to harm her. Not only past experiences of harm but also preexisting affect, amount of time exposed to potential harm, experiences of receiving information about risk objects, experiences of envisioning risks in one's own life, and identity factors like race, age, and gender can make a difference in how likely a person is to perceive risk. None of this is to deny that an individual's experience of fear in the face of perceived risk is real and significant. In fact, I will suggest that it is very important to attend to experiences of fear themselves, even and perhaps especially in cases of misperceived threats.

We will discuss at length in chapter 3 how processes of displacement can function such that an individual genuinely feels fear of, understands and reports herself as feeling fear of, and believes she fears one thing, X, when perhaps this feeling is in fact an expression of a fear of something else, Y. Such cases involve a perceived threat and perhaps the rest of the features of fearing (feeling fear, identifying and reporting that feeling), but they may also reflect a disconnect at the point of *properly identifying* what a fearer is afraid of. Before we can address displacement and possible *mis*identification of what one fears, I have established a distinct and more basic point in this section: perceptions of threat can be wrong.

Think back to the Chapman survey and other measures of what people are afraid of. When we ask people what they fear, they may be right in identifying the objects they are in fact afraid of. But even if very many people perceive some object X as a threat, X may not be threatening. Very many people might be scared of X, and yet it may still be the case that X is not an actual threat if X does not have actual capacity and statistical likelihood to cause harm to them or those they care about. And yet, as is perhaps already coming into view, and as we will discuss at length in chapter 4, what a lot of people *say* they are afraid of, and what a lot of people *act* afraid of, can have serious and damaging effects both on those beings or things perceived as threats and on the likelihood of future perceptions of threat.[11]

We have seen that what we recognize or communicate as the objects of our fears may not be actual threats. If perceptions of threat are not simply *direct perceptions of actual threats in the world*, what is the process by which we arrive at them? The next section further prepares the way for one of the major contentions of the coming chapters: what and how we fear is not chiefly up to individual fearers. Fearing is something we do together—indeed, it is a constellation of relational practices central to our moral lives.

3. Coming to Fear Things Together

We arrive at perceptions of threat in the context of many other fearers perceiving and communicating their own perceptions. All of the ways we ask, tell, and show each other *what we are afraid of*—from large surveys, to other empirical methods, to artistic and fictional depictions, to first-person reports communicated widely or not, to simple actions—shape and direct our fears toward particular objects and not others.

Threat perception is relationally shaped even before we learn from any explicit communication about threat. Cognitive processes of attention and observation are shaped by our relationality. We learn what to pay attention to and what not to pay attention to in part by seeing what others pay and do not pay attention to. Capacities for *joint attention* typically develop early in infants, emerging by nine months, and being well established by eighteen months (Tomasello 1995). Infants learn to follow the gaze or the pointing figure of their caregivers, and this has been recognized as an important indicator of social cognition. From this point on, we learn to pay attention to what others attend to, and we learn that we can shape what others attend to. Attachment relations in infants and young children fundamentally direct and regulate attention (Izard 1984; Waites 1996, 65–66). As psychologist Elizabeth Waites (1996, 66) puts it, "What others notice, react to, talk about, or ignore offers cues to the child developing his or her own capacities to think. . . . By orchestrating attention and establishing the schemas that organize encoding and retrieval, social interactions eventually evolve into personal history." As feminist relational theorist Annette Baier (1985, 84) describes it, persons are *second persons*: those who were "long enough dependent on other persons to acquire the essential arts of personhood." Attention is one of those arts. Whether or not the objects we attend to ever come to be perceived as threats, the fact that we paid attention to them at all is importantly shaped by others.

Among the objects we observe, we learn which to perceive as threats in part by seeing what trusted, significant, or formative others around us do. In developmental psychology, theories of fear acquisition often focused on *conditioning*, where any kind of stimulus can come to be associated with fear or pain and thereby develop fearful qualities, becoming more frightening depending on the frequency or strength of the association (Rachman 1977, 376). We might think of conditioning as similar to the development of food aversions: if I have grape juice as a child and soon after get very nauseous on a carnival ride, I might never want to have grape juice again (Garcia and Koelling 1966; Seligman and Hager 1972). Similarly, when certain stimuli become associated with fear or pain, a person can come to be afraid of those things. But conditioning is not the only path to fear acquisition. Stanley Rachman (1977) proposed a "tripartite theory of fear acquisition," according to which, in addition to conditioning, fears are also commonly acquired by vicarious acquisition (i.e., observing others having fearful responses) and the transmission of information and/or instruction (i.e., others giving information about what to fear).[12] Fears can be vicariously acquired, as well as vicariously reduced (Bandura 1969; Rachman 1972, 1976). Researchers in developmental psychology have attended to the ways parenting can shape threat perception, including in ways that promote hypervigilance in children (Izard and Harris 1995) or atypical capacities for coping with fears (Zahn-Waxler et al. 1990).

Beyond childhood, we commonly gain fears as part of our ways of relating to others we trust, and coming to share another's fears as our own can be an important part of communicating trust in them. The objects we come to fear are partly determined by the involvement of others: in some cases, we see what others fear and might become inclined to fear the same things, or to question ourselves if we do not.[13] If even one person we trust is fearful of an object we had not thought to fear, we might come to fear it on that basis alone. Kasperson and colleagues have noted that perceptions of risk are socially amplified:

> Signals arise through direct personal experience with a risk object or through the receipt of information about the risk object.... These signals are processed by social, as well as individual, amplification "stations," which include the following: The scientist who conducts and communicates the technical assessment of risk; The risk-management institution; The news media; Activist social organizations; Opinion leaders within social groups; Personal networks

of peer and reference groups; Public agencies. (Kasperson et al. 1988, 181)

We have seen already that having certain social identifications makes it more likely that one will fear some things—as in the earlier example that showed women and elderly people as more likely than other demographic groups to fear becoming victimized by crime. But what is not always sufficiently represented in demographic analyses is the ways in which social identifications are themselves a set of relational practices. For example, it is not simply a given that those born with certain primary and secondary sex characteristics will be more fearful of crime than those with different characteristics. Feelings of vulnerability to threat and felt incapacities for self-defense are parts of gender socialization that are learned by those identified as girls and women—they are part of the complex cluster of gendered practices that more feminine people observe, attempt, and are rewarded for attempting, or refuse and are punished for refusing. Gender socialization involves complex relational practices, of which gendered practices of threat perception are one part.

Further expanding the relational dimensions of fear acquisition, the facts of our relationality—the centrality of relationships to our lives—mean that many of our deepest, greatest fears are of threats to our relationships. It is very common for humans to have deep fears of the death of loved ones, harm to loved ones, failing to meet the needs of loved ones, dying and leaving loved ones behind, and the ways future uncertainty and unpredictability may bring suffering and loss to oneself and one's loved ones. I will refer to these in future chapters as our fears of *great threats*. The extent to which these fears are common and shared among many of us is evidenced by all the energy we spend trying to avoid these outcomes—caring for, protecting, meeting the needs of loved ones, and trying to insure our well-being against any number of possible future threats. Consider, for instance, a deep fear of loss of those who have cared for us (our parents/caregivers), or deep fear of loss of those we care for the most (our children, our partners, and closest loved ones). We cannot guarantee that these loved ones will never die, or indeed that we will not "lose" them in other ways, as in the progression of dementia or other illnesses, or by other forms of estrangement. Consider also adjacent fears of relational failure—for instance, fear of one's own failure to successfully protect those loved ones, or failure to anticipate and avoid potential harms to them. An author we will discuss at length in chapter 3, Kim Brooks (2018, 102), notes that humans perhaps gain our greatest fears from "foreseeing things we can't forestall." Further, we might experience fears of other sorts of failures, like moral failures to care for other beings or failures to demonstrate appreciation for the lives and luck we ourselves have had thanks to the work and generosity of others. Many other fears of great threats could be named here, but for now simply note three things: one, these perceptions of the threats of loss, failure, and uncertainty with respect to our loved ones are all very common; two, they all emerge from the facts of our relationality; and three, because they will persist so long as we are in interdependent relations with others, and because interdependence is a condition of human life, perceptions of these as actual threats cannot easily, or perhaps ever, be relieved or discharged.

Many of the most common approaches to understanding how we come to fear certain objects reflect *the presumption of independence* described in section 1: that is, individualistic presumptions about threat perceivers.[14] The general picture we get of fearers as a result is *every fearer for themselves*: each individual has and reports their own fears, and they may or may not report being afraid or very afraid of things of which others are also afraid or very afraid. By contrast, I will take for granted going forward that *threat perception is a relational practice*. This will be part of the understanding of *fearing as a relational practice* I articulate in chapter 2.

4. Conclusion

My goal in this chapter has been to identify and begin to challenge a picture of fearing that overstates the extent to which fears are directly and independently acquired. We have seen that the things we fear are not things we arrive at alone: attention, observation, and perception of threats are processes shaped by those closest to us. And many of the things we fear most stem from our relationships with those others: we fear losing them, failing them, or seeing unpredictable harms befall them. We come to fear what we fear together, in the context of many others perceiving and communicating their perceptions of threat, and such perceptions may or may not reflect actual threats. Having asked and complicated the question of how we arrive at the fears we do, we are now prepared to ask and complicate the question of *what fearing is*. This will be our project in chapter 2.

2
What Is Fearing?

In July 2020, in the midst of the global COVID-19 pandemic—and during the height of a summer of over 7,750 worldwide Black Lives Matter demonstrations in response to the murder of George Floyd by Minneapolis police officers—in the parking lot of a Chipotle restaurant in Michigan's Oakland County (where I live and work), a white woman pointed a loaded gun at a Black mother and her children.

Thirty-two-year-old Jillian Wuestenberg and her husband, Eric, were leaving the restaurant, as Takelia Hill and her children were entering. Hill's fifteen-year-old daughter and Ms. Wuestenberg bumped into each other. Hill's daughter says it was Wuestenberg who bumped into her. Wuestenberg says Hill's daughter started yelling. Hill's daughter started filming on her cell phone. In the footage eventually shared online, we see Wuestenberg and her husband get into their minivan, and Wuestenberg saying to Hill, "You cannot just walk around calling white people racist. This is not that type of world. White people aren't racist. No one's racist."[1] Eric Wuestenberg starts to back out of their parking spot. Takelia Hill is standing behind the van, and Jillian Wuestenberg says that, at that moment, Takelia Hill slapped the back window of the van with her hand. The video then shows the van stopping, and Jillian Wuestenberg getting out of the van, loading a round into the chamber of her handgun, and pointing it at the Hill family. Everyone starts yelling, the children are crying, and the cell phone camera is still recording. Hill screams to call the police. Eventually Wuestenberg and her husband get back in their van, and they are later charged with felonious assault (as of late 2022, they are awaiting trial). Wuestenberg says she pulled the gun on the Hill family because "she feared for her life."[2]

How can we understand Jillian Wuestenberg's claim that she feared for her life? Was she feeling fear or something else as she held a gun in the face of an unarmed woman and her children? If fear, was it for her life? Who will be in a position to answer these questions?

We have so far focused on getting clear on the question of *where fears come from*. This chapter delves more deeply into the question of *what fearing is*. It is clear that fearing involves having certain perceptions and beliefs. We saw in chapter 1 that fearing involves perceptions of threat, beliefs about perceived threats, and beliefs about myself and other fearers. But do we always know what causes us to fear? Do we always know what we are afraid of? It is also clear that fearing involves physiological dimensions that we do not choose and cannot always control. How do these bodily dimensions of fearing shape our perceptions and beliefs?

In this chapter, I explore these questions, drawing on insights from two significant conversations from the last half century: one in the history of philosophy of emotions and the other in neuroscience. These conversations provide two key touchstones to help situate my account of what fearing is: philosophers of emotion help us clarify the relationships between fearing, causes, and objects of fear (section 1); neuroscientists help us clarify the physiological and neurological dimensions of fearing and how they interact in a complex way with other cognitive processes (section 2). In section 3, I lay out the characterization of fearing that will guide my moral and political arguments in the remainder of the book—in particular, about what happens when fearers lack clear understandings of the causes and objects of their fears, and of the ways involuntary dimensions of fearing may shape their actions. We need to properly understand what fearing is—a joint endeavor involving not only fearers and the objects and causes of their fears but also relationships with other fearers—in order to reflect in the coming chapters on how we might better engage in it.

1. Fears, Causes, and Objects

We know from chapter 1 that we arrive at perceptions of threat by complex relational processes and that what we perceive as a threat may or may not be an actual threat. But there are more complexities to consider in these relationships between fearers and the things, beings, events, or facts we are afraid of. To begin, in this section we need to consider the importance of identifying *objects* of emotions for identifying *what emotion we are feeling*. Further, we need to determine how there can be a difference between the *cause* of my fear (the thing/being/event/fact that triggered or provoked my feeling of fear) and the *object* of my fear (the thing/being/event/fact that I feel fearful of or toward). This cause/object distinction begins to help clarify the relationship between fearers and things, beings, events, or facts in the world. It also points to the ways that fearers' understandings of our own processes of fearing are not always transparent to us, even while we might typically believe them to be. It signals again that the points of interaction between fearers and parts of the world are not straightforward. Not only might fearers' beliefs about what is and is not a threat be wrong, as we saw in chapter 1, but fearers might also be confused in their beliefs about the relationship between what *caused* their fears and what they feel fearful *of or toward*.

Part of the way we might tell emotions apart from one another—how, for instance, we might tell the difference between fear and anger even in cases where they might have similar physiological profiles—is by being able to identify the *object* of the emotion. A snake appears on my hiking path. I am not angry at the snake; I am scared of it. In many cases, the object and cause of my fear are the same: I am fearful of the snake (object), and my fear was triggered by the sight of the snake coming toward me (cause). But sometimes the object and the cause of my fear are not the same. Consider the following example:[3] I see a person on the street, and I feel fearful that they may mug me. This is what I am fearful *of*, the object of my fear: the person on the street. But in fact, my fear was triggered by a state of hypervigilance brought about by being sleep deprived and overcaffeinated. The day before, when I had slept well and was less caffeinated, I saw the same person and felt no such fear. The *cause* of my fear is my being short of sleep and overcaffeinated.

I trust that most of us can think of other examples of this type, where the object and the cause of an experience of fearfulness do not align. What's interesting to me about such cases is not simply the fact of the nonalignment: rather, it's that we are not always immediately aware of the nonalignment, and this lack of awareness can have significant consequences for how we relate to the objects of our fears. It is not uncommon for us to assume that the object and the cause of our fears are identical, and to relate to the objects of our fears in ways that aim to *curb their power to cause us to fear*. If I am fearful of the snake, I want to do something about the snake that will prevent it from causing me fear (perhaps to escape it, or even to cage or tranquilize it). Here the cause and the object are aligned, and so whatever we want to say about the moral status of my actions toward the snake, addressing the object is in fact likely to help me fear less. By contrast, if I am fearful of the person on the street who may mug me, and I want to do something about that person that will prevent them from causing me fear (perhaps to escape them, or even to report them to a police officer as suspicious), here the cause and the object are *not* aligned, and so addressing the object is *not* likely to help me fear less. And yet I might persist in believing that if I could just address the object of my fear (the person on the street), I would stop fearing. Not so. I am conflating object and cause.

We do not typically tease apart all these questions about our fears. Am I properly understanding what is *causing* my fear? Is it the same thing that I am fearful of/toward? Even so, they are regular parts of fearing.

To get a sense of how this discussion of objects and causes will help us properly understand fearing, it will help to briefly recall a line of discussion that runs through the history of philosophy of emotion, starting with pragmatists in the late 1800s, and continuing through the 1990s and beyond.

Just before the twentieth century, William James articulated a view of emotions (commonly called the James-Lange theory, given its similarity to the 1885 view of Carl Lange) according to which emotions are simply *perceptions of our physiological responses to some trigger*. As James explains, "Our natural way of thinking about [the] standard emotions is that the mental perception of some fact excites the mental affection called the emotion and that this latter state of mind gives rise to the bodily expression. My thesis on the contrary is that the bodily changes follow directly the PERCEPTION of the exciting fact, and that our feeling of the same changes as they occur IS the emotion" (James 1884, 189–90). Fear comes up often on James's view. On his view, we do not tremble because we are afraid; rather, we "feel afraid because we tremble" (190). According to James, it does not make sense to understand the emotion of fear other than as a perception of the bodily experience triggered by something frightening. James suggests that we can "conquer undesirable emotional tendencies in ourselves" by performing the outward bodily motions of the dispositions we want to cultivate—in anxiety attacks, for example, he notes that regulating one's breathing and slowing down one's heart rate will make the dread depart (199).

James's view has its virtues. It has been confirmed empirically, for instance, that practices of physiological regulation (body scans, deep breathing) can help calm some feelings of anxiety or dread. There is a problem with this view, however, from the perspective of wanting to *individuate* or distinguish between emotions that have similar physiological characteristics. James's view was criticized in this way by Walter Cannon, who worried that the physiological experiences of different emotions (e.g., fear and anger) might be too similar to tell apart, as well as by fellow pragmatist John Dewey (1894, 1895), who argued that we must understand emotions as having more weight in motivating *actions* than James's account suggests.[4] Further, James's view was criticized for not providing sufficient grounds for a common intuition that some emotions are justified and others are not.

Philosophers like Robert Solomon (1973), Amélie Rorty (1980), and Cheshire Calhoun ([1984] 2003) later took up the question of how to individuate emotions, partly by exploring questions of the causes and objects of emotion. They aimed to establish views of the emotions that would allow for differentiating emotions (e.g., fear and anger) and for showing how some emotions might be justified while others were not.

According to Robert Solomon's (1973) cognitive theory of emotions, emotions are judgments. Emotions typically involve feelings but are never simply feelings. The cause of an emotion is always an actual event or state of affairs. The object of an emotion is always an intentional object.[5] Emotion E is a judgment that the formal object of E is instantiated. For instance, my anger at someone is the judgment that I have been wronged by them (Solomon 1973, 27). On Solomon's view, the person with the emotion is in a privileged position to identify the object of their emotion, but their identification may still be incorrect (Solomon 1973, 26). Though I may actually *be* wrong about the cause of my emotion, I cannot *know* that I am wrong about the cause of my emotion while still having that emotion:

> If I am angry about John's stealing my car (the object of my anger), then I cannot believe that the sufficient cause of my anger is anything other than John's stealing my car.... I can only be angry so long as I believe that what has caused me to be angry is what I am angry about. Where the cause is different from what I am angry about, I cannot know that it is.
>
> ... If I can discover the sufficient cause of my anger, in those cases in which the cause and the object are different (and in which the newly discovered cause is not itself a new object for anger, as often happens), I can undermine and abandon my anger. (Solomon 1973, 29)

So on this view, if I fear a snake (the object of my fear), then I cannot *believe* that the cause of my fear is anything other than the snake. I can only be fearful so long as I believe that what has caused me to be fearful is what I am fearful about. If I discover something *else* is actually the cause of my fear (e.g., the fact that I am jittery and underslept) and if that thing isn't a new *object* for fear, my fear will cease.[6]

In many cases, the causes of our emotions are easy enough to clarify, whether they are identical with the objects of our emotions or not. The snake was straightforwardly the cause of my fear. Perhaps it is even easy enough to determine that the cause of my fear of the person on the street is my being underslept and overcaffeinated. According to Solomon, once I have figured that out, my fear of the person on the street will cease. But sometimes the *cause* of our emotions is not just one thing. Amélie Rorty (1980) emphasizes how individuals' emotions should be contextualized not only by *immediate causes*, but also by *significant causes*: an expanded causal history that includes a fuller picture of their past experiences. According to Rorty (1980, 106), the "significant cause of an emotion is ... the entire causal history ... that formed a set of dispositions which are triggered by the immediate cause." When we encounter emotions in others that do not seem to make sense, Rorty suggests we investigate more deeply to understand the full backstory of why an individual might be disposed to pay attention to certain events more than others, how they may have lower thresholds than others for bearing certain events, and how they might therefore be more inclined to have some emotional reactions (e.g., anger at a seemingly insignificant event) than people without that backstory would be.[7]

In "Cognitive Emotions?," Cheshire Calhoun ([1984] 2003) further responds to Solomon and others by arguing that interpretive "seeings as" and their background cognitive sets make up emotion (not beliefs). We can infer from a person's emotions that the world must appear to them in a certain way (Calhoun 2003, 247). However, the person may or may not *believe* that the world is as it appears to them. For instance, Calhoun gives the example of Tess, who was raised to believe that homosexuality is unnatural and immoral, but has later come to believe that in fact homosexuality is neither. Even so, she finds herself feeling shock and revulsion at the news that a good friend of hers is a lesbian. Tess's beliefs do not align with the way the world appears to her—given that her background cognitive set/interpretive framework still "sees" homosexuality as disgusting, and so she still feels disgusted. The same could be true of fears: a person may believe that something is not a threat and yet still feel fearful (e.g., recall Gendler's discussion of alief and the Grand Canyon Skywalk). As Calhoun ([1984] 2003, 247) puts it, "To the acrophobic, heights appear dizzyingly treacherous. . . . We can deny the real treacherousness of heights." This view pushes back on the cognitivist claim that beliefs are constituents of emotion or that emotion ascriptions entail belief ascriptions.

The overview of this discussion of objects and causes of fears in philosophy of emotion helps draw attention to key factors in the ethics of fearing. Fearing involves apprehensions of the objects and causes of our fears and these apprehensions can go wrong in ways which have serious moral consequences. In addition to Solomon's teasing apart the distinction and relationship between objects and causes, and Rorty's and Calhoun's attending to the ways a richer sense of causes and background cognitive sets may be needed to understand a person's fears, philosophers of emotion have offered a vocabulary for understanding the ways fears and other emotions may or may not fit the circumstances. How can we tell if our fears are appropriate? Does it make sense for us to fear the things we do, in the way we do? The book's introduction discussed the ways in which fears can be warranted or unwarranted, depending on whether they reflect actual or statistical threats. We know from chapter 1 that our perceptions of, and beliefs about, the characteristics of supposedly threatening things can be wrong. We might think a thing, person, animal, event, or environment has some characteristic that threatens us, and we may be wrong about that. To put this another way, our beliefs about the *properties* of the objects of our fears may or may not be accurate reflections of reality. In 1963, Anthony Kenny introduced the term *formal objects* to describe the perceived properties of things relevant to our emotional reactions to them, and variations on this term persist through other cognitive accounts of emotion. In the case of fear, the object is anything someone can be afraid of (e.g., a bear), and the formal object is the property of that thing that constitutes *danger* (e.g., its capacity and propensity to harm me).

According to Justin D'Arms and Daniel Jacobson (2000, 73), emotions can be fitting or not fitting, either in *shape* or *size*.[8] They elaborate:

> Envy's shape fails to fit the world: if the thing I envy isn't really possessed by my rival, or if it isn't really good....
>
> An emotion can also be criticized for its size. While such criticism typically implies that it has the right shape, one can nevertheless urge that an emotional response is unfitting because it is an overreaction. Thus your envy might be too large for the circumstances, if what you have is almost as good as your rival's. Then you would not be warranted in being much pained over such a trifling difference. (D'Arms and Jacobson 2000, 73–74)

A feeling is fitting in shape if it reflects something that is true about the world, and fitting in size if it basically matches the seriousness or intensity of the fact about the world. One's fear might be judged fitting in shape when it is a fear of something that exists, does in fact possess some trait or capacity, that is in fact dangerous to me. Fear can be fitting in size when my fear of the threat is neither an overreaction nor an underreaction to the amount or intensity of the danger it poses.[9]

All of this can help us further understand the complexities of how our fears involve perceptions of and beliefs about the world, and of how regularly our processes of fearing can involve misapprehensions. The most important takeaways from this discussion are as follows: fearers can be wrong about the causes of our fears. Sometimes a complex personal history is needed to understand the causes of our fears. We can be wrong about the objects of our fears. We can be wrong about the attributes of those objects. And we can be wrong about whether or to what extent those attributes actually endanger us. If we are to establish an account that does justice to the actual moral complexities of fearing in the coming chapters, we need to hold a steady vision of all these factors, which together establish just how fallible fearers can be.

We have so far learned a great deal about the role of causes and objects in fearing, but we have not yet attended to the potential roles of interpersonal relationships in the identification of causes and objects. More will be said about that in section 3 of this chapter. As we will see at the end of chapter 3, fears persistently involving inaccurate identifications of causes or objects can partly explain morally and politically damaging actions, and successfully mitigating these damages can require, in part, better understanding relational aspects of fearing.

2. Fear and Embodiment

The overall project of this chapter is to work toward a clear understanding of what fearing is. In this section, we turn our attention to embodied dimensions of fearing. We have seen developments in the risk-perception literature and cognitive theories of emotions that established that our perceptions of threat can be out of alignment with actual threats in the world (chapter 1); identifying the causes and objects of our fears may be central parts of identifying our emotion as fear rather than something else while the causes and objects of our fears are neither always identical nor always accurately identified by fearers (section 1 of this chapter). A separate body of research was developing in the same decades as these literatures in risk perception and cognitive theories of emotion, and it pays attention to the neuroscience of fearing. A brief overview of this literature will give context to the instances of fears overriding or bypassing reasoning described in the risk-perception research and in philosophy of emotions.

Over the last half century, neuroscientific research has revolutionized our thinking about fear processes in human brains. In particular, researchers have come to understand the central role of the amygdala (a subcortical structure in the medial temporal lobe) in threat detection.[10] Starting in the 1970s, Joseph LeDoux's research on fear conditioning in rats demonstrated the essential position of the amygdala in threat detection and in triggering the release of stress hormones epinephrine and cortisol. These hormones prompt physiological reactions like rising heart rates, quicker breathing, and higher blood pressure and prepare the body to perform *fight or flight*, a term already familiar from Walter Cannon's 1915 account (see LeDoux 1996).[11] LeDoux's early research showed that in mammals, when a threat is perceived, the amygdala triggers bodily responses that prepare the body to protect itself. All this happens before, in humans, the slower, analytical processes of reasoning might kick in, which might indeed come to reason that the perceived threat is not actually or certainly a threat after all. According to LeDoux, a common chain of events in threat detection is as follows: a stimulus is processed by sensory systems in the brain, nonconsciously determined to be a threat, and this threat detection triggers increased brain arousal and bodily changes. When threat detection occurs in animals with capacities for consciousness, these factors can be integrated and the conscious feeling of fear can be created. For LeDoux, an experience of fear thus often involves the representation of a sensory object or event in the brain, defensive survival circuit activation, attention/working memory knowing the stimulus is present, semantic memory enabling a person to identify what the object is, episodic memory positioning the event as happening to *me, now*, connections from amygdala to long-term memory facilitating retrieval of memories of the threat, and recognition that the ingredients present are indicators of fear and the state is categorized as *fear* (LeDoux 2015, 227–30).

The understanding of the role of the amygdala in threat detection developed over LeDoux's decades of work have paved the way for many advances in understanding fear in relation to the brain. But it is important to note that LeDoux has qualified his position somewhat in recent years. The amygdala is key for threat detection, which is often part of a human coming to feel fear. But on LeDoux's most recent articulation of the view, while threat detection is often one part of a human's fearing, the amygdala and threat detection are not always involved. Not all fear triggers depend on amygdala circuits; there are other parts of the brain involved in defensive behavior, and the amygdala contributes to non-threat-related brain functions as well (LeDoux 2020, R620). As LeDoux puts it:

> The amygdala is indeed wired by evolution to detect and produce body responses to certain kinds of threats, but . . . it is not required to feel fear. For these and other reasons, I have argued that the amygdala's role in detecting and responding to threats is more appropriately considered in terms of a non-conscious defensive survival circuit than a conscious fear circuit. (LeDoux 2020, R620)

From recent decades of research on the amygdala, we have learned a great deal about the ways in which threat detection is embodied. We understand, for instance, how human bodies might react defensively before even knowing that a threat has been identified, as in familiar cases of smelling a scent or hearing a song connected to some past threat. Embodied experiences of threat detection can dramatically shape other cognitive processes in ways that can have significant effects on our actions: these experiences have been shown to shape how and what we see, how we process information, and how we behave in interpersonal relating.

In this line of neuroscientific research, threat detection has been shown to shape other cognitive processes in one way by shaping visual perception (Kosslyn et al. 1996; LeDoux 2002). Some findings suggest that threat detection can *enhance* activity in the visual cortex, for instance, both heightening contrast sensitivity and enhancing attention (Phelps, Ling, and Carrasco 2006). In other words, the presence of a stimulus perceived as threatening may enhance both vision and attention, doubly boosting visual perception. This makes sense from an evolutionary perspective: heightened visual perception would be an advantage in a dangerous environment. Of course, it may also combine with increased risk aversion to make individuals more prone to hypervigilance.

Feelings of fear themselves have been further shown to enhance detailed processing of information in general (Edwards and Weary 1993; Tiedens and Linton 2001) and to increase motivation to learn (Marcus, Neuman, and MacKuen 2000). In 2010, Parker and Isbell (2010, 548–49) found that participants who were prompted to feel fearful by writing about an experience they had that frightened them showed enhanced systematic processing compared to those who had been prompted to feel anger. Fear may also make individuals more likely to be *influenced* by information. In an experiment conducted by Bohner and Weinerth (2001), fearful participants were found both to read information more closely and to be more influenced in response to the information than nonfearful participants.

Beyond enhancing both visual perception and information processing, fear has been shown to also "enhance" risk perception, in the sense of increasing the likelihood that one will perceive risk. The literature on fear and risk perception suggests that "fear causes people to err on the side of caution and not carefully consider all relevant information" (Hunsinger 2010, 8). In much of the psychological literature from the past forty years, we see that, in both human and nonhuman mammals, fear often prompts avoidance and escape (Epstein 1972; Öhman and Mineka 2001; Hebert, Blanchard, and Blanchard 1999; Roseman, Wiest, and Swartz 1994; Zanoveli et al. 2004). As mentioned in chapter 1, in Lerner and Keltner's (2001) series of experiments, fearful individuals were found to be more inclined toward risk-averse decisions and less optimistic about future positive outcomes. "Fearful individuals consistently made relatively pessimistic judgments and choices, whereas both happy and angry individuals consistently made relatively optimistic judgments and choices" (Lerner and Keltner 2001, 154). Fearful individuals are more likely to perceive some object or event as risky than a nonfearful individual. According to the findings of Chanel and Chichilnisky (2009), fear can make individuals so concerned about the possibility of future catastrophe that their processes of decision making and action can become stalled.

Further, fear has been shown to significantly shape how we interact with other people, and the extent to which we feel able to trust them.

Interpersonal trust can be disrupted by all kinds of fear, whether by fears of a person with whom one is in relationship, fears for their safety, or fears of some unrelated danger.[12] As we have seen, whereas anger can promote confrontation, fear is more likely to prompt retreat and withdrawal, including from the risk-taking involved in interpersonal relationships. When experiences of danger or fear are part of interpersonal relationships, those interpersonal experiences have been shown to become persistent parts of individuals' *memories*. As Johnston and Olson (2015, 78) note, "Fear memories are not easily forgotten, and instead, their expression must be regulated or inhibited by further learning." As such, fearers can long remember harms they have experienced, and fearful subjects can be more suspicious and less trusting of others in general than nonfearful subjects are (Ray and Vanstone 2009).

So we can see that threat detection and fear can significantly shape other cognitive processes—in some cases prompting individuals to see differently, process information differently, make decisions differently, and relate to others differently. Notice, too, the ways these shapings might have looping effects: if we see more details or are more attentive to information, we might find more reasons to be fearful. If we feel we cannot trust people, we might perceive their actions as more threatening than they actually are. In other words, unsurprisingly, fear can beget fear.

Anxiety shares some of the features of fear but is not identical. The two are characterized by somewhat different brain mechanisms.[13] In cases of fear, the threat is present and identifiable, the agent's connection to the threat is reasonable, and the experience is episodic rather than ongoing. In cases of anxiety, threats may not be present, identifiable, or likely to occur, and the agent may instead feel a sustained need to be vigilant. Anxious individuals are those with a fairly stable temperament which disposes them both to respond more quickly to threats and to more readily perceive neutral or nonthreat objects as threats than do less anxious individuals (Johnston and Olson 2015, 75). While fear and anxiety are not fully separable, LeDoux suggests:

> In fear . . . the focus is on a specific external threat, one that is present or imminent, whereas in anxiety the threat is typically less identifiable and its occurrence less predictable—it is more internal, and

in the mind more of an expectation than a fact, and can also be an imagined possibility with a low likelihood of ever occurring. (2015, 7)

We might think that anger would share some of the same intensity and effects of fear, but within the neuroscientific literature, fear has been characterized as *low certainty* (fearful individuals perceive future events as unpredictable) and *low control* (fearful individuals perceive bad situations as the fault of circumstances beyond their control). This is in contrast to anger, which is characteristically *high certainty* (angry individuals perceive future events as predictable) and *high control* (angry individuals perceive bad situations as someone's fault) (Smith and Ellsworth 1985). While fear has been shown to increase careful information processing, anger has been shown to decrease it (Bohner and Weinerth 2001, 1427). One research team investigated how fear and anger might incline participants toward particular policy decisions following the 9/11 attacks in the United States. They found that fearfulness was more strongly related to risk-averse responses (like deportations), while anger was more related to confrontational responses (like war). As the subtitle of their article indicates: "Anger wants a fight and fear wants 'them' to go away" (Skitka et al. 2006, 375).

The last several decades of neuroscientific research on fear has brought into clearer focus a great deal about the physiological processes involved in threat detection and in many cases of fear. While the concerted focus on brain processes might seem like a turn toward individual fearers and away from the way relationships shape fearing, in fact many of the physiological processes described are formed and shaped relationally, both by others with whom we share genetic and biological relations, and by all those who interact with us throughout our lives. Our tendencies toward or away from fearfulness are shaped by others and our environments. To be sure, if relational contexts become sidelined in considerations of neurophysiology, this will obscure important dimensions of the fearing brain—but these decades of neuroscientific research need not point us toward that. The more we learn about the neurophysiological processes of individuals, the more we can recognize how foundationally they are shaped by interaction with others and environments.

So far in this chapter I have posed the question of what fearing is, holding in mind cases where we might be unsure that what we or someone else is feeling is in fact fear, and cases where it may be difficult to distinguish fear from other emotions (like anger). I have engaged two distinct traditions to begin to outline an account of what fearing is: cognitive theories of emotion in philosophy, and research on threat detection and fear in neuroscience. I see philosophical psychology and neuroscience as bringing different methods and perspectives to bear on the phenomenon of fearing. As distinct methods of inquiry, they pose different questions, give access to different kinds of information, and are not fully compatible. Each methodological approach has its limits. From cognitive theories, I am informed most by the attention to the distinction between causes and objects of fearing, and by the consideration of how individuals can be wrong about either the cause or the proper object of their fears. These points will be important to hold in mind in the coming chapters, where I explore ways in which individuals might believe their fear to have been caused by X or to be fear of Y, and may be wrong in ways that have serious consequences for action. From neuroscientific accounts, I am informed most by attention to the ways threat detection and/or fear can shape and constrain vision, information processing, risk assessment, and interpersonal trust. I will suggest in chapter 5 that addressing the harmful effects of fears will require taking seriously both the physiological aspects of these experiences and the effects of those aspects on fearers' cognitive processes.[14] As we will see in chapter 5, a number of somatic approaches to responding to fear aim to do just that.

Note that both approaches have something to say about how we can distinguish or individuate fears from other emotions. The question of individuation is a major focus of the cognitive theories, picking up from the tradition in philosophy of emotions that aimed to correct James's failure to show how to distinguish emotions with seemingly similar physiological and behavioral components. On Solomon's view, we can tell the difference between emotions by their distinct objects. Anger is a judgment that someone has wronged me. Fear is a judgment that someone is threatening me. The question of individuation is attended to by LeDoux's model as well: the distinct participation of the amygdala in threat detection as one part of fearing in some cases helps distinguish fear from other emotions. I want to pause here to point out that, on the views we have so far surveyed, the individuation of fear—the determination that an individual's emotion is *fear* rather than something else—is something that happens *in the fearer alone*. I highlight this because, as we will see in the next section, on my view the individuation of fear may turn out to be more dependent on other people than these accounts would suggest.

3. Fearing with Others

The goal of this chapter has been to elucidate what fearing is—what are the cognitive and physiological dimensions of fearing, what roles do causes and objects play in fearing, and how can we distinguish fearing from other emotions? We have engaged conceptual and empirical accounts from philosophy of emotions and neuroscience to begin to understand what fearing involves. I have suggested that each framework can help us see certain aspects of fearing that will help us moving forward.

In the views we have discussed, the focus has been on individual fearers—fear has been positioned as something individuals do alone, though of course their fears are shaped by and can then have effects on others and their environments. Feminist philosopher of emotion Sue Campbell complicates these discussions by highlighting and challenging their individualism.[15] Engaging with her view will help us clarify my relational account of fearing.

It is a deeply held assumption of many philosophical accounts of emotion and expression that our emotions can be *individuated prior to their expression*. Campbell (1997, 51) calls this the *presupposition of individuation*. As we have seen, the presupposition of individuation is present in many of the accounts of fear in the history of philosophy and in neuroscience.

By contrast, Campbell argues that *expression individuates*. It is expressing to others through our language or behavior that actually forms or creates the feelings we have. Campbell argues that "expression is the activity through which our psychological states, including our feelings, become individuated for both others and ourselves. By individuated, I mean formed or created as the particulars they are in such a way that they can then be recognized or identified" (S. Campbell 1997, 48–49): not formed feelings first and expression later—instead, through expression, formation.[16]

Campbell holds that there are many kinds of feelings—classic emotions are only one group of such feelings. Emotions like love, jealousy, or anger are "classic" insofar as they are "a small group of highly conceptualized feelings that might seem to find expression in easily identifiable patterns of behavior" (1997, 165). According to Campbell, not all feelings have objects, but for those that do, as classic emotions do, one clear mechanism by which expression can function in the formation of such emotions is by *establishing their objects*. On Campbell's view, we use various *expressive resources*: "gesture, avowal, involuntary response, action, metaphor, aesthetic creation" (105). Expressive resources are differently available to different individuals. In the case of classic emotions, expression is sometimes but not always needed to identify the object of an emotion, and thereby to individuate the emotion. Expression is not *always* required because sometimes we have already practiced an emotion so much, people can recognize the scenarios and anticipate what it is appropriate for people to be feeling. But in some cases of even very familiar, classic emotions, Campbell (1997, 76) argues that "we must allow expression a role in determining the intentional object of an emotional state, and hence, in determining the character of that state." On Campbell's view, the individuation of an emotion includes a specification of its object, and in some cases, the expressive actions of a person establish that object. Campbell uses the example of "Roxane's Choice" from Edmond Rostand's *Cyrano de Bergerac* as a situation within which the "object of an emotion is established, completing the formation of that emotion, partly through the expression of culturally significant actions that themselves require an object" (S. Campbell 1997, 88). In the case of Roxane, the *object* of Roxane's love is established by expression and action as in fact being two men (87). Love is a classic emotion, and in Roxane's case, the emotion of love is established/formed/individuated by the establishment of the *objects* of her emotion (i.e., the two men Roxane loves), and these objects are established by expression (via language and behavior). So it is because Roxane expresses love for the two men that the *objects* of her love are established, and thereby that her emotion is formed *as love*—through expression, formation.

Moving beyond the role of expression in individuating classic emotions, Campbell (1997, 71) is particularly interested in attending to "free-style feelings" which are "nuanced and nameless feelings that are neither reducible to sensations nor the sorts of states that are adequately captured by the categories of the classic emotions." Freestyle feelings are those which have not yet been adequately identified or recognized, or even named. According to Campbell, the individuation of freestyle feelings is collaborative: it requires expression and interpretation. There are cases in which successfully forming feelings depends on other people's capacities for recognizing our feelings: these are cases where *uptake is necessary* for the formation of these feelings (106). Campbell's account is modeled on Donald Davidson's externalist account of the individuation of propositional states by triangulation, according to which, the individuation of a person's psychological states cannot be accomplished by reference to the person alone but must also reference expressive behavior within the person's environment (S. Campbell 1997, 104). On Davidson's (1991) view, triangulation occurs when people have differential responses to similar stimuli, grounding the possibility of determinate meaning through the possibility of mutual interpretation. To take one of Davidson's examples of triangulation in the creation of *linguistic* meaning, every time a thing appears that I call "mouse," you say "raton." After a while, I conclude that for you, "raton" means mouse. Triangulation occurs when "I respond to a stimulus (the mouse) and to your response to the stimulus (the utterance of 'raton'). You respond to a stimulus and to my response to that stimulus. The speaker's utterance 'raton' and your utterance 'mouse' have the same content or meaning" (S. Campbell 1997, 114).

To demonstrate the function of triangulation in *affective* meaning, Campbell gives the "Pictionary shrug" example. In short, we imagine a game of Pictionary where one player, Sue, fails to draw something recognizable to her teammate, and turns to them and shrugs as the time runs out. In one case, we imagine the teammate shrugging back, smiling sympathetically, and we take both players to understand Sue's shrug as meaning something like an apologetic recognition of her inability to draw the prompt. Everyone understands. In an alternative case, we are asked to imagine Sue doing the same shrug, but Sue's teammate instead responding with "'Look, if you hate the game that much we'll all quit playing'" (S. Campbell 1997, 109). On Campbell's view, such a response can have the power to make Sue unsure of the feeling she has formed. Sue thinks to herself, *Did my shrug express a feeling of impotence in drawing, or did it express frustration or contempt at the game?* Campbell analyzes the example as follows:

> In fairly simple cases of affective communication, someone's response can make me unsure of what I have expressed, and, therefore, of what I feel.
>
> Moreover, in cases where interpreter response makes me unsure of what I feel, the nature of my feelings will become more indeterminate. I wish to argue against a merely epistemological role for uptake in the case described....
>
> ... I am interested in the very common case where the response to an expression begins to make the subject uncertain about what he or she feels. This uncertainty has repercussions for how the subject actually feels. If I become uncertain as to whether I feel impotence or contempt, my affective state itself becomes a more confused one. (109–11)

In other words, when a subject comes to feel uncertain about her feeling as a result of an interpreter's (willful or nonwillful) response, the feelings themselves become indeterminate.[17] We regularly participate in relational interactions where the feelings we have depend on our being enabled to express them to and receive uptake for them from others. Interpreters can give uptake verbally, and they can also provide it in how they *act* in response to the needs of a person expressing emotion. If we face lack of sympathetic interpretation from others—if others dismiss or ignore the feelings—on Campbell's view, we can fail to have the feelings. And if this lack of uptake persists, it can have serious consequences:

> Because of the relation of feeling to significance, when our feelings are trivialized, ignored, systematically criticized, or extremely constrained by the poverty of our expressive resources, this situation

can lead to a very serious kind of dismissal—the dismissal of the significance to a person of his or her own life, in a way that reaches down deeply into what the significance of a life can be to the person whose life it is. (S. Campbell 1997, 188)

Why would theorists like those in the history of philosophy and neuroscience be inclined to unwittingly assume the presupposition of individuation, rather than to emphasize the role of interpersonal expression and uptake in the formation of feelings? In part, Campbell thinks, from a protective impulse: "At bottom, I believe we all wish to guard the idea that our affective lives can be fully formed and remain intact without the interference of others, and even without others' knowledge that we have such lives" (S. Campbell 1997, 62). While Solomon and LeDoux would presume that fearing happens whether it is ever expressed to others, Campbell contests the individualistic framing of what fearing is. In the specific ways I have outlined here, Campbell paves the way for understanding fearing as a kind of collaborative action.

Campbell's corrective is an important one for my project of properly understanding the complexities of fearing. For one thing, Campbell's view helps us see how, for some instances of fear, expression can establish *the objects* of the fear. Some instances of fear align so clearly with paradigm cases (fearing a snake) that it is straightforward to see the object an individual is fearing, and the individuation of the emotion is uncomplicated. But consider other cases where, for instance, a person is feeling fearful but not sure what they are fearful *of*. Imagine the context is sufficiently complicated as to make it not obvious what is triggering their feelings of fear. Recall, for instance, the early months of the COVID-19 pandemic. It was at some points difficult to determine the perceived threats to which individuals were responding. Through an individual's expression—for instance, behavior to avoid talking about the emerging facts about those populations most at risk of negative outcomes, avoiding talking with elderly loved ones, and perhaps through tearing up at every mention of outbreaks at nursing homes—it might become clear that the chief object of one's fear is *loss of elderly parents*. This may not be the only fear a person has in this context, but if it was not immediately clear to an individual, it could become clarified as one of their fears by expression. Some instances of fear, like this one, may be classic emotions where the object is not clearly established, and expression might be necessary for identifying it, and thereby for forming the emotion.

Other feelings might be not well identified by standard understandings of a classic emotion of fear. They may be idiosyncratic and historically situated, and be in need of expression and uptake for their formation. In such instances, expression and uptake in the model of triangulation might establish *what the feeling is*. Imagine a case where an individual, Callie, knows neither *what* she is feeling (whether fear or something else) nor what any potential objects of that feeling may be.[18] Imagine that Callie's partner Eli has announced that an old friend reached out to him on social media just before he left work, and he got distracted while answering and was therefore late leaving work and late getting home for dinner. Now Callie is feeling something, and behaving in some ways toward Eli—short-tempered, sarcastic, insulting, dismissive—but it is not clear what it all means. What is Callie feeling? She herself cannot quite identify it. Eli suggests maybe it is because she is angry that he was late for dinner. That doesn't seem quite right to Callie. Each of them is occasionally late, and neither of them typically cares. Then Eli suggests that maybe it is because she is jealous of the old friend—were they once romantically involved? Callie says that feels closer, but she believes Eli when he denies any romantic interest. Ultimately Eli reminds her that she has always been worried about negative judgment from Eli's longtime friends. Callie has never felt approval from them and has always worried they would convince Eli not to be with her. It begins to come into vision: Callie is feeling *fear of losing Eli*. Fear of losing a loved one is not an uncommon emotion, but this is a case where an absence of expression and uptake, or a dismissal of the feeling, could have both epistemological and ontological ramifications for the formation of feeling—like in the Pictionary shrug case, without expressing and receiving uptake for the feeling, Callie might have been unsure of the feeling, and the feeling itself might have been a more confused one.

Though we may be tempted to interpret a lot of nuanced feelings under the umbrella of a classic kind of fear, Campbell's view helps show how doing so may not do justice to what the feeling actually is. Indeed, my inquiry into fearing is partly an inquiry into feelings that we might tend to categorize as something other than fear, but that should instead be understood as forms of fearing, as well as into instances that we might misunderstand as a simple kind of fear, but that are actually more complex.[19] Further, Campbell's view makes clear how, in many cases, our capacities for fearing will depend on what expressive resources are available to us. As she puts it, "The richer and more discriminating our ways of expression, the richer and more nuanced our affective lives" (S. Campbell 1997, 50). As we will see in upcoming chapters, I think there is something to be said about our having still too constrained capacities for fear expression—and that this can be part of the reason fearing goes badly, in the ways we will see in chapters 3 and 4.[20] Crucially, Campbell's view helps complicate the presumption that fearing is chiefly something individuals do alone. As we have seen, interpreters can play key roles in allowing for the expression, and thereby the formation, of fears.

Recall that we established in chapter 1 that our perceptions of threat are relationally shaped: we perceive threats in the context of many other fearers perceiving and communicating their own perceptions of threat. Attention, observation, and perception of threats are processes shaped by those around us. In this sense, we have already begun to see fearing relationally. Campbell's view shifts us further away from thinking about fearing as an activity of individuals, toward understanding fearing as something we do together. In some cases, the significance of expression and interpretation for emotional experiences will have moral implications—as we discuss further in chapter 5, interpreters may have a responsibility to allow for the expressions of fears and to give uptake (verbally or through behavior) to those expressions in ways that do not dismiss them.

Notice further that not only what we fear (chapter 1) and how we come to form fears (chapter 2) are processes shaped by other people, but even *what fear feels like to us* is an experience shaped by other people. Consider, for instance, how any fear we now have is experienced against the background of our memories of how and what others have feared in the past. We recall the fears our caregivers, family members, friends, and acquaintances experienced—at least the ones they willingly or unwillingly demonstrated or expressed. Those closest to us are likely to have the most direct effects on our own ways of experiencing fear, but even those further from us—public figures, politicians, strangers—may have an impact on the way fear affects us. To some extent, their ways of coping with fears shape our own. If they demonstrated capacities for fearing without being consumed by fear, we may come to experience fear as unpleasant but not all-encompassing. Fear may seem to us tolerable, expected. If, by contrast, those around us have been overtaken, immobilized, or dramatically unmoored by fear, that too might shape the quality of our fearing. Some of what fear feels like to us will depend on contingencies of our personalities and practices, and perhaps on our own choices about the leverage we want to allow fear to have in our lives. But as humans who have been deeply shaped by, and in response to, other people, what fear feels like is not entirely up to us.

I am suggesting we move away from understanding fearing as something individuals do alone, toward understanding our fears as relationally constituted, in the context of other fearers and broader social frameworks of fearing. We have seen that fearing involves perception, belief, expression, and, in some cases, uptake; in other words, fearing involves epistemic dimensions. We saw this already in Solomon, who attended closely to the ways in which causes and objects of fear can be misperceived, and in Campbell, who clarified the key role of expression and uptake in the formation of feelings. We have also seen that fearing can involve complex expressions. Fearers do not always clearly express fear or even always understand themselves to be feeling fear. Individuals can be wrong about the causes, objects, and characteristics of objects of our fears. Perceptions of causes and objects can be shaped by practices of interpersonal expression and uptake. We express, get uptake for (or not), and give uptake for (or not) others' expressions of fears, including expressions of perceived causes, objects, and characteristics of feared objects. In other words, the epistemic dimensions of fearing are relationally complex.

We have also seen that the fearing is not always something we do intentionally. Individuals often feel fearful without having decided they should. And yet, there are facts of the matter about objects in the world and how threatening they are to a given individual. These facts can be determined empirically, though of course we do not always have access to all the information to make these determinations. Sometimes the information has not yet been researched or collected. Sometimes only some people are granted access to the information. Sometimes histories of dismissing some individuals' fears result in a lack of empirical confirmation of the existence and seriousness of threats. For instance, consider documentation of how Black women's fears of adverse outcomes in health-care contexts, and particularly surrounding pregnancy and childbirth, are more likely to be dismissed, while these outcomes have long been genuine and serious threats.[21] The fact of higher likelihood of adverse health outcomes has long existed. Because of a lack of prioritization in research, it has only more recently received empirical confirmation. Black women's experiences of having their legitimate fears dismissed persist long past the point of having the threats empirically confirmed.

We have seen that fearing is *motivational* in a number of ways. Fearing can alter whom, what, whether, and to what degree we trust. Fearing can involve compromised trust of some people or objects, while also prompting increased trust in others. Fearing motivates different ways of processing information and perceiving risk. As we will discuss at length in chapter 4, fearing and individuals' resistance to experiences of fear can motivate actions to address—and often to attack or avoid—perceived threats.

On my view, we are morally responsible for our fearing. By "we," I mean not only those experiencing and expressing fears but also those interpreting expressions of fears, and those involved in a myriad of ways in the broad social contexts that shape fearing. Whether fears are or are not reflective of actual threats, if fearers are not able to live with their fears, these feelings can prompt actions that are morally dangerous (e.g., attacks of various kinds on perceived threats). As we will see more in the coming chapters, and especially in my prescriptive account of fearing better in chapter 5, my immediate priority is harm reduction in the sense of reducing the harms of people *acting* on fears in morally dangerous ways. Prioritizing avoiding the harms of violent fear-driven *actions* informs my account of how we should respond to fears that express morally problematic beliefs and perceptions. As such, the question for me is less whether a fear is morally problematic and more whether a morally problematic action is motivated by fear, and if so, how we can reshape the fearing that motivates it. As we will see in the coming chapters, I am most concerned with intervening in fearing that has a certain form: when fearers cannot bear feelings of fear, including fears of some of the deepest, inextinguishable threats (mortality, uncontrollability, potential harm to loved ones), they sometimes attempt to find some kind of peace by fixing their attention on some other perceived threats that *can* be extinguished or otherwise controlled, and then act in such a way as to control those perceived threats. This form of fearing can result in deeply morally problematic action. Chapter 5 will be my attempt to think through productive disruptions of fearing that take this form.

Before we conclude, let's return to Jillian Wuestenberg, who pointed the gun in the Chipotle parking lot. What was she feeling? Did she, as she claims, fear for her life? Unlike more straightforward cases like the snake on the hiking trail, individuating fear as distinct from other feelings in this situation is likely to be complicated. Wuestenberg clearly perceived the Hill family, an unarmed mother and her two children, as some kind of threat. The eldest child did, after she and Hill bumped into each other, choose to not apologize for the action (which, again, the child claims was in fact Wuestenberg's), and then to criticize Wuestenberg for it on camera. Wuestenberg regards this as threatening, and as part of the Hill family's efforts to block her from entering her vehicle, describes Hill's position behind the quickly reversing van as an attempt to block them from leaving, and the alleged slap of the rear window of her minivan as an attack. None of this amounts to an actual threat to Wuestenberg's life; but as we know, threats are regularly perceived without being actual.

It is a feature of Wuestenberg's case that all claims about what she is feeling must be contextualized within the background of the legal and criminal justice system, within which proclamations of *fear for one's life* are regularly part of defensive strategies that hope to exculpate those who commit violent actions, legitimating them as self-defense. Of course Wuestenberg's claim about her fear must be understood as an action within this context. It goes without saying that in such systems, the claims of defendants with more privilege along racial, economic, professional, religious, and heteronormative lines are likely to be taken more seriously than the claims of those with less.[22]

If Wuestenberg would note the cause of her fear as the *life-threatening presence of the Hill family*, she has misidentified attributes of the cause. We have no reason to think the Hill family had either the will or the capacity to harm Wuestenberg. If she would understand the object of her fear as *fear of her own death at the hands of the Hill family*, she has misidentified that threat as one that is realistic. From this chapter's analysis of what fearing is, we know that Jillian Wuestenberg might accurately recognize that she is feeling fear while being wrong about the cause, object, and/or attributes of the cause and object of her fear. She might believe that she is fearing for her life, while in fact the cause and object of her fear is something else. But it is possible to interpret a different kind of actual threat that Wuestenberg might have been responding to. Imagine Wuestenberg as having something of a freestyle feeling of *fear for white life*. She mentions nothing of a fear for her physical safety on camera during the incident but makes sure to defend herself against the Hills' claims that she is ignorant and racist. Recall her calling out the window, "You cannot just walk around calling white people racist. This is not that type of world. White people aren't racist. No one's racist." In a historical moment when the violent actions and legacies of white people were being uncovered en masse in daily protests around the globe, to be called racist by a Black teenager holding a camera might well be the cause of legitimate fears. One might consider whether the fear was not that of dying at the hands of an unarmed Black family, but instead fear of a loss of supremacy—a loss of the assumed entitlement to move freely, around the world, in and out of restaurants and parking lots, with all Black people giving one the right of way.

We have seen in this chapter that individual fearers are not in every case the authority on whether what they are feeling is fear, on what has caused the fear, on what it is fear toward, or on the characteristics of those causes and objects. I am drawing attention to the fact that we need not simply take Jillian Wuestenberg's word for either what she is feeling or the causes and objects of those feelings. In fact, I think there is reason to contest Wuestenberg's claim that she feared for her life, and noted possible reinterpretations of emotion that could be considered consistent with her expression and behavior. Those who interact with her might suggest alternative reinterpretations to her, and she may or may not be receptive to them—the juridical context she is in as she awaits trial for the charge of felonious assault, and the particular force that claims of *fear for one's life* have been granted within that context, will almost certainly incline her to hold to her professed fear no matter what anyone else says. Features of our legal, political, economic, family, and personal contexts can function as gravitational forces, pulling us toward certain practices and claims of fearing, no matter who contests those practices and claims. Even if alternative understandings of what one is feeling, or of those things that are the causes or objects of one's feelings, are presented, and even if those alternative understandings seem plausible to an individual, it does not automatically follow that the person will easily take up the alternative understandings as their own. The more one has invested in a certain interpretation—*I feared for my life* or otherwise—the more difficult it may be to change it. My goal is not to defend any specific reinterpretation of her feeling. The point is, rather, to show that her claims are contestable: about what she is feeling, what caused her fear, what she is fearful of, and the characteristics of those causes and objects. Fearers can be wrong about these things. There are more and less accurate understandings of these things. Here I am speaking to all of us: coming to internalize a sense of this fallibility and of interpretations of feelings as more of a joint endeavor might reshape how we ourselves are able to understand and reinterpret our own fears in the future. Capacities for such reinterpretation may turn out to be morally and politically vital.

4. Conclusion

The question of this chapter has been, what is fearing? Philosophers of emotion from the twentieth century have helped us understand fearing as partly a relationship between fearers and things outside of the fearer—material things, other beings, events, facts, or concepts—and have helped clarify the potentially complex relationships between causes, objects, and fearing. Fearing is, in part, a response to the world—a response to causes that prompt or trigger fear and a way of relating to objects that we are afraid of, or feel fear toward. These responses have epistemic dimensions since they involve perceptions and beliefs about these causes or objects, and such beliefs may or may not accurately reflect facts about the world. Neuroscientists have helped us understand what is happening in brains and bodies during fearing and how neurological processes can shape the ways fearers relate to things, beings, events, facts, or concepts in the world. Relational theorists have helped us understand how fearing involves, in part, interpersonal expression and uptake. Fearing involves not only relations between fearers and the objects and causes of their fears but also relationships with other fearers.

I have taken up the basic question of what fearing is in this chapter because it is important that the foundational understanding of fearing be properly set if we are to understand (1) the interpersonal dynamics of fearing accurately into the coming chapters, (2) what is happening when fearing goes badly, and (3) what needs to happen if we are to fear better. We need a clear understanding of the way fearing involves causes and objects in part in order to understand the ways it can seem to a person that they are fearing X when in fact they are fearing Y. We need a clear understanding of fearing and brain function in part in order to see how fears with harmful effects can be difficult but also possible to change. We need a clear understanding of the position of other people in our fearing processes in part to begin to understand how relationships and others are involved both when our fearing goes badly and when it goes better.[23]

The first two chapters of this book have characterized fearing as something we do together—what and how we fear is complexly bound up with other fearers. In a not insignificant number of cases our fearing has dangerous and sometimes life-threatening effects on humans, other animals, and environments. As such, the ways we fear together are in need of serious consideration and change. Chapter 3 delves into questions surrounding *how we arrive at fears of perceived but not actual threats*, and chapter 4 considers the moral and political significance of actions motivated by these fears. As we will see, some of the greatest threats may in fact come from actions motivated by fears with which fearers struggle to cope. Fortunately, chapter 5 argues these outcomes are not inevitable.

3
Compelling Fears

As we have seen, fears are pervasive and more complicated than we may have thought. Our processes of identifying and expressing our own fears are shaped by the realities of living in a world with other fearers. As we saw in chapter 1, many individuals experience deep-seated fears of fundamentally unmanageable threats—for instance, fears of an inability to ensure that loved ones will always be safe, or fears of an incapacity to control future events in general. These are sensible fears that reflect accurate, albeit difficult, perceptions of the world. Individuals cannot sufficiently mitigate or manage these threats to the point of no longer needing to fear them.

This chapter turns to one of the major contentions of the book—the threats that individuals perceive as needing to be addressed may not be the actual sources of their feelings of fear but rather substitutes or proxies. We saw in chapter 2 that individuals can be mistaken about the causes and/or objects of their fears. I might believe the cause of my fear is the person on the street who might mug me while in fact the cause of my fear is that I am underslept and overcaffeinated. While we've seen *that* fearers can be wrong about the cause or object of their fears, more remains to be said about *why* and *how* these mistakes happen. Why and how do fearers come to mistake the causes and objects of their fears? Why see the person on the street as the cause of my fear rather than something else? What conditions might make such a mistake likely at all?

Before proceeding, recall the discussion in chapter 2 of how, in some cases, individuals feel fear and have no trouble identifying the threat that has caused them to feel fear: I see a snake, I feel afraid, I describe my experience as *fear of the snake*. But recall that experiences and expressions of fear are not always so straightforward. This chapter delves more deeply into complex instances where an individual feels, and accurately expresses feeling, fearful but fails to accurately identify what has caused their fear.

Following the discussion in section 1 of a number of examples of fears of nonstatistical threats, in section 2, we survey accounts of the culture of fear from theorists who suggest that many individuals, and many North Americans especially, have come to fear too much or to fear the wrong things. Although these theorists in many cases accurately identify problematic manipulations of fearers, I will suggest that their accounts share a problem: they do not consider sufficiently the deeper experiences of fear that come to be expressed in fears of nonstatistical threats, and they do not consider why individuals might be so prone to manipulation of their fears.

Turning to accounts of displacement in the psychoanalytic literature, I suggest in section 3 that in some cases, nonstatistical threats come to serve as proxies for what individuals actually fear most: the great, unmanageable threats we have discussed. I examine how the threats that become such proxies are often suitable alternatives because they are more *manageable* than the great threats described above, such as the threat of an unpredictable future or of an incapacity to protect loved ones. The process of displacement is rarely done deliberately or with awareness but is rather something that happens swiftly and without the consciousness of the fearful individual. Even so, the process raises complex questions of responsibility—though individuals may not displace their fears deliberately, I will argue in chapters 4 and 5 that they can be responsible for the effects of doing so, particularly since such displacement can have serious implications for those beings and entities who are most commonly perceived as substitute threats. I conclude this chapter by contending in section 4 that the process of coming to fear proxy threats is more relational than psychoanalytic accounts of displacement suggest: fears of great threats are not merely ones individual agents displace on their own. We would do better to understand fears of great threats as ones agents *compel*: working together, we push these fears away.

1. Nonstatistical Threats

Recall from chapter 1 that the list of fears held by North Americans is long. Yet some of the most common fears are of things that, statistically speaking, do not pose great risks. We discussed fears of a number of nonstatistical threats: poisoned Halloween candy, road rage, and violent actions against white people by Black men, to name a few.

The number and variety of unfounded fears surrounding the safety and well-being of children should not surprise us since protection of the most vulnerable is a natural concern of responsible adults. We see high levels of fear of kidnapping (when in fact children are more likely to be injured or killed by family members) and fears of video game playing (when a much greater predictor of violent behavior among teens is the accessibility of guns). Yet it would seem that the high stakes of the need to keep children safe can compromise individuals' judgments about what in fact presents the greatest threat to children.

In *Small Animals: Parenting in the Age of Fear*, Kim Brooks (2018, x) examines what the rise of fearful parenting tells us about our children, our communities, and ourselves. In 2011, during a visit to her parents in Virginia, Brooks took her four-year-old to a Target store, to replace a pair of lost headphones for him to use on their plane ride home. In a rush, and judging it safe to do so, Brooks left Felix in the (locked and alarmed) car. It was a mild March day, and with the windows cracked open, it was not too hot to sit in the car. During the five minutes it took her to run into the store and buy the headphones, someone in the parking lot videotaped her leaving Felix alone and called the police. When she arrived back in Chicago later that day, the police had already contacted her to let her know that they would be investigating and potentially charging her with a crime. After two years of limbo, Brooks was ultimately charged with "contributing to the delinquency of a minor" and required to serve one hundred hours of community service and to complete twenty hours of parenting classes. Her book unpacks this experience, and the broader context of how fear and anxiety are interwoven with parenting in the contemporary United States. In the process, she interviews parenting experts, historians, and psychologists whose research focuses on risk perception. She considers the various dimensions of societal pressure and anxiety involved in her own experience of pregnancy and parenting, focusing throughout on a longing to control and protect that expresses itself in parenting contexts. As Brooks describes her experience of early parenthood,

> My days and nights were taken up with protecting my little one from the realities of modern life: its cars; its germs; its hordes of nameless strangers; its overcrowded, impersonal public schools; its processed, sugary foods; its sharp or electrical objects and addictive, digital screens. . . . Were their bodies healthy enough, their minds well nourished, their bedrooms tidy and inviting? Was I cautious enough, protective enough, doing everything in my power to keep them safe? (Brooks 2018, 65–66)

Predictably, the task of protecting children takes a particular toll on mothers, who in two-parent heterosexual households, even with both parents working outside the home, are still by and large the chief caregivers. As Brooks understands it, much of the labor of parenting involves the emotional work of fearing:

> Mothers don't often die of fear. What happens, I think, far more often, is that we simply, slowly disappear. We become something less than we thought we'd be. We see things less clearly, experience things less intensely; as fear expands, the world recedes. The more minutiae a mother has to worry about, the more unlikely disasters she's charged with preventing through her infinite maternal wisdom and foresight, the less mental, emotional, intellectual, and spiritual energy she has for herself, her work, her community. (Brooks 2018, 179–80)

On Brooks's account, an excessive focus on individualized choice and an accompanying false sense of control are integral to the experience of parenting. As she puts it,

> Even before I became a parent, my notions of what it meant *to be a parent*, that this was a fundamentally anxious endeavor that required planning and control at every level, were so deeply ingrained. . . .

... Whether the issue was childbirth or childcare, parenting style or safety protocols, I remained fixated on making the right choice for my children. It was only much later that I began to see how profoundly the choosing itself—the false sense of control and entitlement that choosing entails—had affected my experience as a mother. (Brooks 2018, 47, 54–55)

While relatable, the fearing labor of parents is not reflective of the levels of statistical risk their children face. Lenore Skenazy, creator of Free-Range Kids and Let Grow, two organizations devoted to advocating against overprotective parenting, writes,

The more safe our children became, the more we started to worry about them, because now if anything dangerous did happen to them, it would clearly be our fault.... It is this belief in control combined with the fear of screwing up that is driving us mad. (Skenazy 2009, 97)[1]

Many parental fears for children are a prime example of fears of nonstatistical threats. Children are not as regularly threatened as many parents continue to fear they are.

Fears of nonstatistical threats are also commonplace in many current discussions of migration. Fears of migrants are often articulated in nationalistic, populist rhetoric and policy. We see the rise of such discourse during and following the 2016 Brexit campaign for the United Kingdom to leave the European Union, and in the United States particularly during the 2016 and 2020 presidential campaigns and elections. Discussions of migration in the US context demonstrate deep-seated fear and anti-immigrant anxiety directed against not all migrants but primarily those who are racialized and seen as poor. These fears are not new. As Peter Kwong (2010, 255) wrote over a decade ago, "Anti-immigrant rage in the United States these days is focused mainly on Mexicans who enter the country illegally. In the current post–civil rights era, instead of being portrayed as inferior and unwanted, they are accused of parasitism on our already limited public social welfare and educational resources." Campaigning for the 2016 US presidential election, Donald Trump famously promised to "build a wall" along the southern border of the country to keep such migrants out. Congress subsequently refused to fund that project, and in response, Trump's administration shut down the government for the longest period in US history. All of this occurred despite the fact that the United States is a low-immigration nation.[2] Nonetheless, in nationalist discourse, migrants continue to be cast as unwelcome intruders and parasites, and as posing significant threats to citizens.

Commonly cited concerns about migrants in the United States include fears that they will take nonmigrants' jobs, that they will burden a country's welfare system, and that they will commit violent crimes and property theft.[3] None of these are accurate perceptions of migrants (Budiman 2020). In fact, migrants have been shown not to affect nonmigrant employment in the short term and to *spur* the growth of such employment in the long term. As Amelie Constant (2014) summarizes national labor statistics from North American and European countries,

> Migrants choose locations with available jobs and fill labor shortages. . . . Migrants often complement native workers or accept jobs that natives don't want or can't do. They create new jobs by increasing production, engaging in self-employment, and easing upward job mobility for native workers. The presence of immigrants increases demand and can spur new businesses to open, creating more jobs for immigrant and native populations.

Internationally, migrants have also been shown to receive less welfare than nonmigrants (Giuletti 2014). In the US context, not only are legal immigrants not eligible for welfare programs immediately (or sometimes ever), but it is also true that "immigrant households in poverty consume less welfare than [US-born] households in poverty."[4] Furthermore, neither documented nor undocumented immigration in the United States has been shown to increase crime.[5] Neither rates of violent crimes nor rates of property crimes have been increased by the presence of migrants; in fact, "many studies have established that immigrants commit crimes at consistently lower rates than native-born Americans."[6] So, although migrants are often cited as threats to US-born individuals' security in job markets, welfare systems, and neighborhoods, the facts support none of these perceptions. Migrants are statistically very low threats, and yet many citizens continue to fear them.[7]

The cases of parenting and migrants are just two of many areas where people regularly fear things that pose little or no threat to them. Chapter 1 presented numerous examples of how individuals regularly fear beings and things that pose little statistical threat to them. We know that perceived threats are not always actual threats. To be sure, some fears may be based on misunderstandings of the facts and in such cases might be alleviated by simply coming to learn that something is not in fact threatening. But as we saw in chapter 1, the epistemic dimensions of fear are complicated, and in some cases, individuals may continue to fear that thing even after learning that it poses little or no threat to them.

What explains the origin and persistence of these fears of things that do not threaten us? One set of plausible explanations is that fearers are manipulated by others who have an interest in the generation or maintenance of such fear. Though we will ultimately need to complicate such explanations, I will first survey some accounts that make the case for the central role of politically motivated manipulation in generating fear of nonstatistical threats.

2. Know Better, Fear Less

One explanation for the persistence of fears of nonstatistical threats is that such fears are the result of deliberate efforts on the part of forces who benefit from a broad base of fear in the population. Consider, for instance, how fear of violent crime in residents of family neighborhoods can benefit home security companies who profit from selling alarm systems, corrections corporations that make money from the existence and growth of prisons, or prospective authoritarian governments that may benefit from keeping citizens fearful of life without powerful rulers. Though morally suspect, it would clearly be in the financial and political interests of these companies, corporations, and governments to create or support conditions where such fears arise and persist.

Working with these themes, a number of authors have contributed to a growing literature about the *culture of fear*, focusing on the way populations are led to fear perceived threats that should not in fact seem so threatening. I will very briefly survey accounts from Barry Glassner, Corey Robin, Naomi Klein, and Sasha Lilley to give a sense of this literature here. While the political commitments and specifics of their accounts vary, all these theorists aim to show that by coming to fear particular (non)threats, populations can be influenced by governments, political parties, and corporate agents who stand to gain from their manipulated fears. Part of the goal of each of these accounts is to intervene in the process of manipulation and, by drawing attention to the large patterns of manipulated fears, to help agents come to recognize the ways they may have been manipulated. We might therefore think of these as "know better, fear less" models: they have the goal of raising awareness about manipulated fears, helping agents and communities know better, and thereby hopefully helping them fear less.

Recall the chapter 1 discussion of Barry Glassner's *The Culture of Fear: Why Americans Are Afraid of the Wrong Things*; there we saw that in many cases, individuals fear things that are nonstatistical threats to them. We focused on the content and psychological character of these fears rather than on what external influences may have shaped them. Glassner argues that individuals are regularly manipulated toward focusing on certain threats as part of attempts to redirect their attention away from others. For instance, Glassner reads fears of illegal drug use and the buying and selling of illicit drugs as the result of a coordinated effort of media, political organizations, and others, motivated by financial and political interests. As he writes,

> Scares about heroin, cocaine, and marijuana issue forth continually from politicians and journalists. But except for burps when a celebrity overdoses, they have been largely silent about the abuse of legal drugs....
>
> As a sociologist I see the crack panic of the 1980s as a variation on an American tradition. At different times in our history drug scares have served to displace a class of brutalized citizens from the nation's moral conscience....

Drug scares are promoted primarily by three means: presidential proclamations, selective statistics, and poster children. The first two posit a terrifying new trend, the last gives it a human face. (Glassner 1999, 132, 135, 143)

Glassner considers a number of other cases of fears being manipulated for political reasons; for instance, following mass shootings, fears are directed toward any number of explanations (e.g., violent video games, mental illness) and away from the obvious actual threat of the availability and proliferation of guns. This manipulation is clearly motivated in part by political parties' desire for support and endorsements from pro-gun groups like the National Rifle Association. Glassner notes other politically motivated manipulations of fears about hip-hop motivated by pro-police and pro-incarceration politics (121–27), and fears about teen mothers of color motivated by anti-immigrant and anti-welfare politics (87–95).[8] Financially motivated political manipulation is the central explanation Glassner gives for the prevalence of these and other misplaced fears in US society. As he summarizes, "The short answer to why Americans harbor so many misbegotten fears is that immense power and money await those who tap into our moral insecurities and supply us with symbolic substitutes" (xxviii).[9]

Glassner suggests there is a coordinated effort to convince individuals who might otherwise identify a broad social problem—like mass layoffs or lack of social safety nets—to *neurologize* the problem, coming instead to see it as a failure of individuals. One example he gives is a tendency for workers to express fears of workplace violence (which is in fact a very low statistical threat; see Glassner [1999, 27]) instead of fearing the much more significant threat of insecure employment. As he writes, "Given that workplace violence is far from pandemic, why were journalists so inclined to write about it? Perhaps because workplace violence is a way of talking about the precariousness of employment without directly confronting what primarily put workers at risk—the endless waves of corporate layoffs that began in the early 1980s" (Glassner 1999, 28). Similarly, the interwoven society-level problems of high housing prices in urban centers, extended work hours, long commutes, and failing transportation infrastructure becomes boiled down to a perceived threat at the level of individuals: road rage. Glassner points out that these manipulations of fears mean that, by and large, the greatest threats—poverty and income inequality—go underdiscussed.

In a similar vein, Corey Robin (2004, 16) has detailed cases where fear is used by political leaders or activists to help them pursue particular goals or gain support for their positions. Robin distinguishes two ways political fear can be used. The first way has an outward focus: uniting a populace against an *external* being or thing they should fear. As he explains, "Leaders or militants can define what is or ought to be the public's chief object of fear" (16). He gives the example of how in 2001 the Bush administration in the United States shaped the focus on anthrax as a major external threat, looking for signs of the attack originating in the Middle East (especially Iraq), in support of their existing military goals. The second way fear can be used focuses *inward*: politicians or activists manipulate fears arising from existing social, political, and economic hierarchies within a population (Robin 2004, 18). The purpose of this fear is "internal intimidation, to use sanctions or the threat of sanctions to ensure that one group retains or augments its power at the expense of another" (18). Robin argues that the most significant political fear in the current US context is of the second variety, and in particular involves

> fear among the less powerful of the more powerful, whether public officials or private employers, far-off agents of state or local, familiar elites. . . . This kind of fear is repressive, constraining the actions of the less powerful, enabling the actions of the more powerful. It ensures that the less powerful abide by the express or implied wishes of their supervisors, or merely do nothing to challenge or undermine the existing distribution of power. (Robin 2004, 20)

On Robin's view, fear is regularly used as a tool to ensure the compliance of less powerful groups within a population.

Further developing an account of politicized uses of fear for capitalist development, in *The Shock Doctrine*, Naomi Klein has described a specific way fear is used: when a perceived or actual crisis occurs, political forces seize upon a community's fear in that moment to implement free-market ideas (e.g., privatizing school systems and scaling back regulations on industry). On Klein's account, this strategy is repeated again and again in capitalist contexts: "waiting for a major crisis, then selling off pieces of the state to private players while citizens were still reeling from the shock, then quickly making the 'reforms' permanent" (N. Klein 2007, 7). The changes must happen quickly, while a population is still in shock; the six to nine months of a (perceived) crisis are the ideal time frame (7). She continues:

> That is how the shock doctrine works: the original disaster—the coup, the terrorist attack, the market meltdown, the war, the tsunami, the hurricane—puts the entire population into a state of collective shock. The falling bombs, the bursts of terror, the pounding winds serve to soften up whole societies as much as the blaring music and blows in the torture cells soften up prisoners. Like the terrorized prisoner who gives up the names of comrades and renounces his faith, shocked societies often give up things they would otherwise fiercely protect. (N. Klein 2007, 20)

As Klein describes it, the shock prompted in part in some circumstances by trauma and terror (e.g., the trauma of Hurricane Katrina in the United States) is what facilitates a kind of openness to political shifts that would otherwise be strongly resisted. In the words of Milton Friedman, the speed and suddenness of crises can "provoke psychological reactions in the public that 'facilitate the adjustment'" (N. Klein 2007, 8).

Klein's shock doctrine account has opened up the space for further understanding the political manipulations of fear, which have since been tracked as part of deliberate strategy especially for rightwing political actors. Sasha Lilley and her co-authors (Lilley et al. 2012) have developed a critique of the manipulation of fears in their accounts of *catastrophism*: a presumption that "society is headed for a collapse, whether economic, ecological, social, or spiritual" and an accompanying belief "that an ever-intensified rhetoric of disaster will awaken the masses from their long slumber" (Lilley 2012a, 1). As Lilley explains, the deliberate cultivation of fear is a standard tactic of the political right:

> The strategy of tension is a hallmark of the far right: sowing fear among the public to elicit a general clamor for law, order, security, and a strong authoritarian state to take matters in hand.... By intensifying paranoia and division about immigrants, welfare, external and internal security threats, fiscal crises, morality, and minorities, the organized right works to generate a climate in which the state can "react" to various supposed crises. Indeed, the right often succeeds in generating genuine political crises through agitation and propaganda alone. Border security is just one example where agitation from the right has contributed to the state's militarization of the U.S.-Mexico border, and the growth of a massive internal security apparatus. (Lilley 2012b, 68)

While Lilley makes the case for fear as a hallmark of the far right, she notes that catastrophism can be found anywhere on the political spectrum. The impulse to convince a group that their situation is so dire as to require urgent action toward some change is not unique to conservatives, but she argues that it is most useful in the context of their purposes.

> Whether green, radical, or reactionary, catastrophists tend to believe fear will stir the populace to action. They emphasize panic and powerlessness, and conversely the vanguardist politics of the few. The politics of fear, however, play to the strengths of the right, not the left.... On the terrain of catastrophic fear, the left is not likely to win. (Lilley 2012a, 3)

As we can see, what these "culture of fear" accounts share is an identification of how fear can be a tool used by political or economic forces in advancing their interests. Glassner focuses on the manipulation of populations to fear nonthreats as redirection of attention away from substantial social problems. Robin examines the ways fears are deliberately deployed to unite populations against external or internal threats in a society. Klein develops the shock doctrine account of how moments of crisis are capitalized on by those who will benefit from the implementation of free market ideas. And Lilley and her co-authors (2012) establish the ways in which crises and fear are deliberately generated and/or magnified by right-wing groups who then steer communities toward supporting authoritarian state actions. All of these analyses seem to me accurate representations of the ways fears can be mobilized for dangerous political purposes. I agree with Glassner, Robin, Klein, and Lilley that we are surrounded by influences (corporate, media, state, and otherwise) that redirect and focus our fears in ways that will benefit them. There is no doubt that fear can be deliberately cultivated in populations and that such fear can be useful in profiting industries, state agents, or others. What concerns me about these accounts, however, is that none prioritizes questioning what makes populations vulnerable to feeling fearful and having manipulatable fears in the first place.

Each of these accounts draws attention to how fears are used as tools, in part from the hope that raising awareness will help fearers fear less. But without knowing what makes agents who are vulnerable to having fears prone to redirection in the first place, we are missing an important part of the picture and will not know best how to help individuals and communities prevent or address these misplaced fears.

Moving forward, a central contention of mine will be this: Glassner, Robin, Lilley, and Klein fail to attend to how individuals are vulnerable to coming to fear too much or to fear the wrong things in part because such individuals come to displace their legitimate fears of the great, unmanageable threats onto fears of lesser, much more manageable perceived threats like migrants or poisoned Halloween candy. These fears of nonstatistical threats have not appeared out of nowhere. They are in many cases expressions of deeper, underlying, legitimate fears. Missing in these authors' explanations is attention to the persistent, existing fears that are the raw material that can be deliberately or nondeliberately shifted onto such beings or things as serve various purposes.

Importantly, if manipulated fears are often expressions of fears of the great threats we have discussed, it seems unlikely that simply helping agents come to recognize the manipulative processes underlying their fears will be sufficient to make them less fearful. The "know better, fear less" models will not likely succeed in helping people fear less. Gaining awareness may help agents feel differently—for example, to stop being afraid of poisoned Halloween candy—but the feelings of fear may persist and land (or be deliberately manipulated toward landing) elsewhere. Recall our earlier discussions of Gendler's account of alief and Calhoun's account of background cognitive sets: a person may *believe* that being up on a tall bridge is not threatening while still fearing being up on the bridge as a result of their background cognitive set/interpretive framework. In short, while I agree that fears are often manipulated and that such manipulations can have dangerous political effects and should be addressed in communities, there is a more complex psychological story to tell about how to respond to such fears. Properly understanding the pervasive phenomenon of fears of nonstatistical threats will require understanding that there were fears of great and legitimate threats there to manipulate in the first place. Simply pointing to fears of nonstatistical threats as problematic, as these theorists mostly do, will not address the depth of the problem.

3. Displacement

The central question of this chapter is, how do people come to fear nonstatistical threats—in other words, how do we come to see as critical threats things that are not critical threats?

We have established (section 1) that there are many cases where the perceived threats people report being afraid of are not actual threats, and that (section 2) a number of political theorists point toward external manipulation as the driving force behind our coming to believe nonthreats to be threats. That seems to be part of the picture. But while these accounts of external forces largely reach the conclusion that many of our fears are unjustified, and therefore that we ought not to fear the things we have been manipulated to fear, I now want to reapproach the question of why we persistently fear nonthreatening things.

To begin, recall from the chapter 1 discussion that there are some great, deep-seated fears that, while not necessarily universal, are common to many of us. The facts of our relationality—that is, the fact that our lives are materially created and sustained by the lives of so many others, such that all humans are dependent on, and depended on by, many other humans—mean that potential loss of, or threats to, those foundational relationships are objects of serious fear. The potential for these devastating losses and threats is always *there*.

The persistence and unmanageability of these fears is difficult for many people to cope with. And yet, we need to manage these fears somehow to be able to continue in our day-to-day lives. If we do not find a way to manage them, they may overtake us and make us unable to meet our most basic responsibilities. How can we relate to these fears?

While eventually (chapter 5) I will suggest that more productive relational practices of fearing together are possible, for now I want to suggest that a common coping mechanism involves (largely unconsciously) displacing our great fears onto fears of more manageable perceived threats, which we can then attempt to control in a way that relieves us of the feeling of being pinned under and overtaken by the great fears of loss, suffering, and failure. Psychoanalytic approaches have understood this process as a kind of *displacement*. A brief primer on psychoanalytic understandings of displacement will therefore be helpful as we proceed.

Displacement is one of a number of defense mechanisms described early on by Freud, involving a process of displacing emotional energy from one thing onto another.[10] Various kinds of emotional energy can get displaced: love, desire, anxiety, fear, and other kinds of emotions can be at play.[11] Early writings from Freud discuss displacement primarily in the context of dreams (*Interpretation of Dreams*; *New Introductory Lectures on Psychoanalysis*, Revision of the Theory of Dreams Lecture) and then soon after focus in particular on how anxieties about one thing can come to be expressed as anxieties about another thing (*New Introductory Lectures on Psychoanalysis*, Anxiety and Instinctual Life Lecture). In the context of anxiety, Freud discusses phobias as commonly involving the displacement of a fear of an internal process (e.g., the expression of sexual desire) onto an external thing. He writes, "Suppose that the agoraphobic patient is invariably afraid of feelings of temptation that are aroused in him by meeting people in the street. In his phobia he brings about a displacement and henceforward is afraid of an external situation. . . . One can save oneself from an external danger by flight; fleeing from an internal danger is a difficult enterprise" (Freud 1965, 84). On a basic reading of Freud's early view of mental activity, psychic energy is regularly transferred across ideas. For instance, a person might have a wish to do something that cannot be straightforwardly expressed given social norms and prohibitions. Having the wish therefore triggers anxiety, which disrupts the experience of it. On Freud's view, the wish to do the thing does not simply dissipate but instead is transferred onto associated ideas, which can be experienced in dreams or thoughts. This mechanism works without the person consciously intending it. Displacement can thus occur, for instance, in cases where one experiences desires that cannot be straightforwardly expressed, as in the case of sexual fetishes (Freud 1968).

A classic Freudian case illustrates how Freud thinks displacement works. In *Inhibitions, Symptoms and Anxiety*, Freud discusses the case of a five-year-old, Hans, who was so afraid of horses, and so afraid in particular that a horse would bite him, that he didn't want to leave the house (Freud 1952, 724). Hans was reported to have expressed some fantasies that would indicate incestuous desires for his mother, common (on Freud's view) in boys of his age, thus giving reason to believe his father would be angry with him. On Freud's Oedipal reading, Hans's phobia of horses is merely a symptom of his inability to cope with a more fundamental danger: his fear of castration by his father, as punishment for his expression of desires for his mother. His fear that his father would attack him is too great and constant to live with, and as such becomes reversed as a hostility toward his father. Hans's father used to play horses with him, explaining Hans's association of horses with his father. And, Freud thinks, Hans's neurosis replaces and displaced his father by a horse, but it is further complicated because instead of developing an inclination to hurt horses (as replacement for his father, whom he feels aggression toward), Hans *fears* horses. Freud reads this as Hans's feelings of hostility having been reversed: "Instead of aggressiveness towards the father there appeared aggressiveness from the father in the shape of revenge" (Freud 1952, 726). Freud uses the Hans case as an example of an "anxiety defense" form of displacement: a situation of instinctual danger occurs (in this case, the boy's belief of a castration threat), and because an individual is unable to cope with the danger, the situation incites an *anxiety reaction* that removes the ego from danger by creating *symptoms* (in this case, the horse phobia) that redirect the individual's attention and efforts. Once the symptom is created, all the boy must do is avoid the object of his phobia: horses. While doing so is not without difficulty in the early 1900s, living as he did across from an inn with stables, it is more possible than avoiding the constant and unbearable threat of one of his parents wanting to hurt him.

Before I say what I hope to learn from this interpretation of the Hans case, we need to note a number of serious concerns with Freud's approach. Even before the now widespread feminist criticisms, psychoanalytic and especially Freudian approaches were criticized by analysts themselves, in particular for their phallocentrism, sexism, and gender binarism. Many theorists of analysis have rejected major components of such views: the obsession with penises and castration, the patriarchal assumptions about the power of men/fathers and the deficiencies of women/mothers, the superiority of masculinity over femininity, and the underlying assumption of a gender binary, to name a few.[12] Emily Zakin notes that psychoanalytic and feminist theories can form an "uneasy alliance":

> In developing a theory of the drives and the non-rational forces that move and impel us, the idea that we are opaque rather than transparent to ourselves, incapable of complete self-knowledge or self-mastery, psychoanalytic theory also challenges the rationalist, humanist ego and proposes that our ethical characters and political communities are not perfectable, exposing the precariousness of both psychic and political identity. The unconscious cannot be assumed to be inherently either a transgressive or a conservative force, but an unreliable one, promoting revolt or rebellion sometimes, intransigence and rigid border preservation at other times. (Zakin 2011)

Beyond the many general concerns we ought to have about Freud's approach, the Hans case is analytically peculiar: it was a very early case (in 1909) for Freud, before he had even articulated his view of infant sexuality; Freud did not, as a matter of practice, work with children; he reportedly saw Hans only once; and the story is made even stranger by the history of direct communications between Hans's father and Freud. I raise the case here only because if we can set the specifics aside, it is illustrative of a simple structure of displacement. While there are many things not to like about Freud's approach, psychoanalytic attention to the complexities of unconscious emotional processes, and to the varieties of defense mechanisms in particular, is helpful for understanding why people might be unable to straightforwardly recognize and name their great, unmanageable fears, and why they might instead unconsciously displace them onto more controllable perceived threats.

On Freud's reading, Hans has a great fear, which cannot be coped with (fear of the idea of castration by his father). The fear remains and is displaced onto a more manageable object (a fear of the idea of being bitten by a horse). It is then possible for Hans to feel some relief from his fear, inasmuch as he can control his contact with horses. As Sara Ahmed clarifies,

> Freud argues that this fear is itself a symptom that has been "put in the place" of another fear, one that much more profoundly threatens the ego: the fear of castration as a fear of the father. Hans can "manage" his fear of horses through avoidance, in a way in which he could not manage his fear of the father. . . . The affect of fear is sustained, or is even intensified, through the displacement between objects. (Ahmed 2004, 66)

This account of displacement has been elaborated, detailed, and challenged by Freud and many others. I want to suggest now that many of our expressions of fears of perceived threats are instances of displacement.

Psychoanalytic readings of fear help us understand how we may separate ourselves from unbearable fears by unconsciously displacing them onto other objects and then controlling them. Of course, in some cases, people simply experience great fears without displacing them onto more manageable perceived threats, or simply experience justified or unjustified fears of more everyday perceived threats. Displacement is not always part of processes of fear. But in many of the cases that interest me (e.g., fear of the action of leaving a child in a car for five minutes, fear of migrants), a person may have an emotional experience that is unbearable, not because it cannot be expressed in the context of social norms and prohibitions but because it is so great a fear that both acknowledging its potential and nonetheless going about one's daily life seem impossible. The struggle to cope with the fear disrupts the experience of it. The fear does not simply dissipate but is instead displaced onto associated fears, which *can* be coped with by means of beliefs and actions because they are fears of perceived threats that can to some extent be eliminated or managed (unlike the great threats of loss and failure themselves, which, as described above, are persistent and unmanageable). Displacement happens without the person consciously intending it. It gives indirect expression to the great fears and thereby relieves pressure for needing to cope with them. Everyday life requires some degree of trust and confidence that the world will support rather than constantly threaten oneself and one's loved ones. The fear of loss is too great to bear openly while at the same time acting in the world, but the fear persists, so it becomes redirected, and individuals come to believe some proxy threat is the actual source of their fear.

The psychoanalytic account of displacing fears helps identify how the fears agents express and the things agents identify as being threatening can be expressive—not of a fear of that particular threat but instead of an experience of a deeper fear that is difficult or impossible to recognize or express, perhaps because it is a fear of such a significant threat that an agent does not know how they would survive if the fear were realized (e.g., the loss of a loved one). In reflecting on the Hans case, Ahmed (2004, 66–67) describes something similar as a "sideways" movement where objects of fear become substituted for each other. As we will see going forward, any number of proxy threats might become the object of the displaced fear: the feature they all share is that, unlike the great threats that cannot be managed or extinguished, the proxy threats are things, beings, or phenomena that individuals can in some sense *control*. They are real people, things, or eventualities that are more limited than the great threats, and they can therefore be removed, escaped, destroyed, assimilated, or overpowered. I discuss these common strategies for controlling perceived, substitute threats at length in chapter 4. For now, the point is only to note that I agree with psychoanalytic accounts that the basic psychological mechanism of displacement is functioning in many cases of fear: it allows individuals to displace their great, unmanageable fears of loss or failure onto these more manageable proxy threats and thereby unconsciously attempt to find some relief. As we will see, even when an individual comes to understand that she is living in a time and place with lower rates of violent crime than ever before, or with access to better vaccine technology than anyone before her, *she may still feel fearful of being attacked or giving vaccines to her children*. If such fears are stand-ins for deeper, more unmanageable fears, it can make sense that the feeling of fear would persist, even when reasons to fear these things are dispensed with.

In the case of displacement, the mechanism typically works without the awareness or consciousness of the individual experiencing it. In most of the cases I have described, if it were suggested to someone who has displaced a great fear onto a proxy (non)threat that what they are feeling is a product of this process rather than a response to a genuine threat, the suggestion would offend them. They would typically believe themselves to be responding directly to an actual threat: irresponsible parents, migrants, and so on. But it is important to pause for two considerations here: first, it is at least possible that individuals may in some cases be aware, at least to some degree, that displacement is currently happening while still experiencing the displacement of fears and the full force of its effects. They might even be able to name and describe what is happening (e.g., *I am feeling afraid of _____ not because it is an actual threat, but because I am actually afraid of _____*) while still genuinely feeling fear of the proxy threat as the primary experience. For instance, to take an example that will be discussed at greater length later, imagine I feel genuinely fearful of sex offenders living in my neighborhood. Perhaps I am accurately aware that they do not pose a direct threat to myself or my loved ones, and perhaps I am even able to recognize that I am fearing them as a proxy for great fears of my inability to fully protect my loved ones from harm. Yet my primary experience is still of profound fear of sex offenders in my neighborhood, and I am inclined to do whatever I can to prevent them from being able to live there. This is a case where displacement occurs at the same time as, and in spite of, my awareness. And in other cases, if not in the moment itself, the fact of displacement might later be brought to consciousness. Individuals can come to be aware later of having displaced a great fear onto another, more manageable threat. So although displacement more commonly happens unconsciously, one might be or become aware of one's experience of displacement without thereby overriding or ending the process.[13]

The psychoanalytic account of displacement can thus help us understand why "know better, fear less" models do not fully account for the complexities of fears of many nonstatistical threats. If such fears are in fact displaced by fears of more substantial, actual threats that cannot be fully prevented, then they are one part of an understandable coping mechanism. If, as I will argue in the next chapters, these displaced fears of nonstatistical threats are morally and politically troublesome (e.g., by motivating harmful actions toward the perceived threats), then agents might have a responsibility to work toward alternative ways of coping with their fears of the substantial, actual threats. I will suggest in chapter 5 that such alternatives do exist. But without understanding and addressing the deeper underlying fears, the "know better, fear less" models are not likely to succeed in preventing the harmful effects of displaced fears. These models are treating symptoms without addressing the underlying condition.

While the psychoanalytic account of displacement clarifies a number of significant features of these troublesome processes of attempting to cope with fears of great threats, I suggest that it fails to capture some of the complexities of these processes. Specifically, these coping processes are more deeply relational than psychoanalytic models suggest.

4. Compelling Fears

Even though its nonconscious character might make displacement appear to be a solitary process—one that an individual experiences alone—in fact, like all modes of fearing, it is unavoidably relational. Recall that Glassner, Robin, Klein, and Lilley focused on the role of external influences in what we come to fear, highlighting the role of politicians, political organizations, and media in deliberately swaying our attention toward particular threats. I agree that these can be significant influences in our processes of displacing fears onto proxy objects. More interesting for my purposes than any of these influences, however, is the role others within our personal spheres can play in the fearing process: partners, parents, family members, friends, coworkers, and acquaintances. Recall that I argued in chapters 1 and 2 that all parts of fearing processes—our practices of observing and perceiving threats, feeling fearful, and identifying and reporting our feelings of fear—are thoroughly relational. I now want to add that processes of *displacing* fears are also more relational than psychoanalytic approaches articulate: the particular proxy threats onto which our fears are displaced, our experiences of coming to fear proxy threats, and our experiences of expressing and responding to others' fears of proxy threats are all aspects of the fearing process that are made possible and thoroughly shaped by the involvement of other people. I will outline the relational dynamics of all these parts of the process before suggesting the need for different terminology to better reflect the ways we displace fears together.

A. Fears of Proxy Threats Are Relationally Acquired

What determines the particular objects onto which individuals' fears are displaced? In other words, why are these great fears displaced *onto the specific beings or things they are*, rather than some other beings or things? Recall that in Hans's case, Freud explains why it is *horses* that Hans's fear is displaced onto, rather than tigers or bathtubs or a bigfoot in the basement. Freud's explanation references both Hans's unique psychology and deeper symbolic meanings: Hans sees horses regularly, his father often played horses with him, and horses are not uncommonly substituted as a symbol of powerful masculine sexual and aggressive urges. So it is not an accident that Hans's deeper fear is expressed toward horses. Why is it, then, that in the cases above (fear of children being left alone in a car, fear of migrants taking jobs), *these* rather than other things become the objects onto which great fears are displaced?

One part of the answer is that the objects might have been otherwise—it needn't always be these exact things, so long as there is *some* being or thing that fills the role of the proxy threat, and so long as that being or thing can, at least to some extent, be controlled. At different points in one's life the most salient proxy threat is likely to be different—as a child, I might displace great fears onto a fear of large animals. Later, as a parent of young children, I might displace great fears onto the perceived threat of kidnappers. Later still, as an elder, I might displace such fears onto the perceived threat of random street violence. None of these might be probable threats in actuality, but they may seem threatening to varying degrees at different times in my life. In some cases, a number of manageable threats might serve equally well as a proxy threat in the process of displacement. Think of displacement as involving multiple realizability: just as for Hans, a number of things other than horses might have stood in as proxy threats in the expression of fear that was really fear of his father, so too in other cases of great threats, many other objects might stand in. The point is that *something* often does, and, as I will argue in chapter 4, such proxies share the feature of being to some degree controllable: they can be removed, escaped, destroyed, assimilated, or overpowered.

Another part of the answer to the question of why *these* particular proxy threats are feared is that the particular proxy threats that occur to a person as most salient will depend on a person's particular life circumstances and social position and will vary across social identities. As discussed in chapter 1, one's race and gender affect what one is likely to fear. Women are more likely to fear being attacked on the street than men (Valentine 1989, 385), though they are statistically less likely than men to be attacked by strangers (Timrots and Rand 1987). This fear is not an accident: women and girls are socially conditioned to see our bodies as vulnerable and in need of protection (Young 1980).

A further part of the explanation for which particular proxy threats get the attention of fearers is that fearers are suggestible and ideas of possible threats are widely available. We saw awareness of this suggestibility in the "culture of fear" literature discussed in section 2. I agree with Glassner, Robin, Lilley, and Klein that media sources and political campaigns are effective communicators of many possible threats. I would add that many more ideas of possible threats are made available simply by means of our relationships with other fearers.

What our great fears are is shaped by the position of others in our lives, both because, as described in chapter 1, we learn what to fear most by seeing what those others fear and because often what we fear most are harms to, or loss of, those we love. Our capacities or incapacities to cope with those great fears is relationally determined: to the extent that we do, we learn how to bear the greatest fears by seeing others bear them, and, as will be discussed in chapter 5, by learning to carry them with each other. When we cannot bear the great fears, we are suggestible in our processes of displacement: others can shape (deliberately or not) what proxy threats capture our attention. Building on chapter 1's discussion of the relational dynamics of fearing in general, we can see that others—including family members and friends with whom we are in personal relationships, as well as therapists, politicians, theorists, writers, media developers, teachers, and influencers—can intentionally or unintentionally guide our attention to be wary of certain proxy threats, as well as to be unconcerned about other potential stand-in threats. For instance, if a new parent discovers that a trusted friend does not vaccinate her children for fear of possible side effects, it might make him question his plan to vaccinate his own. As we have begun to see, the particular proxy threats that get our attention are not accidental. Others play a significant role in directing where our displaced fears land.

B. Fears of Proxy Threats Are Relationally Experienced

Beyond partly orienting the proxies onto which our great fears will be displaced, all of our experiences of fear happen in the context of our lives as individuals in relationship with many others. As we discussed in chapter 2, we are always experiencing fears in the context of other people, who are themselves fearers. We saw there that how others experience, cope with, and express their fears shapes how we will experience, cope with, and express our own. This means that what displaced fears feel like to us is also partly shaped by what displaced fears feel like to others. If significant others in our lives have experienced fears of proxy threats without being consumed by them, we may be more likely to do so. If they experience these fears as all-encompassing, we may be more inclined to experience them that way.

C. Fears of Proxy Threats Are Relationally Expressed and Interpreted

Furthermore, our processes of expressing and responding to others' expressions of fears are deeply relational. As we discussed at length in chapter 2, others can need us as interpreters for the expression of their fears, and we can need others as interpreters for our expressions of fear. The process of interpretation can complicate processes of displacement by instigating or spurring the process: if one's expression of fear is dismissed or not given uptake, that in itself can trigger further attempts to express one's fear in ways that *will* be taken up. Of course, the expressions of fear that may be most easily interpretable are those that one's interpreter shares. If I express fear of anti-vaxxers in an area where many people are vaccine hesitant, I may not get uptake. So the relational dynamics of emotional expression can further shape the proxy threats onto which our fears get displaced in the first place.

As we will see in chapter 4, processes of displaced fears are further relationally shaped when it comes to the point of individuals responding to the perceived threats themselves. Many of our responses to these proxy threats take the form of efforts to control them. We neither become inclined toward nor pursue those controlling strategies alone.

D. New Terminology

The relational character of displacement might seem exclusively dangerous. As we have seen, other people, including those with political and financial interests, can sway us toward displacing our fears onto certain kinds of threats. It is true that some of the ways others influence which proxy threats garner our attention might be deliberate and malicious (e.g., a political group wants to motivate hateful actions against a certain community). But the relational dynamics of coming to fear certain proxy threats are not always so pernicious. Part of what might motivate loved ones or friends to sway others' attention toward particular proxy threats (intentionally or unintentionally) is the simple fact that it can be comforting to fear the same things as other people one respects. It can be reassuring to feel confirmed in one's fears, or to see one's fears mirrored in others' lives. And perhaps, if there are controlling strategies to implement, it can be soothing to implement them with others. So the relational dynamics of displacement are not so much uniformly a problem as they are a fact—our experiences of fear, including the displacement of fears, occur always in the context of our relationships with others. Fearers' influenceability is not in itself a dangerous thing. Whether it is helpful or harmful depends in large part on the quality and power dynamics of particular relationships. As such, we must attend to the moral and political complexities of power dynamics and what we owe each other as co-fearers. The thoroughgoing relational character of processes of displacement means in part that, as we will discuss in chapter 5, to the extent that such processes can be morally and politically dangerous, pursuing different modes of coping with great threats will require reorienting not only individuals' ways of fearing but also the ways our fearing processes are intertwined with each other. New ways of coping with great threats will require new ways of fearing together.

To reflect the relational realities of our processes of fearing, I want to augment the psychoanalytic language of displacement as I move forward. Consider instead what it means to *compel* something. Etymologically, compel is from the Latin *compellere*: *com-* (together, with) and *pellere* (to thrust, strike, push, drive). "Pel" appears in words like propel, dispel, and expel. "Com" appears in words like compassion (to suffer together). So, to compel something is to join together in pushing or driving it away. I want to suggest that these fears of great threats are not merely ones individual agents displace. We *compel* these fears: *together, we drive or force them away*.

To return to the description of fears of nonthreats in section 1, we can now see how the extent of fears for our children—that they will be abducted, that violent video games or TV shows will cause them to become violent, or that being left in a cool car for brief moments will put them at great risk—might be a result not of deliberate manipulations but of compelling fears. Instead, we might, together, compel our great fear of our inability to protect our loved ones onto more manageable perceived threats: we come to believe we can protect our children if we simply never allow them to have contact with strangers, do not give them access to violent media, and never leave them alone. Of course, none of these goals are fully attainable, and even if they were, they would not protect our children against any number of other harms. In fact, being committed to these goals will make children *more* vulnerable to other kinds of harms, such as a struggle to trust themselves and their own capacities to solve problems, and the harms of being raised by exhausted, anxious caregivers. In spite of this, the drive can be strong to make more manageable what feel like great fears for the well-being of vulnerable children. If we can instead contain our fears in a more manageable way, we might feel relief. Reflecting on her own experience of the judgment she faced after leaving her son in the car, Brooks also notes that containing fears facilitates a further kind of self-deception: if *others* fail to control the more manageable perceived threats in their own children's lives, we might point to *their* failures as the source of any bad outcomes, relieving ourselves of the sense of how, no matter how much we try to anticipate or forestall them, bad outcomes might also happen to *our* children, to *us*. Similarly, we can see how nonsensical fears—that migrants will take nonmigrants' jobs, burden the welfare system, or bring violent crime and theft—might be a result of compelled fears of great threats: economic and national insecurity, and uncertain access to employment, health care, and social safety nets.[14] Again, I am not disputing the point made by Glassner, Robin, Klein, and Lilley—that when these rather than other threats become the objects onto which our fears are displaced it is partly a result of politicized conditions and the influence of politicized media. My claim is that there is a deeper story about why we come to fear those proxy threats with such force when we do: they can be carrying the weight of great fears that are legitimate and not likely to dissipate if we only come to learn that we have been manipulated or that migrants do not pose the threats we believe them to.

At this point we can begin to imagine how compelling great fears onto objects might be more or less morally troubling. In the case of compelling great fears onto migrants, the outcomes are clearly devastating. Migrants in the United States, many of whom have faced great hardship already, are condemned and attacked as though doing so could free their attackers from their great fears. Humans are caged, abused, separated from families, deported, and sometimes killed for their attempts to migrate. We will discuss the harms of attempts to control threats in the next chapter. But we can alternatively imagine cases where the effects of compelling are not purely harmful. For instance, consider a person whose great fear of the insecurity of the future gets channeled into fear of the particular proxy threat of water insecurity, and motivates her to actively contribute to local water-protection efforts, boycotting Nestlé and other corporations that pose threats to local water supply, and fighting to ensure affordable, clean, and safe drinking water for all. I will suggest in chapter 4 that what follows processes of compelling are often controlling strategies— efforts to *manage* perceived proxy threats—and that such strategies are often harmful in part because the perceived proxy threats are not threats at all. In fact, as we will see, controlling strategies are often not the best for addressing even genuine threats. But it is worth noting at this point that compelling might in some cases result in productive non-controlling attention channeled toward addressing genuine threats.

In cases of displacement/compelling fears, the claim is that while fearers might think they fear manageable threat X, in some cases it is more accurate to recognize that they fear unmanageable threat Y. Even with the caveat that displacement is not always happening, nor always happening unbeknownst to fearers, this is still a rather immodest claim: fearers can think they are fearing one thing while what they are actually fearing is something else. What could justify a claim that an alternative interpretation of their fear as *displaced fear* is more accurate than a fearer's own claim about what they are fearing?

What justifies this claim is partly that some identifications of what people are really fearing are more explanatorily successful than others, and partly that some identifications are more practically useful than others. Identifications of what people are fearing will be (1) better the better they explain the behaviors of fearers; and (2) better the more able they are to help fearers change problematic behavior.

First, an identification of what a person is fearing is more successful *the more it is able to make sense of the fearer's behavior.* As I will argue in chapter 4, fearers very often attempt to control the manageable threats onto which their great fears are displaced. For example, if a fearer has a great fear of economic insecurity and thus their inability to protect loved ones from future possible suffering, they may displace this great fear of an unmanageable threat onto a fear of a more manageable threat—migrants—and then attempt to control this manageable threat to the extent of their powers (e.g., refusing to hire migrants in their business or lobbying in favor of stronger anti-migration policies). Perhaps the fearer herself insists that it is not a fear of economic insecurity at work but simply a fear of migrants. One sign that this person's fear may be not only or chiefly of migrants but of some deeper threat (e.g., economic insecurity) would be if, even when the perceived threat of migrants is totally extinguished, no longer posing any threat to the individual, deep fear and attacks on other perceived threats to economic security persist. If there is a deeper fear being displaced onto migrants, extinguishing the proxy threat (migrants) will not extinguish the fear. If the fearer continues to behave in a way that demonstrates this, by taking up actions to control other perceived threats (e.g., union busting, anti-taxation lobbying, and so on), the explanation of displacement/compelling might be better able to make sense of her behavior than an explanation that takes the fearer's own claim at face value.

Further, an explanation of displaced/compelled fears might help explain the behavior of fearers even when some objects of fears are revealed as nonstatistical threats. Imagine the fearer above is presented with accurate information about how migrants will not threaten job prospects, but in fact potentially increase opportunities for citizens and other migrants, and about how migrants are statistically less likely to commit violent actions than nonmigrants. Imagine this information is presented to them and confirmed by multiple sources they trust (media, family members, religious leaders, and others). Imagine the fearer does not dispute the facts presented, and even notes they have no reason to doubt them. If the person's fear of migrants persists nonetheless, the explanation of displacement might be better able to explain the tenacity of her fear than alternate explanations. It would make sense that this fear is not responsive to the information presented by trustworthy sources because their information does not address the deeper fear that has been displaced.

Second, identifications of what people are fearing are better *the more able they are to help fearers change problematic behavior*. Identifications of displaced/compelled fears can be therapeutically useful in the following sense: when proposed to a fearer, if they provide the fearer with a lens through which to interpret their experience, and in so doing create the possibility for questioning one's fears and/or inclinations to act in light of them, and if the fearer employs the lens and embarks on this questioning, then such identifications will have been therapeutically useful. In cases where an identification of a displaced fear receives uptake in a fearer's life, it may have meaningful practical benefits—allowing fearers to more easily question their own fears of nonstatistical threats and to challenge their actions motivated by such fears, including the controlling actions I will describe in chapter 4. The suggestion that one's fear (e.g., of migrants) is a displaced/compelled fear of something else is not always something a fearer is able or willing to consider. Resistance to the suggestion does not prove that it is completely off base, though it might be. On the flip side, the fact that a fearer *is* willing to welcome such a suggestion *also* does not guarantee its accuracy. In short, a fearer's finding the identification of displacement helpful is not a certain indicator that the identification is accurate, but when we evaluate competing explanations of what a person is really fearing, if a displacement/compelling explanation proves useful in changing problematic behavior, this can speak in favor of such an explanation.

My account of compelling fears builds on the discussion in chapter 2 of how interpreters play key roles in allowing for the expression, and thereby the formation, of fears. In relationships among fearers and interpreters, arriving at an identification of what a person is fearing is already the result of expressive and interpretive work. The identification of the emotion's object, and thereby the formation of the emotion, may depend on the expression and behavior of the fearer. It may be easier in these processes to identify *that* there could be displacement/compelling occurring than to identify *what underlying fear specifically* is being displaced/compelled, but this too could be approached via processes of expression and interpretation. In the above case, I postulate a deeper fear of economic insecurity as having been displaced and expressed as fear of migrants. But in practice, we do not know from the outset that displacement is at play, or what fears are being displaced. Coming to these identifications can be part of the expressive and interpretive work involved in the formation of fears.

5. Conclusion

It is important to understand the process of compelling fears for both ontological/epistemological reasons—so that we can properly understand what we are afraid of and why our deepest fears might be more difficult to identify than one would think—and for moral/political reasons. We have seen in this chapter that, ontologically and epistemologically speaking, we are mistaken if we understand the self-reports of individuals about the things and beings they fear to be in all cases authoritative. Individuals might believe themselves to be fearing migrants when really their underlying fear of an actual threat has been compelled onto the perceived (not actual) threat of migrants. Or they might believe that poisoned Halloween candy is a major threat, when really their underlying fear of an actual threat—their inability to fully shield their children from harm—has been compelled onto the perceived (not actual) threat of poisoned candy.

I have suggested that, contra some contemporary accounts of the culture of fear, the magnitude of fear directed toward things that are perceived as posing greater threats than they actually do is not sufficiently explained as the outcome of susceptible people subjected to powerful manipulation by media and political forces, with the implication being that such people should "know better, and fear less"—should recognize having been manipulated and stop being afraid. Instead, I have described this phenomenon as the result of (1) suggestible people who (2) have great, unmanageable fears of undeniable threats that they cannot cope with, and (3) mostly unconsciously, and always relationally, compel those fears onto more manageable perceived threats, which are (4) made available through personal psychic histories, relationships with other fearers, media, and political forces. Given the substantial role proxy threats play in emotional lives, while it might be morally and politically unacceptable to allow the actions such fears motivate to continue, the path forward is not likely to be so straightforward as commanding that individuals stop being afraid.

In the next chapter, we turn to the moral and political significance of compelling fears and the ways attempts to control perceived threats can have serious harmful effects.

4
Controlling Threats

As we have seen, what individuals perceive to be threats in need of urgent attention can in fact be stand-ins for deeper, less manageable threats. Having come to concern themselves with these more controllable proxy threats, how then do individuals respond?

This chapter outlines five main strategies individuals often use to attempt to control perceived (substitute) threats: (1) removal, (2) escape, (3) destruction, (4) assimilation, and (5) overpowering. As we will see, these efforts may be partially satisfying, insofar as they provide individuals with the experience of being able to *do something*, against the background of a pervasive sense of powerlessness in response to uncontrollable threats. But when used to attempt to control nonthreatening others, these five strategies are morally unacceptable.

1. Removal

Once a perceived threat has been identified, the most obvious first line of defense may be to try to *remove* it. Removal of a threat can involve more or less active tactics, from the creation of spaces where perceived threats are not welcome, cannot enter, or cannot stay, to active eviction or expulsion. If it is possible to do this while keeping the surrounding circumstances intact, removal might seem the most economical approach to controlling such a threat. Consider a low-stakes case: about to leave home, I discover there is a wasp in my car. I might try to remove the wasp as straightforwardly as possible—open the windows, coax it toward the outside. If I succeed, I do not need to employ any other tactics: I don't need to escape from it, destroy it, or overpower it. In the best-case scenario, the wasp leaves of its own accord, and I am no longer threatened. Or think of a bouncer at a nightclub. Typically, as a man with an imposing physical presence, his job is to intimidate, in some cases to refuse entry, and in other cases to forcibly remove people. If a patron has too much to drink, becomes out of control, or threatens violence, the bouncer is there to remove them from the club and maintain a secure environment for staff and other clubgoers. The "threat" is isolated and eliminated when the individual is removed.

As for examples of removal that are common responses to everyday fears, we might picture the use of physical structures designed to keep animals or people out of spaces. Spikes are placed on roofs or fences to keep birds and other animals away. High-pitched sound emitters deter rodents. These devices are not unlike those used to keep humans also out of public spaces, or to keep them from behaving in certain ways within them. Signs communicating what kinds of attire are required (shirts, shoes) are posted so that patrons understand who is welcome in a restaurant. Metal detectors communicate the conditions that a person must meet in order to enter a space. "Hostile architecture" is used in built environments to communicate where people are not welcome, or not welcome to do certain things. Armrests between seats on benches in bus stations or airports keep people from sleeping horizontally across them. Uncomfortable or unhelpful lighting discourages loitering in certain areas. Spikes on windowsills, by doorways, or under overpasses keep people from resting there. Gaps in awnings deliberately allow rain and snow to fall on people who would seek shelter. Raised and spiked subway grates prevent people and other animals from finding warmth.

Larger architectural structures can also be hostile. Walls at the borders of nations are designed to keep residents in and outsiders out, where insider/outsider status is typically multiply policed along lines of class, race, and citizenship. Constructed borders like the Berlin Wall or the Mexico-United States barrier involve erecting full or partial barriers to facilitate the capture and criminalization of unauthorized border crossers. They ease the removal of those who have crossed without permission and attempt to prevent their entry in the first place.[1] All these are examples of structures used to prevent entry into a space or expedite the removal of unwanted individuals who are perceived to be threats.

Sarah Tyson (2014) has focused on another kind of structure built to facilitate the removal of perceived threats of sex offenders from neighborhoods. "Pocket parks" are very small parks designed to be buildable on tiny parcels of land, even in highly populated and crowded areas. They typically contain a compact playscape, and perhaps some grass, for children to play on. Beyond the introduction of play spaces in dense urban areas, these parks serve an additional purpose: they can be used to create zones of exclusion for people who are prohibited from living near spaces where children commonly gather. In one case Tyson describes, a pocket park was built in a neighborhood in Los Angeles with the explicit goal of forcing the eviction of registered sex offenders who lived nearby.

Tyson (2014, 423) calls this tactic of forcibly removing registered sex offenders from a neighborhood an "eliminative strategy." It is an attempt to respond to a potential harm by *removing those who might harm*. Later in the chapter, we will return to Tyson's analysis of why such strategies do not succeed in removing harm. For now, note that the building of pocket parks with the goal of forcing the relocations of some people perceived to be threats is a clear expression of efforts to respond to perceived threats by removing them. Without consideration for where these individuals will end up and without the goal of actually preventing future harms altogether, the strategy is to ensure that these individuals will be less likely to threaten the children in one's own neighborhood because they will have less access to them. Pocket parks are thus another attempt to respond to a perceived threat by controlling it. We might wonder what the actual threat is underlying these efforts—if it is indeed the presence of registered sex offenders in one's neighborhood, some of whom are registered for committing nonviolent offenses like urinating in public outside of a bar in college, or if these are, as was discussed in the previous chapter, instances of compelled threats. We will return to this point in the final section.

Beyond borders, hostile architecture, and pocket parks, all forms of arrest, jailing, and incarceration are strategies of removal. These tactics in every case involve extracting from a community an individual who is perceived to be a threat. In the US context, Michelle Alexander (2010,

185) has referred to this process as the "roundup," during which "vast numbers of people are swept into the criminal justice system by the police, who conduct drug operations primarily in poor communities of color." Angela Davis describes this as a process not only of physical removal but also of removal from the *awareness* of those who are not in prison:

> Prisons allow this society to discard people who have serious social problems rather than recognize that many of them are simply hurting themselves and are in need of help. . . . If poor men and women of color are incarcerated, they belong there, and everyone is absolved of the responsibility of thinking about them. Those who are relieved of the burden of thinking about people in prison are also not obligated to think about the myriad of social problems in the lives and communities of people in prison. They are not obligated to think about poverty, illiteracy, bad school systems, racism, drugs, and so on. (Davis 2012, 50–51)

In other words, by the process of removing perceived threats through incarceration, those on the outside are relieved of thinking about both those individuals perceived to be threats and the larger social threats that underlie criminal actions.

Other forms of nonvoluntary institutionalization also serve as removal strategies, as when people diagnosed with mental illnesses or disorders are kept against their will in psychiatric wards, or when people with disabilities are placed in institutions, or when Indigenous children are forcibly removed from their families and housed in state- and church-run residential or boarding schools. A person with a mental illness might be seen as a threat insofar as they could harm themselves or others. People with disabilities may be seen as a threat to their families' well-being or to the success of mainstream school systems and work environments, insofar as they require more direct care labor and thus are potentially physically, emotionally, or financially costly. More symbolically, they may be seen as a threat to the image of healthy, independent, successful families and communities. Indigenous children have been seen as a threat to the project of colonialism insofar as they can carry on the knowledge of stolen lands and the presence of unfulfilled treaty obligations on the part of settler states, as well as carrying on the self-determining power of Indigenous communities through language, spiritual practices, and governance. All these threats were purportedly controllable through institutionalization.

So far, we have focused on one major strategy of containing and controlling perceived threats: removal. Though I have suggested that removal may often be the most obvious first line of defense, in some ways less effortful and burdensome than the strategies we will turn to next, note that possibilities for removal of threats require that a number of background conditions be in place in order to succeed.

For one, removal strategies require a clear sense of the boundary between *threat* and *nonthreat*. As in the case of another familiar removal strategy—an operation to surgically remove a cancerous tumor—it is important to be very clear on what tissue is tumorous and must be extracted, and what tissue is healthy and must be maintained in order for the organism to function. All processes of removal depend on such clarity about the separation point between threat and threatened. As we will see, clarity about some version of this separation point is a requirement for all five controlling strategies I will discuss. As we can also begin to imagine, such clarity is not always available.

Furthermore, removal strategies also require a distinction between the spaces where threats *cannot* be allowed to exist and the spaces where they *can*. In other words, removal strategies depend on there being some *other place* to which threats can be relocated, without continuing to pose a threat to the would-be protected zone. The other place may be as simple as some other roof for birds to defecate on or some other dance club for a drunk person to go to. Or, as we have seen, it may be as elaborate as a prison. Removal strategies implicitly communicate acceptance of the ongoing presence of perceived threats, so long as they are *there* and not here. But sometimes there is no other place available to house the threats, or sometimes threats are such that they will not ever be securely contained in such a place. Consider contagious diseases that are not fully containable and cannot simply be stored elsewhere. Removal strategies are not likely to help with such threats.

2. Escape

When a perceived threat cannot be removed, individuals may instead attempt to remove themselves from the path of the perceived threat. In such cases, *escape* may be a viable option for avoiding harm. Usually we have some control over our own bodies or over the bodies of loved ones in our care, and the option of removing ourselves from potentially dangerous situations can have the advantage of requiring less energy than approaches that require acting upon a perceived threat against its will.

Think of a tropical storm approaching your area. It may not ultimately threaten your city, but as a precaution, if you have enough notice and the resources to do so, you can remove yourself and your loved ones from its path. Or think of the triggering sounds of loud fireworks being set off in a US city on Independence Day. A veteran with PTSD might remove herself from the threat by retreating to a quieter, remote location for that holiday.

When perceived threats take more protracted forms, escape strategies may become more elaborate. Setha Low has spent years conducting ethnographic research in gated communities in suburbs near New York City, and near San Antonio, Texas. In "A Nation of Gated Communities" (Low 2010), she discusses her findings that people move into gated communities from fear of crime and desire for protection, safety, and security in their financial investments. The idea is that gated neighborhoods will offer a kind of escape strategy, making it less likely that residents will face threats like home invasions or violent crime. Low found that the attempt to escape into gated communities did not, however, have the effect of making people feel safer. Moving into gated communities made people more likely to believe that they were in need of protection, not that they were being well protected (Low 2010, 37). They worried that they had a "false sense of security" (29). They worried about the persistent porousness of their communities, and particularly about the presence of outsiders (often people of color), like nannies, housekeepers, and gardeners. Importantly, they expressed a lack of felt community and, instead, a sense of isolation, even among their neighbors within the gates. As Low writes,

> What is wrong with gated communities is that while residents use gates to create the community they are searching for, their personal housing decisions have unintended negative consequences. Most importantly, they disrupt other people's ability to experience "community": community in the sense of mutual openness of suburb and city, community in terms of access to public open space, and even community within the American tradition of integration and social justice. (Low 2010, 42)

The efforts to escape from potential threats by removing themselves into protected, sealed-off areas does not, by and large, have the outcome residents hope for.[2] Homeowners in gated communities often still feel vulnerable to the threats they worried about on the outside.

Another form of attempted escape follows from a very common set of fears: namely, the fears parents have about potential illnesses that could befall their children. In *On Immunity: An Inoculation*, Eula Biss (2014) offers a reflection on the intensity of fears of disease among especially parents of young children with underdeveloped immune systems.[3] Biss describes how some parents channel intense worries about the survival and well-being of their children into a desire to keep their children pure and free from contamination. So the thought process goes, children are born pure and healthy, and if we can only keep them away from harmful substances and contaminants, they will remain safe. The desire to protect a newborn's closed, secure system can express itself in a variety of ways, including vigilance about whom they come into contact with, what they wear, and what they eat. These are all forms of attempted escape from the potential contamination of the shared world. For instance, there are many reasons behind a desire to breastfeed, but as Biss (2014, 73) writes, "As long as a child takes only breast milk, I discovered, one can enjoy the illusion of a closed system, a body that is not yet in dialogue with the impurities of farm and factory." The same desire to keep one's child pure can make one fearful of possible contaminants in their environment:

> While two-year-olds take bullets in other parts of the city, I worry over the danger embedded in the paint that chips off my child's toys and the walls around him. I fear that it is woven into the clothes he

wears, that it is in the air he breathes, in the water he drinks, and in the compromised food I feed him. (Biss 2014, 132–33).

On one level, Biss's project is an intervention into anti-vaccination practices. In some cases, the need to decide whether or when to allow one's child to be vaccinated is a decision about the risks of possible contamination. The introduction of unknown substances and contagions with the express goal of protecting individuals and populations against dangerous illnesses can make parents apprehensive, even as vaccine science shows repeatedly that such vaccines are safe. As Biss assesses it, part of what underlies dangerous levels of vaccine refusal is parental longing for escape—escape to a space that is imagined to be pure and uncontaminated for one's children—as a path toward protection against any possible sources of disease or harm.[4]

While it is true that escape strategies, whether in response to tropical storms, fireworks, ungated urban neighborhoods, or the potential contamination of children, do not always help individuals avoid threats, in many cases of perceived threats, escape may seem like the most viable option. But like the strategy of removal, successful escape requires the existence of threat-free spaces to which one can escape. And depending what the threats are, ensuring such spaces can prove difficult.

3. Destruction

When possible, the ultimate response to a perceived threat is *destruction*. If a perceived threat can be eradicated, then the most thorough and permanent response to it may be to annihilate it—to reduce it to nothing.

Perhaps the most obvious examples of destruction involve the killing of living things. We might *eradicate*—completely uproot or kill with toxic chemicals—invasive plant species that threaten the growth of survival crops. Or we might exterminate a particular population of some animal that is behaving in some way that threatens us—for example, bedbugs living in an apartment—even if we do not aim to kill all animals of that type in the world. The threat can be eliminated, at least for now, if we can manage to kill the pests directly affecting us.

The killing of living threats extends to practices of killing humans. In criminal justice systems, destruction sometimes takes the form of killing individual persons perceived to be threats—for instance, by capital punishment, police shootings, or neglect of prisoners in need of medical treatment. Or such killing may involve destroying whole groups of people perceived as threats through the use of war, weapons of mass destruction, or genocide. Slower methods of killing groups of people can involve compromising their conditions of life—damaging their supplies of water or food, destroying the land they live on, introducing illnesses into their populations. These have all been effective tactics of colonizers.

It is also possible to destroy *parts* of living things without destroying the entire organism. If the persistence of a community's language is a threat to outsiders' efforts to control that community, the outsiders might attempt to make the language extinct by preventing new generations from learning it. Or if an individual is seen as a threat because of past behavior or current physical strength, destroying their mental or physical capacities might be sufficient to manage the threat without killing the person. Subjecting individuals to combat or torture might cause sufficient mental or physical breakdown to deactivate the individual's threat.

In *Solitary Confinement: Social Death and Its Afterlives*, Lisa Guenther (2013) examines the practice of prolonged solitary confinement as it is widely used in North American prison systems. The practice of solitary confinement typically involves housing a prisoner alone in a cell with a solid door and solid walls, without any contact with other prisoners or prison workers, providing them in some cases with one hour a day outside of the cell, though still alone. This form of confinement is exceptionally effective at destroying prisoners psychologically and emotionally. Guenther argues that solitary confinement is both dehumanizing and de-animalizing—reducing human prisoners to less than animals. As she writes,

> Deprived of everyday encounters with other people and confined to a space with radically diminished sensory stimulus, many inmates

come unhinged from reality. Their senses seem to betray them; objects begin to move, melt, or shrink of their own accord.... They cannot think straight, cannot remember things, cannot focus properly, and cannot even see clearly....

... There is something about the exclusion of other living beings from the space we inhabit and the absence of even the possibility of touching or being touched by another that threatens to unhinge us. (Guenther 2013, 145)

Guenther understands solitary confinement as having the goal of breaking down prisoners' capacities for functioning by removing others who could triangulate, at the most basic level, their perceptions and experiences:

Multiplicity of perspectives is like an invisible net that supports the coherence of my own experience, even (or especially) when others challenge my interpretation of "the facts."....

... Prolonged isolation cuts prisoners off from this network of social, cognitive, perceptual, affective, and even ontological support, turning prisoners' capacity for meaning, and for meaningful relationships, against itself to the point of incapacitation. (Guenther 2013, 146)

Without having to fully destroy prisoners through the use of extreme neglect, facilitated self-harm, direct physical abuse, or capital punishment, prison systems can destroy the perceived threat they pose through the use of solitary confinement.

Nonliving things can be harder to kill, but it can still make sense to understand some responses to such threats as destruction. For instance, ending a toxic relationship and cutting off communication might be an approach to destroying the threat of that relationship. So too would ending a habit of substance abuse or overthrowing a political regime be examples of threat destruction.

There are many reasons that the destruction of threats might be impossible or undesirable. Insofar as destruction is permanent, it allows for less margin of error than other controlling strategies—one may come to question later whether the destroyed objects were really such threats, but there will be no option to reverse one's actions. Further, destruction can be more costly and effortful than other possible responses to threats. Killing individuals or populations is rarely easy.

Many perceived threats are indestructible. Whole species may not be possible to destroy. Texts or writings perceived as threatening (e.g., those on lists of banned books) are not fully destructible since it is very difficult to determine whether all copies have been destroyed and impossible to fully curb the ripple effects of such texts in readers' lives. Even "eradicated" diseases often continue to exist in some form. While many objects seem vulnerable to destruction, in fact not many can be fully and permanently destroyed.

And of course, in the case of many perceived threats, their successful destruction would involve harming other, nonthreatening objects in the process. My neighbor might fully eradicate the prickly thistle growing in his garden but not without harming the edible plants growing there. One could fully eradicate the presence of damaging comments from judgmental family members but not without losing their presence in one's life entirely. In some cases, even considering collateral damages, eradication is worth it. In other cases, it is not. In many cases, other responses to the threats are available to enough of an extent that destruction does not seem the best course of action.

Given this, we might consider it notable how commonly first responses to perceived threats involve destruction: shooting at potential threats, waging wars, using pesticides. We return in the final section to the question of what might be uniquely satisfying about attempts to destroy perceived sources of threat.

4. Assimilation

In some cases, a threat is such that it cannot be readily removed, escaped, or destroyed, but it may still be controllable. Consider attempts to *assimilate* perceived threats: I can attempt to control or limit the perceived threat of some object or agent by forcibly bringing it into alignment with my own values, perspectives, or actions. If I succeed, whatever power the perceived threat had is no longer power working *against* me but is instead now either neutralized or perhaps even power working *with* or *for* me. Think of what an apartment dweller might wisely do before hosting a loud party: invite the neighbors. If they are the types to complain to a landlord about noise, it helps to at least have attempted to bring them onto the side of the noisemakers.

Assimilation strategies may be effective in controlling perceived threats to dominant identity groups. Think of the strategy some religious groups use to attempt to control the perceived threat of queer sexual identifications or desires: conversion therapies. While widely condemned as harmful, unethical, and without scientific validity, and banned in some jurisdictions, conversion therapies persist in the form of psychotherapy, visualization, support groups, and so on, all aimed at changing an individual's sexual orientation from somewhere on a queer spectrum to heterosexual. This is a kind of assimilation strategy: rather than remove a queer person from a religious community (though this is also done), escape them, or destroy them, conversion therapies aim to bring them into the fold of compulsory heterosexuality. If those who receive such therapy stop publicly identifying themselves as queer, they may in fact come to be spokespeople for the efficacy of the approach.

In *Boarding School Seasons*, Ojibwe scholar Brenda J. Child describes the US program of forcing Indigenous children to attend church- and state-run boarding schools as another clear assimilation strategy, aiming to control the perceived threat of sovereign Indigenous nations. Residential school programs in Canada and elsewhere did the same. As Child writes:

> During these trying years for American Indians, some promoters of assimilation still looked to boarding school education as a panacea for many social problems.... Boarding school education, which removed young children from the tribal environment, would "civilize" and prepare Indians for citizenship while providing them with a practical, vocational education....
> Early in the era of forced assimilation, coercion was often used to gather Indian children to the far-away schools. Rations, annuities, and other goods were withheld from parents who refused to send children to school after a compulsory attendance law for American

Indians was passed by Congress in 1891.... Assimilationists argued that the task of "civilizing" Indian children would be easier and lapses into tribal ways less likely if students stayed away from their homes and relatives until their education was complete. (Child 2000, 13)

Boarding schools had the goal of addressing the perceived threat of the so-called "Indian problem"—the multiple implications of Indigenous communities living in poverty and without land—following the US government's refusal to recognize the sovereignty of Indigenous nations and their broken treaties. From the state's perspective, the threat of Indigenous communities with the power to resist the takeover of lands and resources might not be fully removed, escaped, or destroyed, but the threat might be dispelled by assimilating future generations of such communities into US settler culture. The boarding schools were an assimilation strategy with the explicit goal of disconnecting children from their communities and violently mandating their participation in settler institutions. Many children did not survive the abuse of these schools, and so the threat they posed was controlled in another way (destruction), but those who did were subjected to multilevel assimilation strategies. Beyond the core assimilationist strategy of isolating children from their parents, families, and communities, by kidnapping or requiring that they live and work in dangerous and life-threatening conditions, children were also forbidden to speak tribal languages, and those who failed or refused to comply were punished by beatings, having their mouths washed with lye, or being locked in school jails (Child 2000, 28). Children were forced to abandon their tribal names and assume a "Christian" name, and their tribal names were ridiculed (Child 2000, 28–29). They were forced into a rigid, military-like atmosphere and schedule. Children were forced to have their hair cut, required to wear uniforms (in many cases incomplete or unsafe for weather conditions), fed inadequately, and forced to practice only Christian spiritual rituals. Though the boarding schools as a program did not succeed in forcibly assimilating Indigenous communities—we see clearly the resilience and power of all the communities who survived—they were a clear attempt to control the threat the Indigenous communities pose to colonialist governments, and they caused irrevocable damage and loss.

5. Overpowering

As we have seen, many sources of threat do not make it easy or possible to remove, escape, destroy, or assimilate them. There is still an option for responding to these perceived sources of threat resistantly—one can attempt to *overpower* them.

I employ overpowering tactics for responding to perceived threats when I tighten a leash before my dog tries to jump on a stranger, or when I get control of my car before it skids on ice into the middle of an intersection. Overpowering can also be a tactic I use in cases where the threats themselves are more elusive. Think of a smear campaign against a politician running for office, where she is falsely accused of criminal behavior. Though untrue, the accusations pose a threat to her campaign. Such accusations cannot be removed, escaped, destroyed, or assimilated, but they might be overpowered by mounting a public relations campaign to directly confront the accusers and disprove their claims. If the politician's public relations team can cultivate more public trust than the smear campaign has received, they may overpower the threat to the candidate and regain control of her image.

Imagine another threat less tangible than jumpy dogs or icy streets. A mother begins to notice her son expressing nonmasculine gender traits. He wants to wear skirts and dresses, sparkly shoes, and flowery headbands. He wants to play with dolls and read books about princesses. The mother worries her son will be teased and will not grow up to be properly masculine. She worries about what her extended family will say. She is concerned about what she should do to help her son avoid being bullied. The perceived threat in this case is multifaceted, resulting from the child's nonnormative gender performance in a social context where gender norms are strongly enforced, and where nonnormativity is punished, sometimes with violence. Even supposing she would prefer a social context more open to gender fluidity, the mother may feel ill-equipped to change the gendered society surrounding her son in order to try to mitigate the threats of teasing, criticism, and violence her son faces. She may instead try to overpower this threat by managing the aspect of the situation she has most control over: her son's behavior. She may insist that he wear pants and not skirts to school, allow him to play with dolls only at home, and encourage more organized sports and play dates with boys in his class. She may even punish him for acting in feminine ways. She wields her parental power, such as it is, to try to overpower his inclinations toward nonnormative gender performance and steer her child toward a less threatening path.

At the level of perceived threats to whole groups, imagine a situation where members of a community have identified what they see as threatening attempts on the part of pro-choice individuals in their area. Specifically, imagine that some of their progressive-minded neighbors are posting lawn signs and circulating petitions in support of Planned Parenthood and other reproductive-rights organizations, and members of the community group view this as an effort to spread troubling views among, especially, teenagers and young adults in the area. While the community group can neither *remove* nor *escape* the pro-choicers, they can develop a multipronged effort to overpower them. They start letter-writing campaigns against progressive sex education in local schools. They protest outside women's health clinics, and lobby members of their broader church communities to step up and voice pro-life beliefs. Doing this will not destroy their progressive-minded neighbors, but it may chip away at their enthusiasm and persistence over time, at least by requiring that those with the pro-choice beliefs spend some of their limited time and energy engaging with the disputing community group.

Consider another common and pressing threat—in the US context, many face the threat of being without health care because of not having access to health insurance, due to unaffordable premiums, lack of employer support, or federal shifts in allowing for-profit insurance corporations to exclude subscribers who are likely to be costly (e.g., those with preexisting conditions). A federal policy instituted under former president Barack Obama required that all individuals acquire (either purchase, acquire through their employer, or through government support) health insurance that would allow them to access at least basic health coverage, or be penalized. The Affordable Care Act (ACA, so-called Obamacare) was a major shift in the landscape of US society, as previously some 16 percent of the population lacked any health insurance, and millions more were dramatically underinsured.

There were many problems with the Affordable Care Act—it certainly did not make health care truly affordable, as many individuals who were required to purchase health insurance could neither afford the most basic of insurance plans nor even the fine they would pay if they opted to remain uninsured. Universal coverage was not achieved. But the arguable successes of the policy—including instituting some restrictions on a for-profit private insurance industry that could exclude individuals on the grounds that they or a family member have a preexisting health condition—were significant and saved lives. Under Donald Trump's presidential administration, these advances were threatened. The administration attempted to repeal the Affordable Care Act with no replacement, which would amount to loss of insurance for over 20 million Americans. Robert Doherty of the American College of Physicians summarized the likely effects of such a repeal as follows:

> Despite its flaws, the ACA has achieved a historic reduction in the number of uninsured persons in the United States, with more than 9 out of 10 Americans having coverage and 22 million and counting getting their coverage from the ACA. Those who will be most affected by repeal include working-class people, women who are concerned about loss of coverage for contraception, and entrepreneurs with medical conditions who fear they will have to give up their start-ups for jobs that offer coverage—not to mention the many more people with preexisting conditions who may again find themselves turned away by insurers. (Doherty 2017, 145)

The threat of the repeal felt seismic. Many with so-called "preexisting conditions" feared losing coverage if the insurance industry would be permitted to exclude them.[5] Many more would not be able to afford any variety of insurance. Annual and lifetime limits on insurance coverage would prevent even those with insurance from accessing care and would drive some into medical bankruptcy. Fortunately, though part of the law has been changed, the wholesale plan of the Trump administration to repeal Obamacare did not succeed. Even so, as Yamada writes,

> Although the ACA repeal attempts repeatedly failed during 2017 and early 2018, the Congressional deliberations over them were sources of public anxiety across the nation....
>
> ... These legislative outcomes have not been able to prevent widespread fear and anxiety over the possible loss of health insurance coverage for millions of Americans.... Those with limited or no incomes, preexisting health conditions, or major ongoing health care expenses had special reason to be alarmed at the speed and lack of legislative due process driving these deliberations, much less the possible results. (Yamada 2019, 36, 38)

Depending on one's social standing, it may not seem possible to avoid the threat of lacking access to health care. Those without consistent employment, income, or documented citizenship may feel resigned to simply hoping the threat does not become a reality. Others with more financial and social standing may feel that they have some options for responding to this perceived threat. They can train for and seek jobs in fields where employers typically provide health insurance. They can do their best to secure permanent positions with health insurance provision. They can try to make enough money that they could pay out-of-pocket for health care if needed. They can convince themselves that as long as they earn enough, they will be able to afford the care they need. While it is true that others may not be so cared for, these privileged individuals may even convince themselves of a sense of just deserts: those who earn enough will get the care they deserve, and those lacking care have not earned enough. These are all attempts to *overpower* the perceived threat of lacking access to health care: those with some financial standing try to position themselves as more powerful, both materially and psychologically, than the threat. They come to believe that they will be able to act and prepare in such a way as to control how the threat affects them, rather than let themselves be controlled by it. Materially, they try to set up their lives in such a way that there are a number of guards against the threat: a job with insurance, and one where one is unlikely to be fired, and then a backup plan of making enough money to ensure that they will be able to pay for their own care. Psychologically, they may cultivate a kind of denial about how easily they themselves could be in the position of the person without a job, without savings, or with a disability or health condition that allows for sudden exclusion from insurance plans. They know they have not eliminated the threat entirely, or for people other than themselves, but they believe that they have sufficient power to overtake the threat in their own lives.[6]

Even as a last resort in situations when efforts to remove, escape, destroy, or assimilate a threat do not succeed, overpowering strategies are not always successful. They are at best only partially or temporarily effective: if the threats cannot be destroyed, they will continue to exist in some form. Overpowering efforts are also costly: they require that threatened individuals who would seek to overpower have the energy and resources to spare, and such resources may be sapped before the threat is addressed. Some threats may not be overpowered easily or at all.

We have now seen five controlling strategies. Before turning to my arguments for why all of them are morally and politically troubling, I want to note one further feature of these strategies. In most of the examples we have seen, one agent or group of agents sees another object, agent, or group of agents as a threat. The perception of threat is unidirectional. But in some cases, multiple agents can see each other as threats *at the same time*, and they may attempt to employ controlling strategies on each other reciprocally. Indeed, one agent's attempt to control another may trigger that agent to see the would-be controller as a threat and to motivate attempts to control them.

6. Damage of Control

The five strategies we have considered for attempting to respond to perceived (non)threats—removal, escape, destruction, assimilation, and overpowering—are all examples of attempts to control threatening objects. As we have seen, they are tactics that can be mobilized against not only acute, immediate perceived threats (e.g., the wasp in my car), but also more dispersed, longer-term perceived threats (e.g., sovereign Indigenous communities). In all the cases we have considered, the possibility of simply accepting the presence of the perceived threat does not seem an attractive option. Individuals feel they must respond in some way to manage the object.

Recall that the difference between threats and nonthreats is often unclear. As we established in chapter 3, the objects individuals are often attempting to control are *perceived threats*: they are what individuals would describe as threatening them, but they may or may not pose an actual threat. In fact, given processes of compelling threats described there—coming to see more manageable threats as the main object of one's fear, in place of more uncontrollable threats—in many cases, the objects that individuals attempt to remove, escape, destroy, assimilate, or overpower may not be threats at all. An individual's attempt to remove a sex offender from one's neighborhood is an attempt to control a perceived threat that may in fact fail to address an actual threat of unpredictable violence. The perceived threat of the chemicals contained in vaccines may only be a proxy for the actual threat of being unable to protect one's child from unpredictable dangers. The perceived threat of a boy wearing a skirt may be a substitute for the threat of a social world where norms of gendered behavior are violently policed. So when controlling strategies address objects that fears have been compelled onto, rather than objects that are the actual source of deep fears, they affect objects that are not even threatening.

My project in this chapter is not to argue about whether objects are or are not in fact threats. We have seen in chapter 1 and chapter 3 that differentiating actual and nonactual threats can be very complicated. I argued in chapter 3 that in fact many of the kinds of objects described in this chapter are perceived as threats not because they pose any actual threat but because of a complex relational process of displacing fears of great, inescapable, actual threats onto more manageable objects. My concern in this chapter is solely with the practice and the moral status of the controlling strategies we have discussed. I want to make the case for why the five kinds of controlling strategies outlined here can be morally unacceptable.

A. Controlling Strategies Are Attempts to Threaten Objects

First, notice that *nearly all of the attempts to control threats discussed in this chapter are in fact attempts to assuage one's own fears by subjecting others to threat*. The strategy of removal is an attempt to relieve myself from contact with some perceived threat—homeless person, sex offender, migrant—by removing them from my area, and subjecting them to insecurity (e.g., housing insecurity) somewhere else. The strategy of destruction is an attempt to eliminate perceived threats—criminalized individuals, Indigenous communities—by directly destroying them. The strategy of assimilation is an attempt to neutralize perceived threats—queer youth, Indigenous children—by subjecting them to the threat of having their distinct features erased by being absorbed. The strategy of overpowering is an attempt to override perceived threats—gender nonnormative children, pro-choice groups—by dominating them, isolating them, and preventing them from receiving support for their expression. Arguably, escaping as a tactic does not always threaten other agents in the same way as the other four tactics—I remove myself or my loved ones from the context rather than taking direct action against the perceived source of threat. But even in cases of escape, my actions might threaten or harm those I perceive as threats: because of my decision to remove myself, others may be denied my participation in a joint project (e.g., the immunity of a population, or the strength of a neighborhood community beyond gated housing). They may need this participation in order to thrive. So the first thing to notice about all these controlling strategies is that they involve an attempt to threaten some other object or agent.

B. Perceived but Not Actual Threats May Be Controlled, but Attempts to Do So Subject These Objects to Morally Problematic, Unjustified Harms

Now think first of attempts to use controlling strategies against *perceived but not actual threats*. We have seen many relatively uncontroversial examples of these in this chapter already. Loitering people, people with disabilities, Indigenous people, banned books, vaccines, queer-identified people and pro-choice activists clearly belong in this category. What happens when others perceive these as threats and attempt to use controlling strategies against them? The first thing to note is that perceived but not actual threats can, at least in most cases, be controlled to some degree. They are responsive to the controlling strategies of escape, removal, destruction, assimilation, or overpowering, in the sense that *they can be subject to threat*. But I want to argue that these controlling strategies, when leveled against perceived (and not actual) threats are morally troubling examples of harm against these agents or objects.

Making this argument requires two preliminary distinctions: between being harmed and merely being limited, and between justified and unjustified acts of harm.

On being harmed versus being limited: attempting to subject a perceived (not actual) threat to some kind of treatment against their will (e.g., removing them, destroying them, assimilating them, or overpowering them) is inhibiting them without cause. Not all experiences that inhibit an individual's actions are harms: if a child reaches to hit the cat, my stopping their arm from hitting is limiting, but it is not a harm. But removing, destroying, assimilating, or overpowering an individual goes beyond simply limiting them. It is a harm in a sense Iris Marion Young describes: it aims to curb their development and expression of selfhood.[7] So when I use a controlling strategy against another individual, I am harming them.

On justified versus unjustified acts of harm: some would argue that the harms of controlling strategies are sometimes justified. For instance, if an intruder is threatening to hurt me, I may be justified in pointing a weapon at them to threaten them and (I hope) stop them in their tracks before any further harms happen. Both I and the intruder have been threatened in such a case, but we might say that only my threatening of them was justified. (Of course, proponents of nonviolence may not even agree that my actions were justified.) But since the objects we are focused on right now are not even actual threats, but merely perceived threats, I want to suggest, in cases where we attempt to respond to a nonthreat by using one of the controlling tactics we have discussed, we are acting in a morally troubling way. We are unjustifiably harming some other agent or object. Controlling strategies against perceived but not actual threats are attempts to subject these agents or objects to threat, and thereby these strategies are unjustifiably harming them and so are morally unacceptable.

To illustrate this point, recall our earlier discussion of hostile architecture. Imagine a case where residents of a condo building are worried about homeless individuals sleeping in the benches at the doorway to their building. They worry that the people sleeping on benches pose a threat to the security of their building, that they may break in or attempt to steal from them as they arrive home. They pool money to install new benches that are divided with armrests, such that the benches will no longer be comfortable to sleep on. This is a clear case of individuals (the condo residents) responding to a perceived threat (the people sleeping on benches) with a controlling strategy (removal), that subjects the perceived threat to the harm of the controlling strategy (resulting in homeless people having even fewer options for sleeping safely). I would describe this as a morally problematic case of responding to a perceived, not actual, threat with an unjustified harm. The people sleeping on the benches have not actually threatened the condo residents. Rather, they are a perceived threat—arguably a proxy that fears about mugging and theft are compelled onto. By removing them from the benches, the condo residents harm them—they limit them in the development and expression of selves—at a basic level. They make it more likely that they will be hurt or arrested when attempting to rest elsewhere. Even for those who believe that in some cases it is justified to threaten others, threatening those sleeping on benches in this way is unjustified.

So, employing controlling strategies against perceived but not actual threats is morally unacceptable. Perhaps this resonates with many of our intuitions about what we have the right to do to others. I am not allowed to go around harming others when they pose no threat to me. One difficulty with this claim might be that agents are not always skilled at identifying which objects pose threats to us and which do not. My argument about the moral unacceptability of controlling strategies against nonthreats holds whether we perceive them to be threats or not. We established in chapter 1 that an agent's perception of an object as threatening is not sufficient to establish that it is threatening. If an object is not an actual threat toward that agent, they are not morally allowed to employ controlling strategies against it.

C. Controlling Actual Threats

How can we morally evaluate the use of controlling strategies in cases of actual threats? Here the argument is more complicated.

We must first distinguish between kinds of actual (not merely perceived) threats. The "great threats" we have discussed (of loss, suffering, failures to protect loved ones, and uncontrollability) are one kind of actual threat. Beyond great threats there are other kinds of actual threats that are more specific, even if connected to the great threats in some ways. Consider a family member who refuses to respect the bodies and boundaries of others, a large pothole in my driveway, or the development of a pipeline that poses serious threats to environment and health. These are all actual threats. Are controlling actions against them morally permissible or even morally required?

First, let's address attempts to use controlling strategies against great threats. What does it look like to employ strategies of escape, removal, destruction, assimilation, or overpowering against great threats of, for example, loss or unpredictability? The answer is, we do not often directly attempt to control these great threats because they are larger than any material threat. We cannot escape, remove, destroy, assimilate, or overpower them. I have claimed that we do in some cases try to control such threats indirectly via processes of compelling fears and attempting to control proxy (nonstatistical) threats, and I have given the argument above for why doing so is morally unacceptable. It is unjustifiably harming the proxy threats.

Great threats are not the kinds of things that can be eliminated, avoided, or transferred. Recall Sarah Tyson's account of pocket parks and eliminative strategies, discussed in section 1. I underscored her claim that eliminative strategies do not succeed in making communities safer. Tyson turns to Judith Butler's (2009) account of vulnerability in *Frames of War* to make this case. On Butler's view, since vulnerability is an unavoidable part of embodied human life, attempts to prevent or eradicate it, including attempts to prevent the presence of people we perceive to be the sources of violence, are in vain. The fact that we are all vulnerable is not something that can be altered by removing some people we think of as making us vulnerable. In *Precarious Life*, Butler writes:

> The body implies mortality, vulnerability, agency: the skin and the flesh expose us to the gaze of others, but also to touch, and to

violence, and bodies put us at risk of becoming the agency and instrument of all these as well. . . .

. . . Violence is surely a touch of the worst order, a way a primary human vulnerability to other humans is exposed in its most terrifying way. . . . In a way, we all live with this particular vulnerability [to violence]. . . .

. . . To foreclose that vulnerability, to banish it, to make ourselves secure at the expense of every other human consideration is to eradicate one of the most important resources from which we must take our bearings and find our way. (Butler 2004, 26, 28, 30)

Employing Butler's account of vulnerability, Tyson argues that pocket parks as attempted eliminative strategies do not make communities safer. Rather, at their root, eliminative strategies aim to destroy vulnerability by removing select people who are seen as making others vulnerable to harm—but such strategies cannot succeed since, in fact, vulnerability is an ineliminable disposition.

What about the moral status of controlling strategies against other kinds of (nongreat) actual threats? Evaluation of these actions will need to be fine-grained. We need to know how controlling actions potentially affect everyone involved in such cases in order to evaluate them. Consider the difference between (1) my using controlling strategies against actual threats in ways that help others, (2) my using controlling strategies against actual threats in ways that have no effect on others, and (3) my using controlling strategies against actual threats in ways that create threat for (threatening or nonthreatening) others. Each of these will have a different moral status.

For the first case, of using a controlling strategy against an actual threat in a way that helps others, imagine a harassing family member at a holiday dinner. In response to this person persistently touching and hugging other women and children in the family even after they express discomfort and demand that he stop, I might pursue controlling strategies of escape (gathering up everyone else and leaving the event) or removal (insisting that he leave and not come to future family events). Either would be a controlling strategy that would help some others (i.e., all the family members being harassed by him and anyone else distressed by such harassment). I would be *limiting* the harassing family member, but not harming him, since stopping him from acting in harmful ways is not itself a harm. This is a controlling strategy used against an actual threat that should be seen as morally permissible and perhaps even morally required.

For the second kind of case, of using a controlling strategy against an actual threat in a way that does not affect others, imagine I live alone in a remote area and my house is at the bottom of a long gravel driveway. Imagine a large pothole develops in the driveway. The pothole is large enough to do some damage to my car if I drive directly on it, but no one else is going to face the pothole. I might employ the controlling strategy of removal: filling in the pothole. This would be a controlling strategy that has no effect on others. All else being equal, it is morally permissible.

The third kind of case, where I might use controlling strategies against actual threats in ways that create threat for (threatening or nonthreatening) others, is the most complex. Imagine I participate in a blockade preventing the building of a pipeline through unceded First Nations territory. I might be joining with many others in attempting to control the threat of the pipeline with the use of removal: repeatedly removing pipeline developers from the land. Someone might argue that this is a controlling strategy that helps some and creates threat for others, some of whom are themselves threatening (i.e., the pipeline developers) and others of whom are not (i.e., community members who hope the pipeline development will increase options for employment in the area). In such a case, the threats against current and future generations must be understood and evaluated, including threats against those who are threatening (since being threatening oneself does not automatically mean that others are justified in harming you—see the above discussion of self-defense). While it is true that some people may be harmed because there will now be fewer jobs available, the potential current and long-term harms of the pipeline being developed are much greater. And so the controlling strategy can be understood as morally permissible, even if it threatens some others.

In sum, the moral evaluation of controlling strategies against actual threats is complicated. Great threats cannot be controlled, and attempts to do so regularly result in the cases of controlling proxy nonstatistical threats that have concerned me in this chapter. Other actual threats in some cases *can* be controlled, and in such cases we need to employ a fine-grained analysis of whether controlling strategies are appropriate. Do these threats even require a response? If they do, we should ask whether there are options for responding to the threats *other* than controlling strategies, which may well be preferable. We may find other ways to respond to actual threats—ways that do not position us as controllers of them. If other options do not exist, we will need to consider the effects of such strategies on the actual threat, on the person(s) exercising the controlling strategy, and on others, including ourselves. We must consider possible effects the practice of controlling strategies might have on those practicing them. How might practicing controlling strategies in response to actual threats shape the habits and future practice of fearers? We should consider the potential damage of controlling strategies, not only on those things controlled but also on those controlling. Determining whether or to what extent controlling strategies help or harm all these parties will help us evaluate the moral status of such actions. Controlling strategies in response to actual threats can also be morally problematic, and developing capacities for non-controlling strategies in response to such threats can be morally productive.

D. Some Responses

Someone might respond that the controlling strategies I have described in response to perceived (nonstatistical) threats have the merit of making individuals safer, insofar as they make us *feel* safer. But just as we distinguished perceived threats from actual threats in chapter 3, we can distinguish felt safety from actual safety. I might feel safer when in fact I am less safe than I was before. Taking a few swimming lessons might make me feel safer and more confident in the water, when really I am at greater risk precisely because I am now confident enough to go in the deep end without a life jacket. Conversely, I might feel less safe when I am, in actuality, safer: assuming that those in the gated communities Setha Low examined in fact experience fewer threats to their safety (e.g., fewer break-ins than those in surrounding neighborhoods)—a point that would need to be confirmed empirically—they might still claim to feel quite unsafe. So we cannot point to more *felt* safety as evidence of more *actual* safety. Removing, escaping, destroying, assimilating, or overpowering perceived (nonstatistical) threats may certainly make individuals feel safer without in fact making them safer.

I want to pause to return to the point raised earlier about tendencies to respond to perceived threats by employing strategies of destruction. It might seem strange how commonly first responses to perceived threats involve attempted destruction: shooting at potentially threatening figures, using pesticides or herbicides rather than first trying more subtle interventions, and so on. As discussed, tactics of destruction are particularly costly in terms of both risk and energy. Destruction is more final and less correctable than the other potential strategies while also in some cases requiring very high levels of energy output on the part of the destroyer. How, then, can we make sense of the tendency to want to use destruction as a tactic?

I want to suggest it is the allure of complete and final control that makes attempts at destruction particularly satisfying. Even if destruction is very costly, rarely effective, and potentially accompanied by great regret, the belief that one *could* fully and permanently control the source of a threat if one wanted to would bring the ultimate feeling of relief. Successful destruction efforts are potentially the most satisfying antidote to the feeling (of unmanageable, uncontrollable threats) that triggers the process of compelling fears and controlling threats to begin with. Of course, efforts to destroy perceived threats are not always successful, even at managing the perceived threats that may have very little to do with the underlying unmanageable threats individuals struggle to confront.

7. Conclusion

In this chapter, we have examined five common attempts to control perceived (non)threats, after fearers have compelled fears of substantial, uncontrollable threats onto more manageable objects. I have argued that, beyond being largely unsatisfying, these responses often take the form of attempting to transfer threats from oneself to the perceived (nonstatistical) threat and that such attempts are morally troubling.

In *The Fire Next Time*, James Baldwin writes to his nephew that those who are imprisoned cannot be free until those who *believe prisons will make them safer* are free (1993, 9–10). The belief that *threatening others could relieve oneself of threat* is in this case an illusion, and it is one that harms those imprisoned. Those who held onto the belief needed to be freed of it in order that both groups could be freed. But the question remains, what will allow those of us who persist in believing that we could be safer by means of threatening nonthreatening others to be freed of that belief?

In the next chapter, we turn to the question of what other responses to our fears are possible. As Biss writes of her experience of parenthood, as well as of human agency more broadly,

> As Jean-Paul Sartre put it, "Freedom is what you do with what's been done to you." What has been done to us seems to be, among other things, that we have been made fearful. What will we do with our fear? This strikes me as a central question of both citizenship and motherhood. As mothers, we must somehow square our power with our powerlessness. We can protect our children to some extent. But we cannot make them invulnerable any more than we can make ourselves invulnerable. "Life," as Donna Haraway writes, "is a window of vulnerability." (Biss 2014, 152)

The question of what to do with our fears is centrally a question of what to do with our vulnerability. This will be the focus of our final chapter.

5
Fearing Better

I have argued that fears are a central part of our relating to others, that fears of the uncontrollable make up a significant portion of our emotional lives, and that such fears are often compelled onto more manageable perceived threats. Individuals often attempt to control these perceived threats, but such efforts are typically unsatisfying and, in many cases, morally unacceptable. The question remains: how could we experience and respond to these fears differently?

Recall from chapter 1 that the Chapman University Survey of American Fears is one of the best-known surveys specifically designed to reflect patterns of fearing. In addition to reflecting on complications in conducting such a survey and on trends in what survey participants feared over time, survey developers Bader and colleagues have also suggested that fear can have "potentially disastrous social and political consequences" (Bader et al. 2020, 12), that it can have "noxious consequences for health and well-being" (124). As such, individuals should find ways to manage it and resist "its lure" (12). Their suggestions for fear management include avoiding overtly partisan media, limiting screen time and phone use, facing one's fears and learning about the things one is afraid of, planning for future threats within reason, being on guard about the use of fear to manipulate one into purchasing or voting, not allowing fear to undermine one's trust in others, not allowing oneself to be controlled by fear in the absence of imminent danger, and in cases of danger, doing things to ameliorate the threat (132–35). They go so far as to say that "although there are many useful aspects of fear, the greatest danger is ironically posed by fear itself" (136).

It should be clear by now that while I agree that fear can have dangerous consequences for the health and well-being of individuals and communities, I want to suggest that a very different approach to fear is needed. Management of and resistance to fear is not the path forward.

In fact, I will suggest that fearers pursue something closer to the opposite: allowance and acceptance.

In section 1, I consider practices that can support developing awareness of our practices and habits of compelling fears. In section 2, I chart alternative modes of fearing together. In section 3, I situate these in the contexts of crises like the COVID-19 pandemic.

1. Developing Awareness of Our Practices and Habits of Compelling Fears

Part of fearing differently and better will require developing awareness of some facts about fearing—in particular, awareness of how the processes I have described in chapters 3 and 4 play out in our own lives. We have seen that the threats we perceive may not actually be the sources of our feelings of fear but only proxies. We have also seen that our strategies to control these perceived (proxy) threats will not actually succeed in controlling the underlying threats and therefore fail to bring meaningful relief, in addition to being morally and politically troubling. These have been philosophical arguments. What would it be like to gain a personal awareness of these processes and their presence in our own lives?

The experience of gaining this awareness is very likely to be difficult and to trigger defense mechanisms in individuals, not only because many of us would like to believe we have more jurisdiction over our own processes of thinking and feeling than this suggests, and not only because this suggests that we might be failing morally in new ways, but also, and perhaps most of all, because there is a certain amount of trust many of us place in our perceptions of threat and our fear responses. The possibility of a disconnect there—that we might not be able to trust our feelings of fear to tell us what to do—can be deeply disconcerting. If not our feelings of fear, what can we trust to alert us to genuine threats and to guide our actions?

Dissociating from our feelings of fear and perceptions of threat is neither tenable nor desirable. This is not what I am recommending. Yet the arguments in chapters 3 and 4 do suggest that a different way of relating to fears is in some cases needed. We need more ways to respond to the experiences of fear we have now and to consider different practices of relating to fears in the future.

It seems clear that part of what is needed are ways to identify and experience the fears we already have without immediately taking them to be accurate indicators of threats in the world or trustworthy guides for action. If we realize that our individual fearing lives are situated in and shaped by a social context filled with troubling patterns and practices of fearing—that fear is a thing we learn and do with others and that we have learned to fear badly—then we might begin to cultivate a safe way of inhabiting our own practices of fearing, with a capacity to recognize fearing for what it is. In some therapeutic approaches, this recognition is cultivated first through capacities for awareness: to recognize what and how one is feeling, without judgment and without trying to make the feelings go away. These feelings of fear, whatever threats they seem to be caused by, and whatever action they seem to be pointing to are simply the feelings one is having right now. They do not yet tell us any facts, and they do not yet tell us what to do.

Imagine we believe all this about our fears and are committed to responding to fears differently. Still, the actual *experience and practice* of coming to do so is likely to be challenging because doing so will require cultivating new habits of feeling and responding to our feelings. Habits of fearing are hard to break. The solution is not to stop feeling fearful, to deny the fears one has, or to dissociate from them. As we have seen, fears do not always respond to pleas that they go away or that they respond to reason. Fear can be painful and the urge to eliminate perceived sources of fear can be strong. As we saw in chapters 1 and 2, fearing processes in the brain are complicated enough that simply willing oneself to be less afraid is not typically successful. Rather, individuals will need to develop capacities for genuinely experiencing and allowing ourselves to experience feelings of fear while remaining intact as agents who get to perceive and decide how to respond to such feelings rather than simply being at their mercy and under their control. This means we will need to practice new ways of feeling fearful without immediately being drawn into action by these feelings, without rushing to resolve, escape, or otherwise dispel them.

A great deal of work in therapeutic contexts has been done to help identify and understand strategies that can help individuals develop capacities for genuinely experiencing feelings and for responding to them in ways that harm neither those with the feelings nor anyone else. I am thinking mainly of mindfulness-based and somatic-regulation approaches to emotional life. While varying widely, these approaches share a commitment to helping individuals become better able to remain present while experiencing their feelings and to recognize that their feelings are in flux. Feelings come and go, and, with practice, they can be noticed and accepted without one needing to avoid or attack them. The goal of many of these approaches is to give individuals practices that can help them feel secure enough to be able to experience their feelings without being overtaken or controlled by them.

A. Mindfulness

Mindfulness-based stress reduction (MBSR) programs aim to help individuals respond to difficult emotions. One of their best-known popularizers, Jon Kabat-Zinn, defines mindfulness as "the awareness that arises by paying attention on purpose, in the present moment, and non-judgmentally" (Kabat-Zinn 2013, xxxv). The UMass Memorial Health Center for Mindfulness in Worcester, Massachusetts, offers an eight-week MBSR program in which participants commit to daily practices of focusing on their breathing and learn a variety of ways to practice (e.g., eating meditation, sitting meditation, body scans, yoga, walking meditation, and mindfulness in daily life). Individuals are encouraged to come to mindfulness practice with seven attitudinal factors: nonjudging, patience, a beginner's mind, trust, nonstriving, acceptance, and letting go (Kabat-Zinn 2013, 21).

Kabat-Zinn notes that as humans, we are constantly judging our experiences: our thoughts are streams of judgments, liking or disliking things, people, or events. Some thoughts and feelings the mind wants to hold onto—pleasant ones—and others the mind wants to avoid—painful ones. In meditative practice, the task is to simply observe thoughts and feelings rather than judge them. As Kabat-Zinn writes,

> This habit of categorizing and judging our experience locks us into automatic reactions that we are not even aware of and that often

have no objective basis at all. These judgments tend to dominate our minds, making it difficult for us ever to find any peace within ourselves, or to develop any discernment as to what may actually be going on, inwardly or outwardly. (Kabat-Zinn 2013, 22)

In mindfulness practice, we do not need to *do* anything with thoughts and feelings, just notice them, while continuing to focus on the sensations of breathing. Instead of letting our actions be dictated by impulses to avoid our feelings, we can use this practice to create more space for us to respond to those feelings:

> When we are mindful of our breathing, it automatically helps us to establish greater calmness in both the body and the mind. Then we are better able to be aware of our thoughts and feelings with a greater degree of calm and with a more discerning eye. We are able to see things more clearly and within a larger perspective, all because we are a little more awake, a little more aware. And with this awareness comes a feeling of having more room to move, of having more options, of being free to choose effective and appropriate responses in stressful situations rather than losing our equilibrium and sense of self as a result of feeling overwhelmed, thrown off balance by our own knee-jerk reactions. (Kabat-Zinn 2013, 49–50)

Mindfulness practices draw attention to experience in the present moment rather than to past memories or regrets or future plans or worries. They encourage participants to practice responding to stress more mindfully: to pay attention to bodily sensations and to the breath that continues. Doing so can help practitioners turn toward rather than away from stressors. In fact, on this view of mindfulness, practices of noticing sensations of discomfort can give individuals opportunities to develop flexibility and to be able to welcome other uncomfortable experiences when they arise. Mindfulness has been shown to improve physical and emotional health (Kabat-Zinn 2013; Hoffman et al. 2012; Grossman et al. 2004; Hölzel et al. 2011).

We are likely to judge feelings of fear as extremely unpleasant. We might want to move past them and perhaps think that there is something we can *do* to make the fear feelings go away. As Kabat-Zinn understands them, mindfulness practices have direct implications for coming to respond to fears differently:

> The cultivation of greater mindfulness also gives us new ways of working with what we find threatening, and of learning how to respond intelligently to such perceived threats rather than react automatically and trigger potentially unhealthy consequences. (Kabat-Zinn 2013, xxxviii)

The term "intelligent" here is meant to indicate mindful—responsive rather than reactive. Mindfulness practices in part encourage individuals to simply notice the experience and thoughts associated with fear. *There is fear. That's how it feels in my body. There's my body resisting the feeling. There are the thoughts about what I might do to make this feeling go away.* All this can be noticed. No action steps need follow.

In contrast to the controlling strategies discussed in chapter 4, mindfulness approaches aim to cultivate some degree of awareness of the impulse to control and some degree of acceptance of what will not be controllable. As Kabat-Zinn writes,

> Feeling threatened can easily lead to feelings of anger and hostility and from there to outright aggressive behavior, driven by deep instincts to protect your position and maintain your sense of things being under control. When things do feel "under control," we might feel content for a moment. But when they go out of control again, or even seem to be getting out of control, our deepest insecurities can erupt. At such times we might even act in ways that are self-destructive and hurtful to others. And we will feel anything but content and at peace within ourselves. (Kabat-Zinn 2013, lii)

Welcoming sensations of fear may allow us to explore them. This may reduce fear's intensity, and it may not. But it also may help in "becoming more transparent to it, so that it is less eroding of [one's] quality of life" (Kabat-Zinn 2013, 63). And the practice of welcoming sensations of fear, rather than simply acting in some way to make them go away, will, according to MBSR approaches at least, help us "develop some degree of calmness, equanimity, and flexibility of mind" (63), which will help us face many different challenges, stresses, and pains.

When feeling threatened or fearful, we might experiment with noticing and accepting the feeling. Upon noticing the feeling, Kabat-Zinn asks,

> Can you see it clearly as an impulse, a thought, a desire, a judgment, and let it be here and let it go without being drawn into it, without investing it with a power it doesn't have, without losing yourself in the process? (Kabat-Zinn 2013, 95)

Many feelings of fear may be tied to discomfort and pain: perceiving something that causes us pain now, and wanting to feel better in the future. We feel fear, have thoughts about perceived threats, and begin to strategize about what we could do to eliminate those feelings or perceived threats. Instead of saying "I am afraid," Kabat-Zinn suggests we might try saying "I am experiencing a lot of fear-filled thoughts" or "This is the feeling of believing _____ will make me feel safe" (Kabat-Zinn 2013, 445). Having noticed the thought or feeling, we don't need to do anything else with it: "Fear, panic, and anxiety will no longer be uncontrollable demons. Instead you will see them as natural mental states that can be worked with and accepted just like any others" (448).

Someone might resist this approach from a concern about motivation. If we are now simply noticing feelings and letting them go, will feelings no longer be motivators toward action? *Shouldn't* we be motivated by feelings? MBSR approaches are not suggesting that feelings will no longer motivate action. Rather, by creating some space between feelings and automatic action, actions will be motivated as considered responses to some feelings rather than as impulsive reactions to all feelings.

B. Somatic Regulation

In *The Body Keeps the Score*, psychiatrist Bessel van der Kolk (2015) proposes an evidence-based approach to trauma processing focused on improving the regulation of physiological states with the goal of improving cognitive processing.[1] His research and therapeutic practices address and employ various combinations of somatic-focused therapies, all of which have the goal of putting traumatic events into their proper place in the arc of an individual's life and allowing for an individual to "fully feel and befriend the distressing feelings in [their] body" (van der Kolk 2015, 230). Somatic-based therapists can employ a number of questions when considering which therapies may be most helpful:

> What are these patients trying to cope with? What are their internal or external resources? How do they calm themselves down? Do they have caring relationships with their bodies, and what do they do to cultivate a physical sense of power, vitality, and relaxation? Do they have dynamic interactions with other people? Who really knows them, loves them, and cares about them? Whom can they count on when they're scared, when their babies are ill, or when they are sick themselves? . . . How can we help them feel in charge of their lives? (van der Kolk 2015, 351–52)

The practices themselves include mindfulness practices, sensory integration,[2] somatic experiencing (e.g., model mugging programs where people are taught to actively fight off a simulated attack), eye movement desensitization and reprocessing (EMDR), hypnosis, free writing, art, music, dance, yoga, internal family systems therapy,[3] psychomotor therapy,[4] neurofeedback,[5] and theater programs, among other approaches. These programs have various strengths and some are better suited to certain participants than others, but the point of all of them is to help individuals come to be able to experience their feelings related to histories of trauma, which can be very challenging given that a common self-protective mechanism in response to trauma is numbing, strong resistance to embodied experience, and alexithymia (inability to recognize what one is feeling).

Some but not all the experiences of fear I have been discussing throughout the book are tied to traumatic pasts. It is worth recognizing that unbearable feelings of fear or incapacities to allow for one's feelings of fear may be, for many more people than we think, connected to legacies of pain and trauma. It is not the case that everyone has been traumatized, but as we become increasingly aware of the prevalence of trauma in childhoods, relationships, contexts of oppression, and everyday life in militaristic and violent societies, we are right to recognize the breadth of traumatic histories among our communities. In considering the use of somatic-regulation approaches for helping individuals experience fear, I want to suggest that these may be particularly helpful for those individuals who experience difficulties in processes of fear connected to traumatic experiences, there may be more individuals than one might think whose difficulties in processes of fear are (at least in part) connected to traumatic experiences, and these somatic-regulation approaches may be useful also for those whose difficulties in processes of fear are *not* connected to traumatic experiences. Difficulties in processes of fearing are not unique to those with traumatic experiences, but they certainly *can* be familiar to those with histories or continued experiences of trauma, and many more people may fall into that group than perhaps communities might like to admit.

What I find particularly useful about van der Kolk's somatic-regulation approach is its recognition of the many challenges that can be involved in learning to allow for having and experiencing feelings of fear without being overtaken by them. The most significant harms we have seen in this book are outgrowths of fears being so unbearable that individuals prefer taking almost any action—even actions with devastating consequences for themselves and others—to simply sitting with the experiences of fear. What if fear were less unbearable? More to the point, what could *make* fear less unbearable?

Some of the most compelling accounts from van der Kolk's research and practice demonstrate the significance of relationships in making the difference between fears that cannot be borne and fears that can. Fearing with others can make fear more bearable. The physical and verbal presence of loved ones can most powerfully allow us to experience fear without resisting or otherwise refusing it. As van der Kolk writes,

> When we are terrified, nothing calms us down like the reassuring voice or the firm embrace of someone we trust. Frightened adults

respond to the same comforts as terrified children: gentle holding and rocking and the assurance that somebody bigger and stronger is taking care of things, so you can safely go to sleep. In order to recover, mind, body, and brain need to be convinced that it is safe to let go. That happens only when you feel safe at a visceral level and allow yourself to connect that sense of safety with memories of past helplessness. (van der Kolk 2015, 212)

Recognizing the ways fear is embodied can allow us to recognize the ways we can cope with fear relationally. Difficulty allowing oneself to simply experience fear without acting on it can stem from difficulties tolerating the way fear feels in one's body. Fear is hyperarousing. As such, coping strategies that make us feel physically grounded and safe even during experiences of fear can be powerful parts of efforts to build up new capacities for fearing. And, as it turns out, firm, steady, calming physical contact with other people—being held, hugged, and rocked—is one of the things that grounds many people best. Being able to rest and surrender to the embrace of others can calm individuals and thereby allow them to feel more in control, more able to recognize and accept their fears as emotional states that will come and go, rather than feel controlled by them.

In addition to the steadying effects of physical contact, the experience of being able to express feelings and have them understood is profound. This is another way in which allowing ourselves to better experience fear is a relational endeavor. As van der Kolk writes,

Feeling listened to and understood changes our physiology; being able to articulate a complex feeling, and having our feelings recognized, lights up our limbic brain and creates an "aha moment." In contrast, being met by silence and incomprehension kills the spirit. (van der Kolk 2015, 234)

The expression of fears will be an important part of becoming able to experience them without being so overtaken by them that we rush to control anything we perceive as causing fear. Van der Kolk describes in part the importance of relationships with therapists, while also noting that our closest relationships are with people we live with and regularly relate to—family, friends, loved ones, and kin. These are the relationships within which we as individuals are both expressers and (to return to the term introduced by Sue Campbell in chapter 2) *interpreters*. As interpreters, we have the responsibility to listen to the expressions of loved ones with openness. This will mean, in part, allowing for and sitting with the fears of our loved ones, which can itself be painful. Very often, we do not feel comfortable with our loved ones feeling afraid. We would like to reassure them or to prevent them from experiencing fears. We may want to dismiss their fears as unfounded, in part to reassure ourselves and to avoid our own possible fears: there is nothing that will harm them, and none of us has reason to be afraid. As such, developing capacities to allow for others' expressions of their fears depends in large part on developing capacities to accept and allow for our own feelings of fear. If we cannot bear feeling fearful ourselves, we will not likely be able to bear our loved ones' expressions of their fears. To allow for others' expressions of fear also involves a responsibility to become able to experience and accept our own feelings of fear—an ability that itself depends in part on our relationships with others, on others being there to support us in our expressions. We can see again how fearing better is a deeply and complexly relational project.

Van der Kolk's analysis demonstrates the importance of relationships for individuals who are processing trauma and moving toward feeling safe and at home in their bodies and able to simply experience and accept their feelings. As he notes,

> Traumatized human beings recover in the context of relationships: with families, loved ones, AA meetings, veterans' organizations, religious communities, or professional therapists. The role of those relationships is to provide physical and emotional safety, including safety from feeling shamed, admonished, or judged, and to bolster the courage to tolerate, face, and process the reality of what has happened. (van der Kolk 2015, 212)

Given that so many people struggle so much to allow themselves to simply experience fear without rushing to correct or control it, it seems clear that many of us could benefit from strategies for fearing better, in ways that allow us to feel safe and at home in our bodies and able to simply experience and accept our feelings of fear. Somatic-regulation therapies offer potentially helpful strategies, including relational practices of physical contact and attentive listening.

C. Politicized Somatics

Work in politicized somatics shares some of the foundational commitments of somatic-regulation approaches—the fundamental understanding of the need to experience and accept feelings so that we can become able to choose to act rather than be overcome by such feelings, and the need for work at the level of embodied practices in order to both experience our feelings and mindfully choose our responses to them. Generative Somatics is one US-based organization leading work and training in politicized somatics, and they have articulated critiques of some somatic-regulation approaches for lacking an assessment of the social conditions that create the oppressive and individualistic ways of being that we embody (Generative Somatics 2014, 2). Politicized somatics work integrates practices for healing individual and systemic trauma, addressing privilege and oppression, and strengthening movement organizations, potentially shifting from blame, critique, and low emotional capacity to becoming a more attractive presence with a holistic and transformative approach (Generative Somatics 2011, 5–6).

All individuals have default practices inherited through life experiences, and these default practices are embodied. Some may be beneficial to individuals and communities and others may be harmful. As Ng'ethe Maina and Staci Haines explain,

> Violence, oppression, rejection, loss, or other situations that threatened our safety as children (and as adults) all played a role in shaping our default practices. . . . These practices were formed at a time when we needed them—they played a crucial role in our survival and our ability to belong.
>
> However . . . these practices often don't align with our present-day values, politics, and/or what we care most about. . . .

> The good news is that we can learn to observe our default practices, instead of reacting out of them immediately. We can learn ... other ways to deal with conflict, power, our own and others['] emotions and need for safety. (Maina and Haines 2008, 1–2)

Politicized somatics can help us create nonharmful default practices. Histories of trauma are one of a number of causes for individuals struggling to experience and focus on whatever is currently happening. Those who have experienced trauma can find it very difficult to tolerate feelings in the present moment, and they are not the only ones. Generative Somatics supports participants in three major areas: somatic awareness, somatic opening, and somatic practices.

Somatic awareness involves learning to listen to and live inside of sensations and aliveness (e.g., sensations of temperature, pressure, and movement as sources of information). In contrast to dissociation, minimization, and numbing, becoming connected to sensation brings one back into contact with oneself. Participants begin to pay attention to their automatic reactions, seeing whether they can feel and tolerate their own emotions or whether they instead feel a need to rid themselves of their emotions by denying them or taking them out on others. Using meditation, centering practices, and self-awareness, participants "build in time between [the] internal reaction and [the] external action. You can feel more without reacting" (Maina and Haines 2008, 2). The key is allowing oneself to feel the emotions rather than avoiding them. Avoidance is an instance of immediately acting on one's feelings: one cannot tolerate feeling them, and so one *does* something to avoid them. Becoming better able to tolerate and accept the feelings themselves is what creates the space between feeling them and choosing how to act:

> Being present and able to "allow for" sensations and emotions, produces more choice and less reaction. So often what we are fundamentally reacting to is not being able to feel or tolerate what is happening in our own sensations, emotions and experience. Somatic awareness and embodiment ... grows more choice in our responses and actions. (Generative Somatics 2014, 3)

Somatic opening uses touch, massage, conversation, imagination, and emotional processes to work "through the body to access and transform survival reactions, experiences that have shaped us, and emotions or numbing that has become automatic" (Generative Somatics 2014, 3). The goal is to access the ongoing armoring in the body to process the underlying concern (for safety, love, protection, shame). While direct body work like massage is important in these processes, it must work alongside the emotional work of identifying, experiencing, and talking about the feelings that come up in order to be effective over time.

Once space has been created between internal reaction and external action, that space can be used to cultivate different practices that better reflect participants' commitments rather than simply reflecting what they have been accustomed to practicing in the past. *Somatic practice* involves developing new skills like having boundaries to take care of self and others, mutual contact and intimacy, moving toward what is important to you, building trust, and accountability. New practices will lead to change at the level of feelings and embodiment: "As we practice new movements, internal conversations . . . and new emotional states, we are creating new neuronal pathways in the brain and new muscle memory in the body" (Maina and Haines 2008, 3).

Like somatic-regulation approaches, politicized somatics can be helpful not only for healing trauma but also for everyday practices of coming to fear differently.

While mindfulness, somatic-regulation, and politicized-somatics approaches differ in a number of ways, they share a respect for emotional experiences. Fear is not something to be simply dismissed.[6] The controlling strategies that I have argued should concern us grow out of resistance to feelings of fear. They are attempts to do or plan in some way that will *fix* fears. Mindfulness, somatic-regulation, and politicized-somatics approaches ask, what would happen if we instead received the feelings without needing to do anything further? A major goal of these approaches is to develop ways of experiencing fear that do not lead to compelling fears or to resorting to the controlling strategies I have discussed. As such, it seems to me the most pressing question is, *what relational and social conditions could allow us to simply receive the feelings of fear*? How could we come to receive feelings of fear together?

2. Alternative Modes of Fearing Together

Once we begin to understand fear as something we must receive and hold together, we can focus energy not only on criticizing or directly countering the harms of controlling strategies (though this will need to remain a task, for as long as people turn to controlling strategies) but also on what we can do with the fears before we reach the point of compelling or controlling. How do we build different relationships within which fear can be received, instead of ones that contribute to the sense that fears must be acted upon, resisted, or fixed?

We have seen already how an aspect of relationality is contained within some mindfulness-based approaches. As Kabat-Zinn writes,

> I have increasingly come to realize that mindfulness is essentially about relationality—in other words, how we are in relationship to everything, including our own minds and bodies, our thoughts and emotions, our past and what transpired to bring us, still breathing, into this moment—and how we can learn to live our way into every aspect of life with integrity, with kindness toward ourselves and others, and with wisdom. (Kabat-Zinn 2013, xxxvii)

And certainly, within some of the somatic-regulation strategies and the politicized somatics, there is an awareness of the crucial role others play in facilitating our capacities to work with difficult feelings. This points to what I see as a central claim of this book: avoiding some of the major dangers of fearing that I have outlined depends on the cultivation of relationships that help individuals bear their experiences of fear. Fearing better depends on our fearing together.

A. Staying with Fearers

On a June 2019 episode of the parenting podcast *Raising Rebels* entitled "The Wonder of the Unknown," host Noleca Radway (2019) and guest Carvell Wallace have a conversation about supporting their children in times of uncertainty. The conversation suggests that what is most important in learning how to respond to fear as children, or as anyone, is to come to be able to *remain present in our bodies*—to practice focusing on one's breath and feeling grounded in one's current embodiment. This echoes what we have seen in proponents of somatic-based therapies. But Wallace and Radway consistently tie the importance of remaining present in embodiment to core interpersonal relationships. What we need to do to cope with fear is to remain present in embodiment, *and we cannot fully do this alone*. Our capacities to remain present in fear depend on the past and current participation of others with whom we are in relationship: how we are present in their fearing, and how they are present in ours. The focus of the episode is parent-child relationships, but its lessons are far more expansively applicable.

Radway raises the example of how she felt as a child when her mother was unable to pay the electric bill and the power would temporarily be turned off in her home, and yet she was for some reason not afraid. Wallace notes that this experience was also common for him as a child, and he too was not afraid: "There was something about those nights . . . it didn't bother me. . . . Just the pure fact of walking through those candlelit nights with my mom. . . . We were in a thing together." Radway agrees, "There is something about the role my mother played in that space which was like, safety." They reflect together: this felt okay because they were present together with their mothers, and that felt like the antidote to fear. The future unknowns persist (Will the power come back on? Will we be okay?), but the present is fine—it is calm, even—because we are here together. Notably, this is the perspective of Wallace and Radway *as children*, not the perspective of their mothers. Now, as parents themselves, they each acknowledge the ways helping one's children remain present does not always translate into a relief from fear for the parents.

Of course, parent-child relationships are not the only ones that allow for this. Many other people can help us to remain present in our fear, by remaining present there with us, and we remain present for many other sorts of people beyond any children we may care for. Contra images of meditation involving hyper-alone individuals going deeply within themselves, by themselves, this isolated state is not typically where we learn to stay present while fearing. Others tether us and allow us to be present while fearing with them. This is not to say that others are fearing *for* us or fearing the same things as we are, or that we are aligning fully in fearing. The "staying with" is more complicated. Fearing together is so fundamental to our emotional well-being that there are disorders that arise from having to fear alone. Sometimes it was someone's responsibility to be there with us in our processes of fear, and they were not. In fact, this failure of presence is not at all uncommon because the weight of fully being there for all those for whom we need to be present, while also holding our own fears in social contexts that fail to ensure our basic needs are met, is impossible for any one person to bear. So it is the norm that we will fail each other sometimes. We must ask what we can do to sometimes succeed.

What does it mean to stay present with others as they fear? The fearing-together relationships I have in mind are fundamentally those that, as Radway and Wallace discuss, allow parties to remain present while fearing rather than experience fears and immediately need to avoid, attack, or fix them. As such, these are relationships that in any number of ways allow us to *experience and express* fears openly and in ways that help fearers simply *have* the experiences rather than need to do anything about them.

Sometimes this means that individuals will feel fearful and be able to express that verbally or in other kinds of actions, with those around them being able to perceive and accept that they are feeling fear, and to hold steady with them through that experience, rather than reacting in some negative way (e.g., with judgment, blame, dismissal, shame, or other modes of communicating that the feelings of fear are unacceptable). In the simplest terms, staying with fearers requires effort to listen to, otherwise perceive, or potentially anticipate a fearer's expression of fear, and it requires effort to relate to that fearer verbally and in behavior in ways that communicate that their fears are recognized, held, and accepted. The goal is to make it possible for fearers themselves to simply have the feelings of fear, potentially also employing mindfulness or somatic-regulation strategies, without immediately needing to avoid or fix the feeling, by use of controlling strategy or otherwise.

The actions involved in this "staying with" are complex and in some cases will require a significant effort on the part of those committed to staying with the fearer. Though I refer to people who stay with fearers as "interpreters," as we will see, the roles of "fearers" and "interpreters" are not always—perhaps rarely—fully distinct. For the most part I am describing relationships where all parties within them are at some times expressing fears and at other times being present as interpreters for others' expressions of fears—and sometimes these instances overlap. Of course, relationships within which people express fears are not always so symmetrical. For better or worse, sometimes (e.g., in professional therapeutic relationships or in other relationships with asymmetrical dynamics) only one party does the expressing, and another party does the interpreting.

Staying with fearers will require self-awareness and self-regulation on the part of interpreters. Whatever feelings the interpreters themselves experience while attempting to stay with fearers—and it would be a rare case when interpreters would not have feelings come up during the process—will need to be recognized but not allowed to eclipse the experience of the fearer. Interpreters need to be able to hold the space for fearers' expressions, even if they too have fears or other feelings that will also properly need to be expressed.

Interestingly, as in Wallace and Radway's electricity examples above, fear does not always quite come to the surface because, by inhabiting potentially threatening situations together, at least *some* of the parties are able to feel present rather than overwhelmed by fear of future possibilities. Much more could then be said about the emotional toll on those (in this case, mothers) who work to help others regulate their fear and about what supports they might need to help experience and express their *own* experiences of fear. The importance of interpreters cannot be overstated.

The goal of staying with other fearers in their experiences and expressions of fears is not to make the fears go away, though of course fears are dynamic and sometimes they will dissipate. Neither is the goal to endorse anything and everything a fearer might express. Rather, the goal is to help make the experience of fearing more bearable so that fearers are not driven by the suffering of fearing to do whatever is necessary to avoid or fix their fears. This "staying with" can involve curiosity, openness, and the creation of common ground between fearers and interpreters. As we saw in the discussion of Freud in chapter 3, different people have different dynamic thresholds for how much fear they can bear before fleeing from it. The shifting limit points of different people will need to be part of what gets recognized and accepted in these relationships.

B. Complications of These Relationships

Though I am making the case for why these relationships of staying with fearers will be necessary, they are at the same time complicated for a number of reasons: (1) relating to others whose threats and fears we do not share is difficult; (2) relating to others whose fears we *do* share can be dangerous; and (3) fears themselves are constantly in flux.

i. Relating to Others Whose Threats and Fears We Do Not Share Is Difficult

As we know, what fears people have depend on a great number of factors, different people fear different things, and it can be challenging to understand or relate to fears others have that we do not share.

We saw in chapter 1 that different individuals will have different senses of what is threatening, for many reasons. Many fears do not reflect statistical threats (e.g., a white person's fear of being attacked by a Black person does not reflect any statistical threat). Some things are statistical threats to some people and not others (e.g., the fear of job loss is reflective of a statistical threat to some people and not others; one person who fears job loss may not actually be likely to face that threat, while another person who does not fear job loss may actually be more likely to face it). When I suggest that individuals must work together to create relationships that will help us receive rather than resist fears, inevitably individuals will be in relationships where there will be different levels of statistical threats. Some individuals will be actually threatened by certain things that pose minimal or zero threat to others. So we can imagine that we will be in relationships where perhaps everyone fears X but where X is more likely to be a threat to some of us than others, or perhaps X is not likely a threat to some of us at all. And we will also be in relationships where not everyone fears the same thing. If, as I suggest, we in some cases have a responsibility to help create space for others to experience and express their own fears (with caveats to be discussed in section 2.C), this means we will need to prioritize understanding others' experiences and expressions of fear and others' perceptions of threat, even when they do not align with our own. In real-life relationships, this can be complicated. It might mean struggling to understand how someone could fear some object in the first place, when the same object strikes us as harmless or even pleasant. It might mean resisting the impulse to dismiss others' fears as irrational. It might mean having to listen to someone fear something that I know *is not* a statistical threat to them yet at the same time *is* a statistical threat to me, and deprioritizing communicating that difference (again, with caveats to be discussed). It might mean feeling angry at the fears that someone else is articulating and still trying to allow them to express them. Ultimately, the fact that we are diverse as fearers—and that I am suggesting we should relate as interpreters to others' fearing lives—can introduce possibilities for all manner of thoughts and feelings on the part of interpreters. It is unlikely that the process of attempting such interpretation will be easy going.

ii. Relating to Others Whose Fears We Share Can Be Dangerous
Perhaps even more complicated than relating to others whose fears we do not share is relating to others whose fears we *do* share, because of the ways doing so can introduce particular hazards.

Though it will not always be the case, in many situations the people to whom we are most likely to be expressing our fears are people we already trust—people with whom we are already in relationship, and perhaps people who feel *safe* to us, like they will not unleash harsh judgments or criticisms of our emotional lives. We are more likely to be in trusting relationships with people who, at least to some extent, share our values and agree with us on important things. These are points of commonality that bond us and create trust. As such, the people to whom we may be most likely to open up about our fears may also be people who *share our perceptions of threat and our fears*. This fact introduces several risks for the kinds of relational practices I have been espousing.

There are a number of major risks that come with relating to others whose fears one shares. In short, there are risks that individuals will (1) become more convinced that their perceptions of threat are accurate, (2) be bolstered in not only fearing but enacting controlling strategies against perceived threats, (3) come to fear additional nonstatistical threats simply by having been more exposed to these fears in the lives of others they trust, and/or (4) be even less inclined to engage with others who fear different things than they do.

For one thing, having these sorts of relationships—in which we express our fears to people whom we already trust and who might already be inclined to share our perspective on threats—can more forcefully convince us that our perceived threats are actual threats. The experience of having one's perception of threat confirmed as aligning with others' perceptions of threat can be very affirming—to the point of convincing a fearer that their own perception of threat reflects reality. This confidence can persist even if other sources deny that the fearer's perception is accurate, particularly if those challengers seem to the fearer less trustworthy. If another person whom the fearer trusts is backing up their perception, telling them it aligns with their own, why attend to the opinions of less trustworthy challengers? This kind of danger can come up in ways that are politically concerning—for instance, in anti-vaccination movements, pro-gun movements, anti-universal health care movements, and the like. But the risk I am identifying is not itself partisan. It is present across political contexts.

A related risk of relationships in which we express fears to those we already trust is the fact that expressing fears to those who share them with us can tip us over the edge from simply having and expressing such fears to wanting to act against underlying perceived threats. In other words, these relationships can have exactly the opposite effect as I have hoped—that they might help us have and express the fears without needing to act to control or fix them. Hearing that *you fear the same thing* can embolden and hasten action against the thing we both perceive as a threat. Take the example of the condo residents from chapter 4. Some residents feared the homeless people sleeping outside their building. We can imagine they first or only ever expressed their worry to those other residents whom they anticipated would agree with them (not first or perhaps ever to those they knew would certainly not agree). It is possible all the residents of the building agreed with the worries, and this shared perspective might be all the more likely if the residents were similar in terms of race, class, income status, educational background, political commitments, and so on—the more they share social and demographic identifications, the more their perceptions of threat might align. Their agreement—that the homeless people sleeping on the benches posed a threat—may have emboldened them to use a controlling strategy (removal by installing new benches) against that perceived threat. Even if not all the condo residents agreed, the group in favor of new benches might have been emboldened by the fact that *some* others agreed.

Adding a further risky dynamic to this idea, relationships in which we express fears most to those we already trust can incline us to fear additional new things that we previously had not, just by virtue of having been exposed to those as fears of others whom we trust. Think of how websites try to sell us on additional goods by noting that other customers who purchased the things we are purchasing *also* purchased these other things. "You may also like" X, Y, or Z. There is a parallel "you may also fear" phenomenon. If I fear X and a friend I trust also fears X (and perhaps our trust is partly built on the knowledge that we share this fear), and then that friend comes to express also fearing Y and Z that I had not even considered, I may come to fear Y and Z too. I also may not come to fear them—my personality, identity, and unique background all play into what I will actually come to fear—but the point is, I may come to the point of seeing new objects as *potential threats* in ways that I would not have otherwise.

And finally, the fact that we often have these fearing-together relationships with people whom we already trust or who already agree with us can mean we are less likely to have, pursue, or keep relationships with others who do not share our perceptions of threat. This means we can become isolated in echo chambers, and we lose the potential benefits of being in trusting long-term relationships with those who don't perceive the same threats that we do.[7]

iii. Fears Are Dynamic

The relational dynamics of fearing together are further complicated by the fact that fears do not hold constant—they shift and change over time. The perceived threats that most hold our attention at some times can come to seem less pressing at others, or we can come to no longer fear them at all after time passes or we gain more experience. So this can mean that we move in and out of alignment with what and how others are fearing, such that our ways of relating to and providing interpretation for others' expressions of fears can become newly challenging over time.

To take a benign example, when I first moved to Michigan, I had never before owned a car or needed to drive. I had lived in walkable cities with functional public transit systems. In fact, I only got my driver's license in my twenties and had barely driven at all. Upon arrival in Michigan, I needed to commute thirty-five minutes on hectic highways with short on- and off-ramps, among aggressive drivers. I was frightened of driving for much of the first year, and I used to commiserate with another newly arrived friend who was similarly frightened. While I had to drive a lot and eventually became comfortable with it, my friend avoided driving as much as possible (and still does). Eventually we stopped talking about fears of driving. Our relating about what once were shared fears faded away. This is only one of the ways shifting fears can trigger shifts in ways of relating to fears over time. Fears might wax and wane, and not always in a linear direction—my fear of driving could return or intensify in future, hers could lessen. Relationships where we express fears to each other will need to be flexible enough to allow for this dynamism.

Although these relationships are complex and, as we have seen, they are not without dangers themselves, I am suggesting that they are necessary parts of any approach to reducing the harms of compelling fears and controlling threats. Our capacities to experience fears without being driven to harmful avoidance of them depend on relationships with others who stay with us in our fearing. These relationships do not always come easily. I am suggesting we have responsibilities to create and sustain them.

Of course, some perceived threats are accurate reflections of actual threats. Feeling fearful of the effects of ongoing climate crises or police violence are fears based on a perception of an actual threat. Relationships between fearers and interpreters are also important in these cases, since it is still true that creating space between fear feelings, perceived threats, and actions will be helpful. Even in cases where the threats I perceive and fear are actual, controlling strategies may not be the best response to them. So it is still helpful to have the help of others who can hold fears with us and allow us to experience and express them without doing anything about them. Coming to determine how to act will be supported by this process of being able to respond rather than react to fears. And then the specifics of what we decide to do in response to actual threats will likely be strengthened by the involvement of other people—others who can help flesh out the perception of the threat and possible strategies for response based on their own unique experiences and social locations. Diversity in approaches to threats can be a very helpful thing.[8] In other words, the relational processes I have described are necessary *both* for avoiding the dangerous consequences of compelling fears (chapter 3) and controlling strategies (chapter 4), *and* for developing productive responses to actual threats. Responding well to actual threats will in the best case involve working together to sift out what are merely our perceptions, what are problematic inclinations to control those threats, and then what are possibly productive responses to actual threats.

Part of my goal has been to shift the focus from determining exactly how best to respond to actual threats, to exploring how best to respond to *fear*. If we cannot respond well to fear, we are almost certain not to respond well to actual threats. Part of practicing responding well to fear involves taking seriously the possibility that there may not always be an effective response to actual threats. Many of the great threats I return to throughout the book—the threat of loss, failure, suffering—are realities of human life that cannot be fully prevented, avoided, or solved. I am not suggesting that when a bear charges toward me, I should do nothing about it. I am suggesting, rather, that even in contexts of actual threat, all my options for action may have their own dangers attached, and that the goal of my response to the bear should not be in the spirit of being able to control those threats completely. When we become less attached to controlling strategies in response to nonactual threats, our dedication to the presumed efficacy of such strategies in response to actual threats may also be more open to question.

My argument here might be thought of as a hypothetical imperative: if we care about reducing the harms of controlling strategies, we must help each other bear our fears. The call to "stay with fearers" is a strategy for short-circuiting the connection between fear and controlling actions. Within this hypothetical formulation, if controlling strategies are not in fact harmful, if we no longer care about reducing these harms, or if it turns out empirically that "staying with fearers" is not an effective strategy for reducing such harms, then the argument is easily abandoned. I hope to have made the case for why controlling strategies are in fact often harmful and why we should care deeply about these harms. For now, I think we have sufficient empirical support for thinking both that challenging, criticizing, or commanding the end of fears is not reliably effective in helping people stop fearing or enacting attempts to control perceived threats, *and* that approaches that prioritize staying with fearers (relational approaches to mindfulness, somatic regulation, and politicized somatics) can help fearers bear their fears rather than try to control perceived threats. The data we have do not support believing these points to be true of all people at all times. Some people more than others may be responsive to being told to stop being fearful. Others may never be responsive to the relational strategies of "staying with." Perhaps one day we will be presented with empirical support for thinking that staying with fearers is no longer helpful. At that point, I will be open to revising my view.

C. Concerns and Caveats

Perhaps the greatest concern about this account of the need to stay with fearers is this: it so far seems to acknowledge neither the potential hazards of interpreters responding to expressions of fears that are likely to prompt morally dangerous actions nor the question of whether the call to "stay with fearers" might apply differently to different agents at different times.[9] As discussed in chapter 2, I am chiefly concerned with morally problematic actions motivated by fears, and particularly with times when fearers cannot bear feelings of fear, including fears of some of the deepest, inextinguishable threats (mortality, uncontrollability, potential harm to loved ones), attempt to avoid their feelings by fixing their attention on some other perceived threats that *can* be extinguished or otherwise controlled, and then act in such a way as to control those perceived threats.

I am suggesting that an interpreter has a responsibility to allow for the expression of fears, to stay with a fearer as they experience and express fears, and to position those fears as acceptable rather than respond in ways that judge or shame the fearer. I have suggested that this kind of relational involvement will be an important part of allowing fearers to practice remaining present, noticing and accepting their fears, without feeling so unable to bear them that they compel them or move to control the perceived threats associated with them. But what happens if the fear a person experiences and expresses seems likely to lead to morally problematic action? Or what happens if a fearer expresses such a fear to a person likely to be harmed by the actions it might motivate?

Take the following case. What if I am attempting to be an interpreter for a family member who is experiencing and expressing fear of migrants taking jobs from her and her family? I know this is a fear that is out of alignment with statistical threat—we saw in chapter 3 that migrants have been shown not to affect nonmigrant employment in the short term, and only potentially positively affect it in the long term (Constant 2014). But here my family member is expressing to me her fear of migrants taking "our" jobs. How should I respond? Should I, as I have suggested, be an interpreter for her expression of these fears? Should I instead challenge her with facts about why her fears are not reflective of actual threats?[10]

It is complicated. There is a place for my own awareness of statistical threats, of the facts about how her fear is out of alignment with them, and of the likely sources of her misaligned fear. These facts may, and perhaps should, come to be part of my interactions with this family member at some point. But the approach I have been describing in this chapter prioritizes harm reduction in the sense of reducing the regularity of the harms of compelling fears—the ways we, together, displace great fears onto fears of people, objects, or eventualities that are more manageable—and controlling perceived threats. I have been committed throughout to the goal not of ensuring that people fear the right things in the right ways for the right reasons, but rather of ensuring that people's fears, when (as they too often are) misdirected, do not as commonly have such devastating moral and political effects as they currently do.[11] To put it plainly, I care most that fewer people point guns at harmless others perceived as threats, that fewer prisons are built, and that fewer migrants are encamped. I am in favor of tactics that will help interrupt these things from being natural outgrowths of all-too-common fears. In short, on my view, staying with fearers as they express fears *not acted on* can be important for avoiding the harms of *fears acted on*.

To this end, I want to defend the view that I, someone in a long-term, trusting relationship with my family member, should *at least in the first place* be an interpreter who stays with her expression of these fears.

First, we should consider empirical support for thinking that pointing out to a fearer that theirs are fears of nonstatistical threats is not likely to make the person stop fearing them. Part of what sustains fears of nonstatistical threats are individuals' inabilities to comprehend differences in statistical likelihood that we will be endangered by something (Belling 2012).[12] Simply pointing out that the odds are low that some perceived threat will actually harm someone who fears it may not be enough. The fearers may not understand the numbers, and they may not be inclined to trust reports of numbers that they do not understand. Furthermore, there may be constant sources of information from media and from other people that overrepresent certain perceived threats (e.g., of migrants) and thus make them appear to be constant dangers. The influence of these sources cannot be undone simply by pointing out that they are misinforming. Traumatizing events can further attune one to being hyperaware of some sources of threat.[13] While in some cases it may be enough to simply point out to a fearer that their perceived threat is not actually a threat, in many cases just hearing this fact will not be enough.

Furthermore, we should consider a possible harm of simply shutting down the conversation by pointing out that my family member's fears are not reflective of statistical threats. In certain circumstances people may be less likely to want to continue to engage with people who have given dismissive responses to their fears. Having one's emotions dismissed can also feel like being dismissed as *who one is*—for some, it can be a serious enough insult to signal the end of a relationship.[14] Besides the possible general harms of ending the relationship for both of us, ending the relationship closes down any possibility of future engagement with the family member. I will no longer be someone she turns to with emotional expression. And this means I will not be in a position to offer support in a way that might allow for the expression (and not enactment) of her fears, nor be able to have distinct conversations more focused on statistical facts.

And furthermore, this refusal of recognition of what is significant to my family member could also make her more eager to search for other interpreters who will affirm her fears and her identity. So, a refusal of recognition can mean that a fearer both turns *away* from those with beliefs that challenge their own and turns *toward* others who share her beliefs. As such, it can further intensify the problem of echo chambers, where those who fear a particular nonstatistical threat communicate about that fear only with people who share it. As discussed above, this can have dangerous effects: individuals may become more convinced that their perceptions of threat are accurate, may be emboldened in not only fearing but enacting controlling strategies against perceived threats, may come to fear additional nonstatistical threats, and may be even less inclined to engage with others who have different fears.

These are some practical reasons to think that the goal when encountering an expression of fear that might be acted on in morally dangerous ways should not be to immediately challenge the fearer for the content of their fear. We might understand my view in chapters 3, 4, and 5 to be suggesting that we have responsibilities to recognize and respond well to fears *not based on their particular content*, where the content of some fears reflects statistical threats and others do not, and the content of some fears are more morally acceptable than others; rather, we have responsibilities to recognize and respond well to fears based on their *form*, where the form of some fears is morally problematic, regardless of content.[15] Displacing and compelling fears and then trying to control the perceived threats that deeper fears have been compelled onto is in all cases a troubling thing. I have argued that different ways of experiencing, expressing, and responding to expressions of fears have the potential to disrupt this process and thereby prevent the attempts at controlling strategies, which can be seriously harmful.

How can parties within relationships acknowledge that there are facts of the matter about how accurately fears reflect statistical threats, while maintaining that, at least according to my view, the most important response (from the perspective of avoiding the harms of compelling and controlling fears) is not to fact-check each others' fears but instead to find a way to experience them and allow them to shift over time without needing to enact avoidant modes of controlling them in the meantime?

I am motivated by the work of Detroit-based artist and educator Sterling Toles, who has been quoted as saying, "We must not only heal the suffering that oppression causes, but we must also heal the oppression caused by suffering."[16] In short, I think a focus on healing and a focus on moral responsibility need not be exclusive. We can hold people responsible for moral failures and morally dangerous actions. But I think doing so exclusively, without any attention to trying to attend to the experiences of fear/suffering that motivate them, is shortsighted.

There are ways to reduce the potential harms of the process of such healing. For one thing, we need to attend to who should be responsible for attending to morally troubling experiences of fear. It must not be the job of those most adversely impacted by these expressions of fear and the actions they might motivate. A migrant worker should not be asked or required to bear witness to my family member's unsubstantiated fear of her. Other people are better positioned to not be harmed by the emotional labor this situation might call for. Though I mainly have in mind the ways in which ordinary other people can be interpreters for each other, people can also be paid professionals who inhabit these roles (e.g., therapists, and researchers like Hochschild).

Healing these processes of fearing requires also recognizing that they do not start with individual people simply deciding to be afraid. They are most often generated by multiple apparatuses (media, policing and prison systems, and histories) that should be challenged and dismantled. Changing harmful practices of fearing need not wait for these things to happen, but it also cannot fully happen without addressing these larger forces.

Healing should be understood as ongoing and not as only worthwhile once complete. As we have seen in the mindfulness, somatic-regulation, and politicized-somatics approaches above, practicing simply having and noticing emotional experiences can have important effects on creating distance from feeling like they define us. These approaches can allow for the feelings to come and go without dictating what we as agents do. And the feelings, as feelings, are likely to wax and wane, come and go, and change over time, especially once we can practice not clinging to them as though they are telling us the truth or showing us what we must do. This does not mean the feelings go away for good. They may, and they may not. The goal is not to make them disappear but to develop our capacities for responding to them in nonreactive ways when they arise—as we have seen, getting to that point can require practice and a great deal of relational involvement. From this perspective, healing should not be expected to be a process that eventually eliminates all fears that may motivate morally problematic actions. Rather, the hope is that healing will create space between having the fears and being driven to identify with them and act on the basis of them.

I say that I should be an interpreter for my family member's fears "at least in the first place," because I do think that there may be space thereafter for engaging more directly with her inaccurate beliefs. It is by no means the case that facts about statistical threats are irrelevant, and not all perceptions of threat should be believed. My point is more that the order of priority when responding to perceptions of threat (our own and others) should be to first separate out (1) the feeling of fear, (2) the perception of threat, and (3) attempts to act upon or against perceived threats. And since this is a difficult process—our inclination may be just to get rid of feelings of fear by acting directly on perceived threats—the difficulty of the process can be eased somewhat by holding our fears within relationships, not being expected to hold them alone. The danger in thinking that others' fears of nonstatistical threats (even very offensive ones) should be simply dismissed as unacceptable is that it will not help at all with efforts to separate out feelings, perceptions, and actions, and may instead actually tighten or speed up those connections by adding additional difficult feelings of being dismissed, hurt, isolated, or angry. So it may be possible within relationships to both hold the feelings of fear, with the chief goal of disrupting the path from perception of threat to action, and in some cases, at some times, also to question and rework the perceptions of threat themselves. This reworking may involve questioning inaccurate beliefs, as well as questioning with a fearer whether their fear is really *fear of X* (as they believe) instead of perhaps *fear of great threat Y*. But prioritizing contestations of the perceptions of threat, especially when done so from an outsider's perspective (i.e., as someone without an existing level of trust) can backfire and cause hastened moves toward the path of action.

If and when such space becomes available, the goal can be to change beliefs, ideally by individuals coming to better beliefs not by forceful criticism from without but by more careful reflection on their own experiences and what sources of information they trust. Moving away from hierarchical, didactic modes of changing minds requires some degree of optimism and trust in individuals to come to better ways of being. Whether space to have these interactions ever becomes available or not depends in large part on how my family member feels and how she feels about me. If she is defensive, angry, or ashamed, she may not be in a mental space where her beliefs can be open to contestation. If she feels that she can no longer trust me or endure talking to me, I may not be in a position to contest her beliefs.

It may seem to some readers that most of the fears I am talking about here are unrelatable. Perhaps you do not fear migrants or sex offenders or vaccines. It might seem that I am criticizing examples of fear-motivated actions that are more common to those with right-leaning political commitments than to those with left-leaning ones. In fact, I do not believe that it is only those with right-leaning commitments who act in morally problematic ways motivated by fear. Processes of compelling fears and controlling threats cut across political commitments.

Examples come to mind of my students, from a variety of political backgrounds, expressing to me their fears of the future. In 2012 when I began teaching in Michigan, a number of my students expressed their fears about the Affordable Care Act, that it would damage the healthcare system, that health care and taxes would become too expensive, that they did not want their freedoms to choose whether or how to have health insurance to be violated. While such fears were foreign to me as a newly migrated Canadian, I could understand how a person might have such fears as a young adult, in many cases raised in families impacted by severe economic insecurity due to the auto industry crisis, and already in debt and facing unclear prospects for future employment. A few years later, during the 2016 election cycle, other students expressed to me their fears for LGBTQ rights and protections. These fears were more relatable to me, and certainly understandable, but also in some cases they motivated actions (e.g., political will to toughen up legal responses to hate crimes and discrimination) that we might see as problematic controlling strategies that will not ultimately benefit all marginalized groups (see Spade 2015). Fears of Obamacare and fears of attacks on LGBTQ rights were on different sides of the political spectrum, but both had the potential to motivate controlling strategies that would not ultimately address the greatest threats. I took it to be my position in both cases to allow the fearers to have and express the fears, and to hold space for deeper expressions of how they might reasonably connect to fears of underlying great threats (in a way appropriate within my position as a professor)—both in fact connected to fears for the unpredictability of the future security of oneself and one's loved ones.

Think further of an example of a parent of a child with a disability expressing fears about whether that child will ever live up to some vision the parent had once held of their future. Even if the parent's particular vision embodies values we might rightly interrogate—for instance, assumptions equating success with individualism, financial autonomy, property ownership, or professional achievement—the fear of the underlying threat such a parent might articulate—*Will my child be okay?*—deserves space and uptake. Such parents might *themselves* be critical of the values they find expressed in their fears. They might be of any political orientation and still have and express such fears. Their interlocutors can create space for such expressions and perhaps also establish common ground with them in a way that can be healing. Of course, they worry for the well-being of their child. What parent doesn't? It does not mean that the best approach is to try to control the (perceived, not actual) threat of their child's potential failure to be fully independent, economically autonomous, or academically or professionally validated. Even so, *the parent can have their fear*. They may well need to have and express it in order to avoid the potential harms of attempts to control these perceived threats.

My claim is that people can *have* the fears. The real concern for us should not be in the having of the fears; it should be in the action that can come from them. Prioritizing preventing the action can require relating to the fearer in a way that helps them have the fear without acting on it. An approach that prioritizes correcting the belief or critiquing the fear is not always or often the way to go.

In this section, I have suggested that an approach of staying with fearers, with all its challenges and caveats, will help reduce the harms of controlling strategies. In many cases, the practice of staying with fearers and sitting with fears may lead to coming to terms with the persistence of great, underlying, uncontrollable threats. The great threats of loss, suffering, failure, and uncertainty are not fully avoidable. They are part of the conditions of our lives but fortunately not ones we need to hold alone.

3. Fearing Crisis Together

A. Fearing Pandemic

The global pandemic has disrupted nearly every aspect of life in recent years: physical and mental health; practices of relating to family members, friends, partners, and colleagues; workplaces and daily schedules; capacities to travel, cross borders, and move around communities; what food we can access; and much more. The weight of pandemic fear landed differently on different people. Many of us have been occupied with the COVID-19 pandemic: trying not to get sick, caring for those who are sick, anticipating and preventing the ripple effects of economic devastation, coping with job loss, deciding how to get food or determining how to afford it, and creating new modes of being isolated in our homes with, or without, others. Tensions of privilege and precarity have been exacerbated.

Early on, climate justice essayist Mary Annaïse Heglar compared her experience of the pandemic to climate grief: "This is painful. It's supposed to be. We are suffering through a collective trauma. We're watching our world change, and it feels like it's falling apart. That's not supposed to feel OK: It's not OK."[17]

On March 15, 2020, Sean Illing drew insights from Albert Camus's novel *The Plague* to understand the COVID-19 crisis just getting started. He wrote,

> The key is to recognize the universality of suffering. A plague is an extraordinary event, and the horror it unleashes is extraordinary,

too. But suffering is anything but extraordinary. Every single day you leave the house, something terrible could happen. At any moment, you could get mortally sick. The same is true for everyone you know. All of us are hostages to forces over which we have no control. A pandemic simply foregrounds what's already true of our condition.[18]

B. Compelling Fears and Controlling Threats during COVID

I suggested in chapter 3 that our greatest fears emerge from the facts of our relationality. We very commonly fear potential loss of, or threats to, our foundational relationships. At the best of times, we fear loss of our parents, children, partners, and kin. We fear suffering for ourselves or our dearest loved ones. We fear our potential failure to protect them, and failure to anticipate or avoid harms to them. We fear our failures to care for other beings and to appreciate our lives and luck. These fears will persist as long as our interdependence does—which is to say, as long as we are alive.

Notice that in the COVID-19 pandemic, all of these great, unmanageable threats have seemed nearer than usual. Many of us lost loved ones because of the virus or because of any number of related harms.[19] If we were spared this loss, we know others who were not. Many of us have been far from loved ones and feel unable to protect or comfort them. Many areas have faced worries about health-care systems being overwhelmed and uncertainty about whether there will even be sufficient hospital beds for all who could need them; and so besides the suffering of the illness, we have some reason to fear the death of those who fall ill. Many of us fear our own potential failure to protect loved ones or to be able to anticipate or avoid all harms to them. Even now, years into the pandemic, we are still learning new things about the virus and its effects. In the United States, all this has taken place in a context where racialized communities are hardest hit by the health-related, social, and economic effects of the virus and at the same time under conditions of continued state-sanctioned violence.

We have very likely, at least some of the time and to some degree, channeled our great fears into fears of people, objects, or eventualities that were more limited and controllable—displacement—and our processes of displacement are, as I have argued, best understood more relationally. We have acquired, experienced, and expressed fears of proxy threats always in relationship—we have compelled our fears together.

In one sense, perhaps we can think of the virus itself, COVID-19, as having served as a proxy threat. Great threats of loss and suffering of course extend beyond COVID-19. Even if we were to completely eradicate this virus, those threats would continue to exist, because other harms may befall us and our loved ones, people will continue to die of and suffer from other causes. So there may be a sense in which our grander fears of loss and suffering are compelled onto COVID-19, and there are some controlling strategies we may have attempted to apply to the virus itself as a current proxy for other threats that will never be controlled.

We might also note how communities employed controlling strategies during this time. Some of us attempted to *escape* the effects of COVID: we managed our own bodies in order to remove ourselves and our loved ones from the path of the perceived threat. We worked from home. Perhaps we kept our kids out of school, nursery, and preschool. We stayed away from public indoor spaces. Some people with the option even left hotspot areas entirely, fleeing to properties in less populated areas or places where virus transmission has been better managed by communities. If we did not manage to do these things, perhaps we fantasized about it. *What if we could just entirely escape this?*

Attempts to destroy the virus itself, remove any objects or others that may introduce it into our homes, or escape spaces where it may be present all channeled an accurate recognition of the genuine threats of suffering, loss, and death into efforts to control more minor, more manageable perceived threats. We cannot control the virus itself or the great threats of loss and suffering it poses, but we can control what we do with our own bodies while the virus persists.

At times, some alternative responses to COVID have seemed to compel great fears onto perceived (but not actual) threats. For instance, in Michigan, right-wing armed protests against our Democratic governor's stay-at-home orders were widely publicized.[20] These protesters embodied attempts to *overpower* the perceived threat: one might suggest that the protesters displaced fears of economic collapse onto the perceived threat of a Democratic governor using her authority to issue executive orders, and they then attempted to overpower that threat, demanding entry into the State Capitol building, armed with the intention of threatening the governor into easing her orders.

To be sure, armed protest is an extreme example of attempted overpowering. But it embodies a kind of overpowering/denial that became somewhat common as the pandemic stretched into its sixth and seventh months in the United States. We saw many people trying to convince themselves that while others may have been harmed by this, *they themselves would not be*. They positioned themselves as sufficiently young, healthy, protected, or invincible as to not fall seriously ill. Media sources downplaying the seriousness of the virus supported these ways of thinking. Fear of the actual threat of COVID-19, which we know is a threat to all humans regardless of age and background health, was displaced onto a perceived threat of not quite the same illness, but instead a version of it that was imagined to only affect the very old or those with preexisting conditions. This too was a sort of attempted overpowering.

Arguably even the kinds of institutional reopening plans that relied completely on temperature checks, health screening forms, or "social distancing" rules that required six feet of space between desks or cubicles (but failed to account for the eventual admission that the virus is airborne) were all kinds of demonstrative practices that embody a kind of overpowering. Fear of the actual threat of COVID-19 was displaced onto a perceived threat of an illness that could be fully controlled just by controlling symptomatic bodies and controlling the distance between bodies. Although these practices prevented some instances of transmission, there was a kind of magical thinking involved in claiming that safety would be ensured by these practices. Ultimately some such practices were instituted in a clear-headed way, with the understanding that they could reduce risk of transmission without eliminating it, from the judgement that the benefits accrued from having people physically present in schools and workplaces outweighed the risks. By contrast, something more like overpowering occurred when people attempted to convince themselves that such practices somehow overcame the risks of the virus.

Again, it is important to note the complex effects of these controlling strategies. Many of the strategies I discussed in chapter 4 had no positive effects. They were exclusively harmful. But at least some of these controlling strategies in the context of COVID-19 had some positive effects while perhaps simultaneously having other harmful effects—and still not necessarily being a productive response to the great fears themselves.

The case of controlling strategies in COVID-19 is interesting for a few reasons. For one, it demonstrates how the difference between actual threats and perceived threats can be complicated and slippery. What the threat of COVID-19 actually is and what I might perceive it to be may be identical, or close but not quite identical (as in cases where an individual maintained an understanding of the virus as containable if we just stay six feet apart), or radically different (as in cases where an individual believed it is only something that infects people over sixty-five). Sliding between accurate and inaccurate understandings about threats is common and certainly understandable when we were regularly learning new things about new threats. It is also understandable, given the burden of all the fears associated with COVID (e.g., fear of death, illness, suffering, unemployment, mental illness), that many of us would have compelled our great fears onto apparent threats that seemed more manageable—which can sometimes mean we gravitated toward (mis)understandings of actual threats that downplayed or minimized their actual danger. In other words, we do not always displace fears of X onto fears of Y or Z (completely different threats). Sometimes we displace fears of X onto fears of X^1 or X^2 (slightly or dramatically different imagined versions of the original threat).

The case is further interesting because evaluating the moral status of the controlling strategies is complicated. Unlike many of the cases of controlling strategies discussed in chapter 4, where their harms were clear, in the case of COVID-19, some of our controlling strategies were at the same time both arguably *not good ways of coping with our fears* and also *morally acceptable or even morally desirable actions*. It is clear that we should continue any and all practices that have been demonstrated to reduce the harms of this virus. But it can be harmful for us and others if we do these practices in an attempt to fix or avoid the great fears triggered by this virus. Doing so means that we are not allowing ourselves and others to have, express, and respond to the great fears themselves. Not being granted the space to have and express our fears in this process can mean that the fears are more likely to get rerouted in nonproductive or harmful ways.

For instance, early pandemic obsessions with cleaning and sterilizing surfaces were likened to "security theater" after 9/11, where efforts to ensure physical safety (using methods that were not necessarily effective at making anyone safer) were obsessively performed, especially at borders and airports.[21] Hygiene theater is an example of a rerouted fear with harmful effects. Where schools opened, they in some cases were closed for extra amounts of time (e.g., in some areas, for an extra day each week), burdening parents (and especially those lower-resourced to begin with) and potentially harming children. Public transit systems spent more money on cleaning and had less money to pay workers or provide masks. And perhaps worst of all, hygiene theater in some cases both created a false sense of security and exacerbated "prevention fatigue," where already overwhelmed people began to cut corners when feeling overwhelmed by all the information and recommendations about what they had to do.[22]

Beyond these harms of attempted "removal" strategies, attempts at escape, where individuals flee hotspot areas to those less populated, might subject those in the less hard-hit areas to increased risk and perhaps burden their more easily overwhelmed health-care systems. Certainly the examples of overpowering I describe, from armed resistance to stay-at-home orders to the more personal denial of one's own risk, all posed potentially serious harms. Stay-at-home orders proved essential in reducing transmission in some of the most hard-hit areas. Jurisdictions that delayed introducing such orders saw astronomically high rates of transmission, illness, and death. Individuals who were cavalier about their own susceptibility to the virus drove transmission by refusing to wear masks, ignoring recommendations about social distancing, and introducing the virus to new areas through travel. And businesses and institutions that only minimally attended to the likelihood of virus transmission regularly became sites of outbreak.

C. Fearing Together in Crisis

Chapter 4 concluded by noting that the question of what to do with our fears is centrally a question of what to do with our vulnerability. What did we do with our vulnerability to this new virus, to all the effects of a crumbling economy, and to severely undercut public goods?

Of course, there was much to be done about COVID-19 itself: research, vaccines, and stay-at-home orders; individual practices of social distancing, mask wearing, and reducing risks in other ways; allocating state funds to protect economically vulnerable individuals and organizations; developing social supports for individuals and families; and so on. My interest here is not in enumerating or evaluating the strategies we saw for addressing the actual threats themselves but in what we did and should have done with the feelings of fear during pandemic time, and in what we might do with feelings of fear in future crises.

Later in the chapter, I present a table that can remind us of some of the main strategies I highlighted from the mindfulness, somatic-regulation, and politicized-somatics approaches as well as the main relational strategies that might help us better express and interpret fears in the context of interpersonal relationships. Responding well to fear should be one of the central tasks of life in future crises. It should not be made an afterthought. My hope in detailing some of the ways fearing together can and should work now is that this thinking can help us respond when we find ourselves in the midst of serious threats to come—climate crises chief among them.

As discussed above, fears during the pandemic were numerous and intense. They no doubt infused many of our daily lives. They might have constrained how gently and generously we interacted with others, how focused we were in our work, how physically and emotionally healthy we were, how thoughtfully we were able to process the myriad sources of information we encountered, how mindfully we were able to plan for the future, and so on. But crisis conditions do not negate the insights from mindfulness and somatic-regulation approaches about the need to become able to simply have feelings of fear. Making space for these feelings in our experience, paying attention to them in a mindful way, allows them to co-exist with other feelings, allows them to change over time, and affords us the capacity to experience them without being controlled by them. The option of simply not fearing future crises at all is not on the table. We do not escape fear by attempting to avoid it. In the best-case scenario, we come to understand fears as *only one part of our emotional lives*, and a bearable one.[23]

Contexts of crisis might complicate mindfulness practices in a number of ways. The call to mindfulness practices means that we should set aside time and space to practice mindfully focusing on our breath, simply observing thoughts and feelings, and noticing experiences of and thoughts about fear. In these dedicated times, we practice welcoming sensations of fear, accepting those as feelings, and recognizing that these thoughts and feelings do not define who we are. Concretely, one of the difficult things about some crises is a lack of time and space to practice mindfulness alone. Those with increased caregiving responsibilities, or increased responsibilities to do paid work inside or outside the home, can find themselves with very little available time or space to have protected meditation time. For others, motivation to commit to mindfulness practice can be difficult. In the pandemic, we saw rising rates of mental illness (depression, anxiety) that made it challenging to commit to mindfulness practice. Within mindfulness practice itself during crises, we might find feelings and thoughts about illness, economic insecurity, and loss showing up in ways that are difficult to simply notice and accept. Some of our thoughts and feelings might be surprising to us. We might be surprised to find how much our thoughts turn to some kinds of fears and not others. We might find the experience of the crisis bringing up past feelings we did not know were still affecting us. All of this can complicate mindfulness practices.

Contexts of crisis might further complicate *somatic* practices in a number of ways. In cases like the pandemic, we might be able to access somatic-regulation practices that are only possible while we are in social/physical isolation. We might need to recognize how fears related to particular new crises feel different in our bodies. We may need to develop new methods and technologies that allow us to access the grounding presence of others and that allow us to be a grounding presence for others.

Contexts of crisis might also complicate relational practices. Our needs (e.g., for reassurance, relationship, comfort) are higher because we are stressed. The decisions we have to make about whether or how to meet those needs might be weightier if they have far-reaching implications for the well-being and safety of others. We might have little trustworthy guidance on the decisions we should make.

On my view, when in crisis, we need to understand fears as things to receive and hold together. We need to build relationships where fear can be received. These might be not the relationships we expected. People we were very close to before might not be the same people we are closest to in crisis now. We need to help each other remain present in bodies. This might become challenging, since for a number of reasons our bodies might come to not seem the same or trustworthy. If you've been sick, you might not feel comfortable in your body. If you worry that your body might be unsafe for others to be near, you might not feel you can trust your body. I have claimed that we should make efforts to stay physically present or available to fearers. We have learned that some kinds of crisis make such physical presence unsafe or impossible. We should find ways to support and provide relief within those relationships so that they do not become overburdened.

I claimed that part of fearing together requires allowing others to experience and express fears openly and in ways that help fearers simply have the experiences of fear without acting on them. Being able to show up as an interpreter in this way can require work to allow one to have and express one's feelings at other times, with other people, or alone. Interpreters need to practice self-awareness and self-regulation, including recognizing one's own feelings of fear when they come up and recognizing the need for expressing them in ways that still make space for other fearers.[24] In the kinds of mutual-fear-calibration scenarios I am describing, where another person might express an object or level of fear I had not yet shared, my first reaction to another's expression of fear might involve significant resistance: *You are wrong to fear that. You are overreacting. Stop saying that.* These may be understandable reactions, and interpreters can certainly feel and notice their feelings of resistance to others' expressions, but there are harms that come from dismissing others' expressions in this way. It can be challenging to remember that another person's expression of *fear does not need to make them do anything, and it does not need to make me do anything*—it does not need to make me fear that thing or to that degree. We need to relate with fearers with the goal of making it possible for fearers to have fear and potentially to use mindfulness or somatic-regulation strategies, calming impulses to fix or attack the fears. As we have seen, one of the risks of communications about fears among those who share the fears is that all parties can feel bolstered in enacting controlling strategies against perceived threats. It is imperative that we hold space for all of us to fear without letting that fear determine how we will act.[25]

4. Conclusion

At its core, this book has been about uncontrollability and the lengths to which some of us will go to resist it. As we have seen, our greatest fears are often emotional responses to the fact that we cannot control the future, with its potential suffering, loss, and failure. We (accurately) recognize this uncontrollability as a threat. But anyone who has ever benefited in a major way from a happening beyond their control—landscapes and opportunities and families and friendships and life histories and even the very fact of our births—knows that the uncontrollable presents not only our greatest threats but also, in some cases, our greatest luck. Uncontrollability may appropriately be the object of both our deepest fears and our deepest gratitude.

Table 5.1 Approaches to Fearing Better

1. **Mindfulness Approaches:**
    - Do mindfulness practices with seven attitudinal factors.
    - While practicing, focus on sensations of breathing; simply observe thoughts and feelings.
    - Simply notice experiences of and thoughts associated with fear.
    - Welcome sensations of fear and accept the feeling.
    - Recognize that one's thoughts and feelings do not define who one is; try saying "I am experiencing fear-filled thoughts" rather than "I am afraid."

(continued)

Table 5.1 Continued

2. **Somatic-Regulation Approaches:**
   - Employ somatic-regulation practices: mindfulness practices, sensory integration, somatic experiencing (e.g., model mugging programs where people are taught to actively fight off a simulated attack), eye movement desensitization and reprocessing (EMDR), hypnosis, free writing, art, music, dance, yoga, internal family systems therapy, psychomotor therapy, neurofeedback, and theater programs.
   - Recognize how fear feels in one's body.
   - Rest and surrender to the grounding presence of others.
   - Develop capacities for accepting and allowing for our own and others' feelings of fear.

3. **Politicized-Somatics Approaches:**
   - Listen to and live inside bodily sensations.
   - Practice centering and meditation.
   - Engage in touch, massage, conversation, imagination, and emotional processes.
   - Have boundaries, build trust and accountability, and move toward what is important to you.

4. **Fearing-Together Approach:**
   - Understand fear as something to receive and hold together.
   - Build relationships where fear can be received.
   - Help each other remain present in bodies.
   - Stay physically present or available to fearers.
   - Allow others to experience and express fears openly and in ways that help fearers simply have the experiences of fear without acting on them.
   - Perceive or perhaps anticipate that others are having or may have the experience of fear, and hold steady with them rather than reacting negatively.
   - Communicate to fearers that their fears are recognized, held, and accepted.
   - Relate with fearers with the goal of making it possible for them to have fear and potentially to use mindfulness or somatic-regulation strategies to move beyond impulses to fix or attack the fears.
   - Practice self-awareness and self-regulation as interpreters, including recognizing one's own feelings of fear when they come up and recognizing the need for expressing them in ways that still make space for other fearers.

Notes

Introduction

1. Which of these become publicly accessible often partly depends on the class, economic, and educational status of the fearers. Many more personal accounts of fear exist than those we can access. Recent accounts which come to mind include *Our House Is on Fire: Scenes of a Family and a Planet in Crisis* by climate activists Greta Thunberg, Svante Thunberg, Malena Ernman, and Beata Ernman (2020); *Small Animals: Parenthood in the Age of Fear* by writer Kim Brooks (2018); and *Being Mortal: Illness, Medicine, and What Matters in the End* by surgeon and writer Atul Gawande (2015).
2. Think of the films *Mad Max: Fury Road* (Miller 2015), *Contagion* (Soderbergh 2011), *The Road* (Hillcoat 2009), *Children of Men* (Cuarón 2006), *28 Days Later* (Boyle 2002). For depictions of life under a state-sanctioned temporary state of nature, think of *The Purge* (DeMonaco 2013) and its sequels. For a depiction of life under racism, think of *Get Out* (Peele 2017). One film that is not best known as an account of fear, but that I think is an exceptional portrayal of some of the nuance of the experience, is *99 Homes* (Bahrani 2015). This film follows a family evicted from their home in Orlando when their house is foreclosed on by a real estate broker. The film features the crisis of middle-class families who are trying to keep their houses (and school districts and sources of security), while they are fundamentally insecure—at the mercy of banks, courts, and real estate brokers, in the midst of a financial crisis. It can seem that the best provider of security will be property, and it can seem that families and individuals are alone in protecting themselves. The film shows how the main character becomes willing to put other families at risk to try to bring some security to his own.
3. For instance, Arlie Hochschild's (2016) *Strangers in Their Own Land: Anger and Mourning on the American Right* draws on interviews

with individuals in Louisiana who fear for their health and well-being after the destruction of their environments and health by chemical and oil companies, and who defend right-wing capitalist approaches as potential solutions. Marianne Cooper's (2014) *Cut Adrift: Families in Insecure Times* follows how households of diverse class statuses respond to the individualization of economic risk and lack of social safety net in US society. Setha Low's (2003) *Behind the Gates: Life, Security, and the Pursuit of Happiness in Fortress America* considers the fears expressed in the drive of wealthy families toward gated communities. Hugh Gusterson and Catherine Besteman's (2010) edited volume *The Insecure American* includes contributions from a variety of perspectives, including Joseph Dumit's (2010) examination of the "double insecurity" of health in America (people always being at risk, and never being sure of what to do to keep themselves healthy), and Peter Kwong's (2010) reflection on fear-driven attacks on migrants.

4. In *Small Animals: Parenthood in the Age of Fear* (2011), Kim Brooks describes being charged with "contributing to the delinquency of a minor" for doing just this. I discuss Brooks further in chapter 3.

5. I follow the risk perception literature's use of the term 'nonstatistical threats' to indicate perceived threats that *statistically unlikely* to pose actual threat to perceivers.

6. An alief, according to Gendler, is a "mental state with associatively linked content that is representational, affective and behavioral, and that is activated—consciously or nonconsciously—by features of the subject's internal or ambient environment" (Gendler 2008a, 642). Gendler calls them *a*liefs because they are *a*ssociative, *a*utomatic, *a*rational, *a*ntecedent to other cognitive attitudes, *a*ffect-laden, and *a*ction generating. Gendler is especially interested in *belief-discordant aliefs*.

7. To take another example, in "Fearing Fictions," Kendell Walton (1978) describes a case where a man watches a movie about a green slime and shrieks and grips his chair at one point in the movie. He does not *believe* that the slime is going to harm him. But, as Gendler describes it, he alieves something like "dangerous two-eyed creature heading towards me!" While the man believes he is not in danger, he alieves that he is. On Gendler's view, some unwarranted fears are ones fearers themselves believe to be unwarranted: actions based on these fears are *belief-discordant behavior*. But other unwarranted fears are ones a fearer would deny are unwarranted. Perhaps some fearers really do believe that the Skywalk is likely to collapse the minute they step on it, and refuse to visit. This would be a false belief, but belief-accordant behavior.

Chapter 1

1. See the website for the Chapman University Survey of American Fears at https://www.chapman.edu/wilkinson/research-centers/babbie-center/survey-american-fears.aspx. See their published list of America's Top Fears 2020/2021 at https://www.chapman.edu/wilkinson/research-centers/babbie-center/_files/Babbie%20center%20fear2021/blogpost-americas-top-fears-2020_-21-final.pdf. In *Fear Itself: The Causes and Consequences of Fear in America*, Chapman survey developers and administrators Christopher Bader, Joseph Baker, L. Edward Day, and Ann Gordon reflect on the process and results of having conducted the survey annually for (at that point) five consecutive years. The book is advertised as "an antidote to the culture of fear that dominates modern life." They describe the goal of the survey as follows: "Where neuroscience has advanced our understanding of the biological dimensions of fear, our goal is to advance the social psychological, sociological, and political understanding of fear among Americans in the early twenty-first century." (Bader et al. 2020, 5)
2. These findings show significant shifts from surveys of the recent past. Most pronounced are shifts in fears of loved ones dying, becoming seriously ill, or contracting COVID-19; and fears of a pandemic, which ranked not nearly so high in previous surveys. In the years since 2016, respondents have noted being more fearful of pollution, climate change, and other environmental issues. Also notable are shifts in fears regarding health care. While in 2016, the Affordable Care Act (Obamacare) was noted as the tenth top fear, in 2017 (following the election of President Trump), the American Health Care Act (Trumpcare) was noted as the second top fear; and then in 2018, neither specific health care plan appeared, though fear of "high medical bills" was tenth on the list.
3. Reflecting a more global perspective, the Pew Research Center conducted an ambitious Global Attitudes survey in spring 2018. The survey was conducted among 27,612 respondents in twenty-six countries from May 14 to August 12, 2018. The top four perceived threats overall for the twenty-six countries surveyed were as follows: (1) Global climate change (top choice for most major threat in thirteen countries); (2) The Islamic militant group known as ISIS (top threat in eight countries); (3) Cyberattacks from other countries (top threat in four countries); (4) Russia's power and influence (top threat in one country) (Poushter and Huang 2019, 2). Focusing on a younger global population, in fall 2019, Amnesty International conducted a *Future of Humanity* survey. They

asked over 10,000 eighteen- to twenty-five-year-olds across twenty-two countries about their greatest fears about issues facing their countries and the world. Climate change was the number one issue they feared the world was facing, and pollution, loss of natural resources, lack of access to safe water were among the top ten. Violent crime and violence against women were seen as the sixth and seventh top threats. Issues related to poverty—income inequality, lack of access to health care, and poor education—were all listed within the top twenty. See "Climate Change Ranks Highest as Vital Issue of Our Time—Generation Z Survey," Amnesty International, December 10, 2019, https://www.amnesty.org/en/latest/news/2019/12/climate-change-ranks-highest-as-vital-issue-of-our-time/. Of course, in the time since the Pew and Amnesty International surveys, the global spread of COVID-19 has significantly shifted what are seen as top threats.

4. See also German Lopez, "The Myth of Poisoned Halloween Candy," *Vox*, October 31, 2018, https://www.vox.com/science-and-health/2018/10/31/18047794/halloween-candy-poisoned-needles-pins-razors.

5. For one thing, crimes against black victims are underreported, making crimes against white victims appear more ubiquitous than they are (Azi Paybarah, "Media Matters: New York TV News Over-reports on Crimes with Black Suspects," *Politico*, March 23, 2015, https://www.politico.com/states/new-york/city-hall/story/2015/03/media-matters-new-york-tv-news-over-reports-on-crimes-with-black-suspects-020674; see also Glassner 1999, 113). Furthermore, in 2015, black men made up 52 percent of all murder victims in the United States (National Center for Victims of Crime 2017; see also Glassner 1999, 112).

6. Many US residents also describe their fears of use of illicit drugs, when in fact "more Americans use legal drugs for nonmedical reasons than use cocaine or heroin [and] more than half of those who die of drug-related medical problems or seek treatment for those problems are abusing prescription drugs" (Glassner 1999, 131).

7. In contrast to scientists and state agents who were invested in these developments, communities in many cases perceived nuclear technologies as posing dangers to environments and public health. Researchers who were invested in the development of these technologies were motivated to try to understand and address this difference in assessment of risk. In 1969, Chauncey Starr, an engineer with expertise in nuclear energy, proposed that individuals would be much more likely to accept risks if they emerged from actions they themselves had decided to perform (e.g., driving a car), and much less likely to accept risks generated by external actors (e.g., nuclear technologies). He focused on the need to provide

individuals with more information about the risks from factors outside their control, with the thought that individuals would then be more willing to accept those risks.
8. Though these will not be approaches I follow, it is worth noting that approaches in social psychology prioritize the understandings of threats in line with in-group/out-group status. According to realistic conflict theory (D. Campbell 1965), realistic threats are threats that pose a danger to an in-group's survival (e.g., threats to the health, safety, or existence of a group). Realistic group conflict theory focuses on threats posed by groups' competition for resources (Sherif et al. 1961). And symbolic threat theory focuses on outgroup threats to the values of an in-group (Sears 1988). All these approaches try to understand how perceptions of threat can be shaped by the interests of a group, concerns about others outside of one's group, and concern for the long-term fitness, survival, or strength of one's own group. Members of a group might perceive those outside the group as threats to one or more of these things (whether they in fact pose such a threat or not) and express and enact prejudice and attacks on those outside the group.
9. The risk-perception literature is very interested in determining what capacities are needed to accurately identify threats and the likelihood of them occurring. Some within the field have argued that the line between perceived risks and actual risks is not fully identifiable—not to say there is no fact of the matter about what is and is not a threat, but just that there is no fail-safe way for any expert to identify that distinction (Shrader-Frechette 1990, 345). Others within the literature are more optimistic about objective standards for evaluating risk when sufficient information about particular conditions and statistical likelihood of perceived threats is available. Even those like Shrader-Frechette who are most cautious about capacities for fully distinguishing risks and risk perceptions take as foundational that there are standards of objectivity in light of which a perception could be judged more or less accurate.
10. While previous research had suggested that the individuals *most* fearful of crime were actually those *least* likely to be victimized, Stafford and Galle (1984) argued that the victimization rates used in such analyses failed to take into account not only actual victimization but also exposure to risk (i.e., amount of time spent outside of the home and workplaces and thus exposed to risky conditions). When adjusted in this way to include exposure to victimization experiences, Stafford claims that we see a high degree of correspondence between victimization and fear of crime.
11. It is worth anticipating that chapter 2 will introduce further complexities in thinking about the relationship between the *things we fear/perceive*

as threatening, the things that have *caused our fears*, and the things our *fearful actions may be directed toward*. So far, we have only talked about the first of these—the things we fear/perceive as threatening—and I have used language of "objects of fear" and "what we are afraid of" interchangeably to refer to these. The next chapter will get into more detail about distinguishing between the "objects" and "causes" of fear.

12. As an example of vicarious acquisition, Rachman describes mothers who were fearful of air-raids during the war being an important determinant in whether their children became fearful of air-raids (John 1941), research demonstrating correspondence among the fears of children within a family (May 1950), correspondence among the total number of fears exhibited by children and their mothers (Hagman 1932), as well as examples of combat aviators who acquired fears after observing other mates expressing fears (Grinker and Spiegel 1945).

13. Some researchers in behavioral and psychiatric genetics have considered how genetic factors can play a significant role in an individual's tendency toward general fearfulness, and then that environmental factors (including family environments) might play a significant role in an individual's tendency toward a specific feared object—though according to some twin studies, perhaps not so much in the sense of parents teaching fears to their children, but in some cases more in the sense of siblings observing and learning from each other's fears (Carey 1990, 629; see also Hettema et al. 2003).

14. Arguably these approaches also reflect nonrelational understandings of threats themselves. On this point, recall that quantification is the key goal of the Chapman survey. It seeks to identify how much one individual fears X, Y, or Z, what they fear more or less, in order to report on what the *participant population as a whole* fears most and least, on how demographic subsets of the population compare (e.g., do women fear X more than men?), and on how these whole and partial demographic sets' greatest fears change over time. Notice that this takes as given, at least for the purposes of the survey, that the fears themselves can be individuated. It takes for granted that fears of different objects can be identified at least to the extent needed to evaluate how much or how regularly each individual fear is felt by a participant. I am asked to report the extent to which I fear (A) *catching the seasonal flu* separately from the extent to which I fear (B) *catching the flu from a flu vaccine* and both separately from the extent to which I fear (C) *harmful side effects from the flu vaccine*. No one would deny these fears could be related, and we might expect some of those who report a high level of fear of one of these things to also report fears of one or both of the others. And no doubt these are in fact meaningfully distinct

fears, since a person could understandably fear one without fearing the others. The point I want to make here is not to say they are *not* ontologically distinct—in some sense, they must be—but instead just to note that the research design is more interested in and able to attend to *the separateness and ranking of these fears* than to *their relation and the context which might make some people more likely to experience them as related*. For instance, we might wonder whether those who reported being afraid of all of A, B, and C were more likely to be part of anti-vaxxer social circles. To some extent, the survey data could allow for a focused reporting about the relations among just these fears. The Chapman survey could, say, pull data and produce a report just noting how many people reported being afraid or very afraid of all of A, B, and C, and it could report on how common or uncommon that was compared to the whole population of participants. It could even look for demographic trends among those people. But to my knowledge, the researchers have not focused on these types of smaller reports, likely because that is not the goal of the survey. The goal is the bigger picture: what are Americans *most* afraid of, and how does that change over time? Focusing on that goal means that the distinctness and quantifiability of fears are prioritized over the connections between such fears and the contexts that might make some fearers more likely to experience some perceived threats as connected.

Chapter 2

1. WXYZ-TV Detroit Channel 7, "Wife, Husband Charged with Felonious Assault after Pulling a Gun on a Woman with Her Children," posted online July 2, 2020. Cell phone video recorded by Makayla Green on July 1, 2020, in Orion Township, Michigan. YouTube video, 3:08, https://www.youtube.com/watch?v=skGh_5tVJZg.
2. *Good Morning America*, "Couple Speaks Out after Wife Pulls Gun on Family in Parking Lot," reported by Alex Presha, aired July 11, 2020, on ABC. YouTube video, 2:39, https://www.youtube.com/watch?v=6h36cu_96CY.
3. The example is inspired by one from Robert Solomon (1973, 25) but modified significantly.
4. Out of his critique of James's view, Dewey (1895, 15) developed his own account according to which an emotion is a "mode of behavior which is purposive." For him, emotions are basically states of preparedness to

act; any given emotion is identified by the emergence of the behaviors it prompts (Scarantino and de Sousa 2018; English and Stengel 2010). So, the emotion of fear specifically might be identified by the emergence of flight, fight, or paralysis behaviors (English and Stengel 2010, 530). In *Human Nature and Conduct*, Dewey notes that in all cases of fear, we are able to identify "contractions, withdrawals, evasions, concealments . . . evasion or running away or shrinking up . . . gestures of hesitation and retreat" (Dewey 1922, 154–55).

5. As Solomon (1973, 22) writes, "It is not simply the fact that John stole my car that is what I am angry about; nor is it, as I said above, my belief that John stole my car about which I am angry. I am angry about the intentional object 'that John stole my car.'"

6. Ronald de Sousa's (1987) view is relevant to note here. I do not engage it at length since it is more of a perceptual theory with the goal of positioning emotions as helping shift our attention to some features of the landscape, determining salience and thereby helping individuals sort and attend to the relevant information. But in the process of his argument, de Sousa distinguishes a number of terms that further detail various parts of objects: *target objects* (the entity the emotion is about), *motivational aspects* (attributes apprehended about the target object that form the basis of an explanation of the emotion), and *formal objects* (the second-order property ascribed to the motivational aspect if the emotion is to be intelligible). On de Sousa's view, when I have an emotion (e.g., anger) the target of an emotion (e.g., David) is apprehended as having some motivating aspect (e.g., did me harm), which instantiates the formal object (e.g., is harmful toward me; when people are harmful toward me, it is fitting for me to be angry) (de Sousa 1987, 131–33). For my purposes, distinguishing between causes and objects as Solomon does is sufficient—but this further detail is available on de Sousa's view.

7. This does not give carte blanche to individuals or suggest that any emotional responses are acceptable, since Rorty also holds that individuals may come to be aware of the ways their histories are shaping present emotional responses and may, with sufficient self-awareness, work toward changing their own "emotional repertoire" (Rorty 1980, 121).

8. For language of fittingness/unfittingness, see also Broad (1954) and Brandt (1946).

9. D'Arms and Jacobson's main project is not only to say what would make a feeling fitting or not but also to argue that the fittingness and moral acceptability of a feeling do not always align. A feeling may be morally objectionable while still being fitting. So, there can be a difference between "the

right way to feel" morally speaking and whether a feeling "gets it right" in terms of fit (D'Arms and Jacobson 2000, 66). Both of these might further diverge from what is pragmatically most useful to feel.

10. LeDoux's early research investigated how rats would respond when an auditory tone was paired with a brief electric shock. Rats learned to react to the tone. As Johnston and Olson explain, "LeDoux's seminal discovery was that more than one auditory pathway leaves the thalamus.... The auditory pathway that carried information about the fear-conditioned tone projected from the thalamus along a previously unidentified pathway to target a subcortical structure called the amygdala, a collection of forebrain nuclei buried in the medial temporal lobe.... The auditory information entering the [basolateral complex] is quite distinct from that traveling in the cortical pathway; it has not been highly analyzed.... This makes sense if the amygdala functions as a threat detector.... The amygdala has been built to be safe rather than sorry; responding to any tone that is somewhat similar to a learned threat keeps one safe, even if frequent mistakes are made" (Johnston and Olson 2015, 69–70). For a helpful overview, see Hartley and Phelps (2012, 113).

11. In his 1915 book *Bodily Changes in Pain, Hunger, Fear, and Rage: An Account of Recent Researches into the Function of Emotional Excitement*, physiologist Walter Cannon coined the now commonly known term "fight or flight" to describe how animals respond when seriously threatened. In response to acute stress, the body releases adrenaline and noradrenaline, which trigger increased heart rate, blood pressure, and breathing rate, preparing the animal to either fight the threat or flee from it. In more recent developments, Bracha et al. (2004) suggest that research to date more accurately reflects a four-part reaction to fear: freeze, flee, fight, and "fright," in the sense of "tonic immobility," like playing dead. But Cannon's early characterization persists in many popular understandings of fear responses.

12. See Ray and Vanstone (2009).

13. On LeDoux's view, it is important to note a feature that fear and anxiety share: both are *conscious feelings*. As he explains, "Fear, anxiety, and other emotions are, in my view, just what people have always thought they were—conscious feelings.... Feelings of fear, in my view, result when we become consciously aware that our brain has nonconsciously detected danger.... Research on fear and anxiety disorders in animals, and also in humans, that I and others have conducted is often focused on how the brain detects and responds to threats, processes that operate nonconsciously. Although this work is very relevant to understanding

conscious fear and anxiety, it has to be understood in its proper context. Responses to threats, in spite of common practice, are not foolproof markers of conscious feelings, even in humans, and likewise should not be assumed to be so in animals" (LeDoux 2015, 19–21).

14. LeDoux and Hofmann (2018) have recently suggested that those who wish to treat and relieve excessive fear in clinical settings understand that subjective dimensions of fear (i.e., human feelings of fearfulness) and objective dimensions of fear (i.e., biological processes of threat detection in the brain) need to be addressed separately. As they put it, "Subjective fear does not require the amygdala, and medications that target the amygdala do not necessarily relieve subjective fear" (LeDoux and Hofmann 2018, 70). LeDoux and Hofmann argue that relieving fear can require cognitive behavioral therapy and/or pharmaceutical treatments to dampen the amygdala central state and verbal strategies to relieve subjective experiences of fear.

15. I have elsewhere articulated my position on emotional expression and uptake, following the work of Sue Campbell (1997), Naomi Scheman (1980, 1996), and Elizabeth Spelman (1989) on the importance of processes of emotional expression and interpretation (Harbin 2016, 156–58; 2014). Campbell, Scheman, and Spelman have clarified in various ways how centrally our emotional lives depend on the participation of other people.

16. As Campbell (1997, 165) puts it, "Theorists, in neglecting expression, have neglected the role of interpretation in the formation of affective meaning and have failed to account for the many ways in which individuals and groups are emotionally manipulated through the unsympathetic or hostile interpretive practices of others."

17. In the Pictionary shrug example, Campbell (1997, 117) states that "the model of triangulations does not locate a stimulus under a single stable description, and I become confused about the meaning of my own response. . . . If I am confused about my feelings, those feelings are themselves confused." She continues, "Instability at one apex of the triangle produces instability at the others. But this means not that we just can't tell which of two or more alternative meanings a person's utterance or gesture has, but that there may be no clear truth to the matter" (118).

18. Recall that on Campbell's view, while all instances of classic emotions have objects, not all feelings do.

19. "Interpreting others within the narrow range of categories set by emotion types will restrict the range of affective significance that can be determined and the significance to people of their own lives" (S. Campbell 1997, 136).

20. Partly it seems that it is difficult to express and receive proper uptake for the depth of feelings of fear—how deeply the richness and vibrancy of our lives are paired with fear. The luckier, the more to lose. And it is difficult to express fear I think, and to receive uptake for it, given current social norms, informed as they are by legacies of positive psychology emphasizing strength, resilience, clarity, and growth. The more capacities we can develop for expressing and giving uptake to complicated fears, perhaps the more we will be able to avoid some of the (unsatisfying) efforts to push past, bury, or overcome those feelings.

21. Amy Roeder, "America Is Failing Its Black Mothers," *Harvard Public Health*, Winter 2019, https://www.hsph.harvard.edu/magazine/magazine_article/america-is-failing-its-black-mothers/.

22. This explains in part why sympathetic media and crowd-funding campaigns in support of the Wuestenbergs ("Stand with Eric and Jillian," 2020, https://standwithjillian.org/; Nicole King, "Drop Charges against Jillian Wuestenberg and Eric Wuestenberg—Charge the Aggressors!," Change.Org petition, 2020, https://www.change.org/p/jessica-cooper-and-michael-bouchard-drop-charges-against-jillian-wuestenberg-and-eric-wuestenberg) emphasize Eric Wuestenberg's veteran status and the couple's happy marriage, four children, and participation in their church community.

23. The question of *what fearing is* is addressed by many more perspectives and research methodologies than those I engage here, and I have not aimed to provide a comprehensive view of everything fear is and involves. For some of us, the ways fear is characterized here may be a reorientation; for others, it may not. I touch on the perspectives I do because I believe they are the views most needed for establishing a secure-enough account of what fear is in order to move forward with the moral and political claims I make in the coming chapters.

Chapter 3

1. As Skenazy adds in a conversation with Brooks, "This shift that's taken place, this idea that it is not safe for children to be out of our sight at any moment, this idea that a good parent is a parent who watches and manages and meddles and observes ceaselessly. This is not insignificant. This has profound consequences in the lives of parents and children.... This is a shift that is not rooted in fact. It's not rooted in any true change or any real danger.... It's rooted in irrational fear" (Brooks 2018, 76).

2. As of 2019, the Pew Research Foundation reported that only 13.7 percent of the US population is foreign born (Budiman 2020). Even conservative editorials have suggested that the United States should strive to welcome *more* migrants if gross domestic product is to be maintained; e.g., see Shikha Dalmia, "Actually, the Numbers Show That We Need More Immigration, Not Less," *New York Times*, January 15, 2019, https://www.nytimes.com/2019/01/15/opinion/trump-immigration-myth.html.

3. See IZA World of Labor (2017). According to a Pew Research study conducted in January 2019, 36 percent of US residents surveyed said that immigrants burden the country by taking jobs, housing, and health care. Among Republicans and Republican-leaning independents, the belief is even more prevalent: 58 percent say immigrants burden the country (See "In a Politically Polarized Era, Sharp Divides in Both Partisan Coalitions," Pew Research Center, December 17, 2019, https://www.pewresearch.org/politics/2019/12/17/views-on-race-and-immigration/).

4. And this according to right-wing think tank the Cato Institute. See Alex Nowrasteh, "CIS Exaggerates the Cost of Immigrant Welfare Use," *Cato at Liberty* blog, May 10, 2016, https://www.cato.org/blog/cis-exaggerates-cost-immigrant-welfare-use.

5. See Anna Flagg, "Is There a Connection between Undocumented Immigrants and Crime?" *New York Times*, May 13, 2019, https://www.nytimes.com/2019/05/13/upshot/illegal-immigration-crime-rates-research.html.

6. Ibid.

7. It should be noted that while migrants pose none of these threats, they *may* pose a threat to the identity and perceived homogeneity of a nation. Thus, if individuals fear that migrants will contribute to a nation's identity diffusion—though such a fear is morally problematic—that fear may be justified.

8. Roger Lancaster (2010, 74) emphasizes a similar kind of manipulation on the part of political forces as the cause of misplaced fears: "Forbidden to critically contemplate the very real, very high risks associated with neoliberal economic policies—currency crises, job loss, capital flight, reduced health care insurance, underfunded retirement plans, environmental degradation—John and Jane Q. Public are induced to fear instead far less consequential hazards to life and limb, they substitute various forms of pseudopractice (vigilance, show trials) for meaningful social involvement."

9. Sometimes Glassner gives something closer to an explanation based on individual psyches. For instance, when discussing misplaced fears of violent media and stranger danger, he claims that fear can be a way of

mishandling guilt: "Our fear grows, I suggest, proportionate to our unacknowledged guilt. By slashing spending on educational, medical, and antipoverty programs for youths we adults have committed great violence against them. Yet rather than face up to our collective responsibility we project our violence onto young people themselves, and onto strangers we imagine will attack them" (Glassner 1999, 72).

10. Philosopher and psychoanalyst Jonathan Lear (2005, 253) defines displacement as "a hallmark of unconscious mental functioning; psychic energy flows loosely among ideas according to primary process, and thus energy can easily move from a forbidden idea or wish onto another idea that is innocuous in itself. The forbidden idea loses its intensity, the innocuous idea gains its intensity. But the innocuous idea comes thereby to stand for the forbidden one."

11. Freud (1965, 74–75) describes displacement as a process characteristic of the id: "The id of course knows no judgements of value: no good and evil, no morality. The economic or, if you prefer, the quantitative factor, which is intimately linked to the pleasure principle, dominates all its processes. Instinctual cathexes seeking discharge—that, in our view, is all there is in the id. It even seems that the energy of these instinctual impulses is in a state different from that in the other regions of the mind, far more mobile and capable of discharge; otherwise the displacements and condensations would not occur which are characteristic of the id and which so completely disregard the quality of what is cathected—what in the ego we should call an idea."

12. Much feminist critique is focused on challenging the Freudian Oedipal narrative about how people become subjects and in doing so become sexually differentiated. On Freud's account, all children are born emotionally attached to the mother, not yet sexually differentiated. For a boy, the attachment to the mother continues and develops into a sexual desire for her, and eventually into a jealousy of his father and a fear that his father will overpower and castrate him. For a girl, this pre-Oedipal attachment eventually switches to the father, because of a realization that the mother is castrated (without penis), as she too will be. So for Freud, femininity is marked by wanting to be the object of a man's desire. Freud understands there to be no feminine libido—the only libido on his view is masculine. All of this has been criticized by feminists: his lack of attention to mothers, the heteronormativity at the core of his account, the claim that there is no feminine libido, and much more. While rejecting important elements of Freudian and psychoanalytic approaches, a number of feminists have attempted to make use of others. For instance, Karen Horney argued for a

distinct feminine disposition that does not develop just in response to castration and penis envy, and for a biologically based feminine sexuality (see Paris 1996; Westkott 1986). Simone de Beauvoir claimed that Freud was not able to account for women's distinct libido. On Beauvoir's view, Freud's account troublingly pits femininity and subjectivity against each other. Though there are points of contention between Beauvoir and Freud, they both hold a view in which becoming gendered is a social process rather than a biological fact. And Beauvoir also appreciates the attention psychoanalysis pays to understanding the emotional complexity of lives. Some Anglo-American feminists have worked to make use of some of Freud's and Lacan's central analyses. Lacan was a major interlocutor for French feminists Luce Irigaray and Julia Kristeva. Irigaray was a student of Lacan who eventually broke with his views. Among many other departures, she highlighted relationships between mothers and daughters and the important role of mothers in society. Kristeva too had psychoanalytic training (though she was not a student of Lacan) but maintained an Oedipus structure in her view. Lacan too has been criticized for maintaining phallocentrism in a different and more symbolic way than Freud—he doesn't maintain Freud's obsession with the actual penis but instead understands "phallus" to mean a signifier within a system of other signifiers. Other feminists have instead taken starting points from British object-relations theory (especially Melanie Klein [1984] and Donald Winnicott [2005]) and its attention to the bonds between mothers and children. For instance, Jessica Benjamin has used psychoanalysis alongside insights from Foucault to attend to women's experiences of domination in patriarchal society and the way such experiences can shape erotic attachments to patriarchal power. Benjamin and some other Anglo-American feminists have attempted to use psychoanalytic approaches to diagnose and reduce the harmful emotional effects of domination.

13. Note that I am here diverging in a specific sense from Solomon's account, discussed in chapter 2. Solomon held that I can only be fearful so long as I believe that what has caused me to be fearful is what I am fearful about. If I discover something else is actually the cause of my fear, and if that thing isn't a new object for fear, my fear will cease. Calhoun gave us reason to think things might be more complicated, since on her view the background cognitive set could sustain my fear of X (e.g., heights), even if I came to no longer believe that X was threatening. I am suggesting here that it is possible a fearer might become aware that their fear of X is actually a displaced fear of Y and still feel fearful of X. If grown-up Hans later comes to believe that his fear of horses was really a fear of castration by his father, he might then no longer feel fearful of horses, *or* he might still feel

fearful of horses as he always has, *or* he might fear horses in a qualitatively different way (to a different degree, or with different intensity).
14. As Peter Kwong (2010, 255) notes, "In the United States, immigrant bashing has become a ready-made tool used by politicians to stir up popular support and distract attention from problems that are much more difficult to solve."

Chapter 4

1. There are also less formal or elaborate walls, like the various recent iterations of a boundary wall erected in Michigan between a majority low-income and Black area of the city of Detroit, and its wealthy, whiter neighbor community of Grosse Pointe. This barrier, established at one busy entrance to Grosse Pointe from Detroit, has taken various forms, from a gigantic plowed pile of snow, to a number of Farmers Market sheds, to a row of large trees planted in oversized clay pots that the Grosse Pointe community had shipped in from California.
2. As Low (2010, 34) writes, "At a societal level, people say they move because of their fear of crime and others. . . . At a personal level, though, residents are also searching for the sense of security and safety that they associate with their childhood. The gates are used symbolically to ward off many of life's unknowns, including unemployment, loss of loved ones, and downward mobility; but of course gates cannot deliver all that is promised."
3. Biss describes the fear she felt for her son when he was young: "There are many explanations for the extreme fearfulness I felt in the weeks after my son's birth—I was a new mother, I was far from my family, I was anemic, I was delirious with fatigue. But the true source of my fear eluded me until months later, when I went out on Lake Michigan in my little canoe made of bent wood covered with a transparent canvas. I had been on the lake many times before in that boat and I had never been afraid, but this time my blood was pounding in my ears. I was newly aware of the immensity of the water under me, its vast cold depths, and I was painfully aware of the fragility of my boat. *Oh*, I thought to myself, with some disappointment, *I'm afraid of death*" (2014, 79–80). Her new fear of death is both for her child's death and also her own, as she is part of her child's survival.
4. Someone might wonder whether parents who have been misinformed about vaccine safety and choose not to vaccinate for that reason would be exempt from responsibility for their failure to vaccinate—they did not

know better. I would not accept this: such misinformed decision making is culpable ignorance.
5. See Reed Abelson and Abby Goodnough, "If the Supreme Court Ends Obamacare, Here's What It Would Mean," *New York Times*, June 17, 2021, https://www.nytimes.com/article/supreme-court-obamacare-case.html.
6. Beyond the threat of lacking health care, the threat of having ourselves or our loved ones face serious illness is always present. Joseph Dumit (2010) has argued that fear of illness is one of the most unrelenting in the landscape of American insecurities. Even when individuals are healthy, the specter of illness is a constant component of one's plans and considerations for the future. Individuals have a sense of a perpetual responsibility to do everything in their power to avoid illness, as though all illnesses can be avoided by individuals' efforts. As Dumit (2010, 163) writes, "Health in America today is defined by this double insecurity: never being sure enough about the future (always being at risk) and never knowing enough about what you could and should be doing." As we saw with Biss's discussion of vaccines and children, the threat of illness is not one that can be removed, escaped, assimilated, or destroyed. The only partially effective option is to try to overpower it—to employ preventive measures more tenacious than prospective illnesses, or treatment protocols more potent than the actualized ones. As in the case of health insurance, much of the overpowering of illness is psychological—though one's body may become susceptible to illness at some point, individuals attempt to convince themselves that they will be able to power through.
7. In all cases, *the experience of being threatened is a harm*, using the term "harm" in the sense Iris Marion Young (2011, 40–41) does to identify limits in the development and expression of selves.

Chapter 5

1. It is necessary to note that the van der Kolk's writing and practice has been called into question following his being fired in 2018 from his position at the Trauma Center he founded after he had been accused of bullying employees. Van der Kolk has denied these charges. A lawsuit was filed and settled without extensive public discussion. Somatic regulation as a set of practices far outreaches van der Kolk's work, but since *The Body Keeps the Score* remains a foundational text within the practice community, I have chosen to continue to cite it here to outline the foundations of the practice, not as an endorsement of all its claims or its author's actions.

2. Kaiser, Gillette, and Spinazzola detail their "Sensory Learning Program" (SLP) as follows: "According to SLP theory, systems are inhibited by trauma but retain the potential for being restored; therefore, the creation of an environment for the brain to 'relearn' adaptive internal structure is possible.... During the SLP process, the participant lies on a trochoidal motion table that slowly rises and descends in a circular pattern, providing vestibular stimulation. At the same time, the participant's eyes follow a stationary light instrument that provides predetermined frequencies of colored light in accordance with syntonics theory. Gated music is introduced through headphones that are worn during the session" (Kaiser, Gillette, and Spinazzola 2010, 704).
3. Internal family systems therapy identifies different roles within a single person—protector, exile, and others—and establishes therapy to help individuals realize when the balance between these roles may be out of whack, potentially in response to past events that have required, for example, more intensive efforts at self-protection than would ideally be necessary. As van der Kolk (2015, 283) writes, "The mind of each of us is like a family in which the members have different levels of maturity, excitability, wisdom, and pain"—some parts act as protectors for others.
4. Van der Kolk describes Pesso Boyden Psychomotor therapy as a kind of individual therapy involving a group of people, which involves creating structures/tableaus of a person's past enrolling other people as actors and witnesses—the protagonist is in charge of placing enrollees in particular roles, recreating scenes where past harm has happened, and correcting that harm in a re-performance of the scenes. (For more information, see "What Is Pesso Boyden Therapy?," Pesso Boyden Training Institute, 2016, http://pessoboydentraininguk.com/what-is-pesso-boyden-therapy/.)
5. In the cases van der Kolk describes, neurofeedback involves something like computer games that encourage some brain wave patterns and discourage others: "When the fear patterns relax, the brain becomes less susceptible to automatic stress reactions and better able to focus on ordinary events. After all, stress is not an inherent property of events themselves—it is a function of how we label and react to them. Neurofeedback simply stabilizes the brain and increases resiliency, allowing us to develop more choices in how to respond" (van der Kolk 2015, 316).
6. In an episode of her podcast, author Elizabeth Gilbert (2016) points to the importance of respecting and receiving fear: "A lot of the trouble that people get into with fear is that they hate it so much and they want to fight it and they want to battle it and they talk about kicking it in the ass and punching it out and dominating it, which only makes it more insecure

and only makes it fight back more. And my experience is, the more respect and kindness and gratitude even that you can show to fear, the more it quiets down."

7. See Nguyen (2020) for a helpful discussion of echo chambers and epistemic bubbles.
8. I say these decisions and responses will "likely be" strengthened by the involvement of others, because of course with more participants can also come conflict that, if not well handled, can be counterproductive. So it is not a given that relational processes for determining responses to threats will be effective. But nonrelational processes that depend solely on one person's perspective and ideas are certain to be more anemic.
9. My thanks for Susan Sherwin and Constantin Mehmel for these concerns.
10. We might also imagine how this could play out in larger interpersonal settings, with different calibrations of power dynamics, and infused with institutional constraints. For instance, think of a university classroom situation, where perhaps a student is expressing fears and a professor is in the role of educator and also potential emotional interpreter, and where there are many others (students) around as witnesses/interpreters/other fearers. Because the case of the family member is complex enough, I focus on it here. But questions of whether and when to prioritize interpretation versus correction of false beliefs come up in many different interpersonal contexts.
11. An Aristotelian might object, is there really no such thing as a virtuous fearer, who fears the right things in the right ways for the right reasons? If such a fearer exists, perhaps they don't have so much need to create distance between feelings and actions. While I can think of examples of people whose fearing I trust more than others, both in the sense of likelihood of aligning with actual threats and in the sense of not inclining toward controlling strategies, I would suggest that these people too would not be harmed by a pause between fearing and acting, nor by the presence of others who would stay with them as fearers.
12. See also Olga Khazan, "The Psychology of Irrational Fear," *The Atlantic*, October 31, 2014, https://www.theatlantic.com/health/archive/2014/10/the-psychology-of-irrational-fear/382080/.
13. For example, past experience with severe illness can make a person overly fearful of illness in future (see Melissa Dahl, "Ebola Fears Are Triggering Mass Hypochondria," *The Cut*, October 7, 2014, https://www.thecut.com/2014/10/ebola-fears-are-triggering-mass-hypochondria.html). In Kellner's (1982) study of treatment options for hypochondria, it was

found that with many participants, an approach that combined following up on the participant's perception of possible illness after a physical exam (i.e., taking them seriously rather than dismissing them out of hand) with psychotherapy that helped participants learn about selective perception and the connection between psychological and somatic experiences, and anti-anxiety drugs. It was not effective to simply tell participants that their fears (i.e., that they were ill) were unfounded.
14. Of course, sensitivity and responses to these dismissals will vary among individuals.
15. Thanks to Duncan MacIntosh for formulating the point in this way.
16. See Marcia Lee, "Four Thoughts on Hope and Resistance," *Radical Discipleship*, October 30, 2020, https://radicaldiscipleship.net/2020/10/30/4-thoughts-on-hope-and-resistance/.
17. Mary Annaïse Heglar, "What Climate Grief Taught Me about the Coronavirus," *New Republic*, March 25, 2020, https://newrepublic.com/article/157059/climate-grief-taught-coronavirus.
18. Sean Illing, "This Is a Time for Solidarity: What Albert Camus's 'The Plague' Can Teach Us about Life in a Pandemic," *Vox*, March 15, 2020, https://www.vox.com/2020/3/13/21172237/coronavirus-covid-19-albert-camus-the-plague?fbclid=IwAR2kHkNRWOQJp8X1teFs9Z2dCkP3HeKW8KaYsFb4yMXGdsNV2PMtfmxQ4Vo.
19. See, for example, the American Medical Association (2021) brief on the exacerbation of opioid and substance use issues during the pandemic.
20. See Lois Beckett, "Armed Protesters Demonstrate against Covid-19 Lockdown at Michigan Capital," *The Guardian*, April 30, 2020, https://www.theguardian.com/us-news/2020/apr/30/michigan-protests-coronavirus-lockdown-armed-capitol.
21. Derek Thompson, "Hygiene Theater Is a Huge Waste of Time," *The Atlantic*, July 27, 2020, https://www.theatlantic.com/ideas/archive/2020/07/scourge-hygiene-theater/614599/.
22. Tess Wilkinson-Ryan, "Our Minds Aren't Equipped for this Kind of Reopening," *The Atlantic*, July 6, 2020, https://www.theatlantic.com/ideas/archive/2020/07/reopening-psychological-morass/613858/?utm_medium=social&utm_source=facebook&utm_campaign=the-atlantic&utm_content=edit-promo&utm_term=2020-07-06T10%3A30%3A31&fbclid=IwAR3cIbFj9nJgIiZ1mLbQfuut7QZp77saIfHwFPHk3FZzMCdd4PS7MiMKiWw.
23. My thanks to Linda Diaz for this point.
24. I explore other aspects of these calibrating relationships in Harbin 2022.

25. As in the concerns discussed earlier, someone might wonder, should we really be willing to hear all crisis-related fears? In the pandemic, recall fears of government overreach expressed by those protesting the stay-at-home orders. What about fears of the perceived harms of wearing masks, which cited the (thoroughly debunked) possibility of carbon dioxide poisoning? I maintain that yes, interpretation of fears not acted on is important for avoiding the harms of fears acted on. We should not respond sympathetically to attacks on stay-at-home orders or refusals to wear masks. But we should, to whatever extent we have opportunities to do so, make space for expressions and interpretation of underlying fears in future crises (including those of economic insecurity, in these examples).

References

Ahmed, Sara. 2004. *The Cultural Politics of Emotion*. Edinburgh: Edinburgh University Press.

Alexander, Michelle. 2010. *The New Jim Crow: Mass Incarceration in the Age of Colorblindness*. New York: New Press.

American Medical Association. 2021. "Issue Brief: Drug Overdose Epidemic Worsened during COVID Pandemic." https://www.ama-assn.org/system/files/2020-12/issue-brief-increases-in-opioid-related-overdose.pdf.

Bader, Christopher, Joseph O. Baker, L. Edward Day, and Ann Gordon. 2020. *Fear Itself: The Causes and Consequences of Fear in America*. New York: New York University Press.

Bahrani, Ramin, director. 2015. *99 Homes*. Broad Green Pictures. iTunes, MPEG video, 112 minutes. https://itunes.apple.com/us/movie/99-homes/id1062167116.

Baier, Annette. 1985. *Postures of the Mind: Essays on Mind and Morals*. Minneapolis: University of Minnesota Press.

Baldwin, James. 1993. *The Fire Next Time*. New York: Vintage Books.

Bandura, Albert. 1969. *The Principles of Behavior Modification*. New York: Holt, Rinehart & Winston.

Belling, Catherine. 2012. *A Condition of Doubt: The Meanings of Hypochondria*. New York: Oxford University Press.

Biss, Eula. 2014. *On Immunity: An Inoculation*. Minneapolis: Graywolf Press.

Bohner, Gerd, and Thomas Weinerth. 2001. "Negative Affect Can Increase or Decrease Message Scrutiny: The Affect Interpretation Hypothesis." *Personality and Social Psychology Bulletin* 27 (11): 1417–28.

Boyle, Danny, director. 2002. *28 Days Later*. Fox Searchlight Pictures.

Bracha, H. Stefan, Tyler C. Ralston, Jennifer M. Matsukawa, Andrew E. Williams, and Adam S. Bracha. 2004. "Does 'Fight or Flight' Need Updating?" *Psychosomatics* 45 (5): 448–49.

Brandt, Richard B. 1946. "Moral Valuation." *Ethics* 56 (2): 106–21.

Broad, C. D. 1954. "Emotion and Sentiment." *Journal of Aesthetics and Art Criticism* 13 (2): 203–14.

Brooks, Kim. 2018. *Small Animals: Parenthood in the Age of Fear*. New York: Flatiron Books.

Budiman, Abby. 2020. "Key Findings about U.S. Immigrants." Pew Research Center, August 20, 2020. https://www.pewresearch.org/fact-tank/2020/08/20/key-findings-about-u-s-immigrants/.

REFERENCES

Butler, Judith. 2004. *Precarious Life: The Powers of Mourning and Violence.* London: Verso.
Butler, Judith. 2009. *Frames of War: When Is Life Grievable?* London: Verso.
Calhoun, Cheshire. (1984) 2003. "Cognitive Emotions?" In *What Is an Emotion? Classic and Contemporary Readings,* edited by Robert Solomon, 2nd ed., 236–47. New York: Oxford University Press.
Campbell, Donald T. 1965. "Ethnocentric and Other Altruistic Motives." In *Nebraska Symposium on Motivation,* Vol. 13, edited by David Levine, 283–311. Lincoln: University of Nebraska Press.
Campbell, Sue. 1997. *Interpreting the Personal: Expression and the Formation of Feelings.* Ithaca, NY: Cornell University Press.
Campbell, Sue. 2003. *Relational Remembering: Rethinking the Memory Wars.* Lanham, MD: Rowman and Littlefield.
Cannon, Walter B. 1915. *Bodily Changes in Pain, Hunger, Fear, and Rage: An Account of Recent Researches into the Function of Emotional Excitement.* New York: D. Appleton and Company.
Carey, Gregory. 1990. "Genes, Fears, Phobias, and Phobic Disorders." *Journal of Counselling and Development* 68 (6): 628–32.
Chanel, Olivier, and Graciela Chichilnisky. 2009. "The Influence of Fear in Decisions: Experimental Evidence." *Journal of Risk and Uncertainty* 39 (3): 271–98.
Chapman University, Robyn Rapoport, and Kyle Berta. 2019. *Methodology Report: American Fears Survey.* SSRS. https://www.chapman.edu/wilkinson/research-centers/babbie-center/_files/full-survey-methodology-2019.pdf.
Child, Brenda J. 2000. *Boarding School Seasons: American Indian Families 1900–1940.* Lincoln: University of Nebraska Press.
Constant, Amelie. 2014. "Do Migrants Take the Jobs of Native Workers?" *IZA World of Labor* 10 (May). https://doi.org/10.15185/izawol.10.
Cooper, Marianne. 2014. *Cut Adrift: Families in Insecure Times.* Berkeley: University of California Press.
Cuarón, Alfonso, director. 2006. *Children of Men.* Universal Pictures.
D'Arms, Justin, and Daniel Jacobson. 2000. "The Moralistic Fallacy: On the 'Appropriateness' of Emotions." *Philosophy and Phenomenological Research* 61 (1): 65–90.
Davidson, Donald. 1991. "Three Varieties of Knowledge." In *A. J. Ayer: Memorial Essays. Cambridge,* edited by A. Philips Griffiths, 153–66. Cambridge: Cambridge University Press.
Davis, Angela. 2012. *The Meaning of Freedom: And Other Difficult Dialogues.* San Francisco: City Lights.
DeMonaco, James, director. 2013. *The Purge.* Universal Pictures.
de Sousa, Ronald. 1978. "Self-Deceptive Emotions." *Journal of Philosophy* 75 (11): 684–97.
de Sousa, Ronald. 1987. *The Rationality of Emotion.* Cambridge, MA: MIT Press.

REFERENCES 185

Dewey, John. 1894. "The Theory of Emotion. (I) Emotional Attitudes." *Psychological Review* 1 (6): 553–69.

Dewey, John. 1895. "The Theory of Emotion. (2) The Significance of Emotions." *Psychological Review* 2 (1): 13–32.

Dewey, John. 1922. *Human Nature and Conduct: An Introduction to Social Psychology*. New York: Henry Holt.

Doherty, Robert. 2017. "The Demise of the Affordable Care Act? Not So Fast." *Annals of Internal Medicine* 166 (2): 144–45.

Dumit, Joseph. 2010. "Normal Insecurities, Healthy Insecurities." In *The Insecure American: How We Got Here and What We Should Do about It*, edited by Hugh Gusterson and Catherine Besteman, 163–81. Berkeley: University of California Press.

Edwards, John A., and Gifford Weary. 1993. "Depression and the Impression-Formation Continuum: Piecemeal Processing despite the Availability of Category Information." *Journal of Personality and Social Psychology* 64 (4): 636–45.

English, Andrea, and Barbara Stengel. 2010. "Exploring Fear: Rousseau, Dewey, and Freire on Fear and Learning." *Educational Theory* 60 (5): 521–42.

Epstein, Seymour. 1972. "The Nature of Anxiety with Emphasis upon Its Relationship to Expectancy." In *Anxiety: Current Trends in Theory and Research*, Vol. 2, edited by Charles D. Spielberger, 291–337. New York: Academic Press.

Farrall, Stephen, Jon Bannister, Jason Ditton, and Elizabeth Gilchrist. 1997. "Questioning the Measurement of the 'Fear of Crime': Findings from a Major Methodological Study." *British Journal of Criminology* 37 (4): 658–79.

Fattah, Ezzat A. 1993. "Research on Fear of Crime: Some Common Conceptual and Measurement Problems." In *Fear of Crime and Criminal Victimization*, edited by Wolfgang Bilsky, Christian Pfeiffer, and Peter Wetzels, 45–70. Stuttgart: Ferdinand Enke Verlag.

Fingarette, Herbert. 1969. *Self-Deception*. London: Routledge and Kegan Paul.

Fischhoff, Baruch, and John Kadvany. 2011. *Risk: A Very Short Introduction*. New York: Oxford University Press.

Flores, J. Robert. 2002. "NISMART Questions and Answers." *NISMART: National Incidence Studies of Missing, Abducted, Runaway, and Thrownaway Children* fact sheet. US Department of Justice, Office of Justice Programs, Office of Juvenile Justice and Delinquency Prevention. https://www.ojp.gov/pdffiles1/ojjdp/fs196760.pdf.

Freud, Sigmund. 1952. *The Major Works of Sigmund Freud*. Translated by Alix Strachey. Chicago: Encyclopedia Britannica.

Freud, Sigmund. 1965. *New Introductory Lectures on Psychoanalysis*. Translated by James Strachey. New York: Norton.

Freud, Sigmund. 1968. "Fetishism." *The Standard Edition of the Complete Psychological Works of Sigmund Freud*, Vol. 21 (1927–1931). Translated by James Strachey. London: Hogarth Press. 147–158.

Freud, Sigmund. 1985. *The Interpretation of Dreams*. Translated by A. A. Brill. New York: Buccaneer Books.

Garcia, John, and Koelling, Robert A. 1966. "Relation of Cue to Consequence in Avoidance Learning." *Psychonomic Science* 4: 123–24.

Gawande, Atul. 2015. *Being Mortal: Medicine and What Matters in the End*. New York: Henry Holt.

Gendler, Tamar S. 2008a. "Alief and Belief." *Journal of Philosophy* 105 (10): 634–63.

Gendler, Tamar S. 2008b. "Alief in Action (and Reaction)." *Mind & Language* 23 (5): 552–58.

Generative Somatics. 2011. "Why Somatics for Social Justice and a Transformative Movement?" GenerativeSomatics.org. https://generativesomatics.org/wp-content/uploads/2019/10/WhySomaticsforSJ.pdf.

Generative Somatics. 2014. "What Is a Politicized Somatics?" Generative-Somatics.org. https://generativesomatics.org/wp-content/uploads/2019/10/Copy-of-What-is-a-politicized-somatics.pdf.

Gilbert, Elizabeth. 2016. "Dear Creativity and Fear." *Magic Lessons*, July 24, 2016, season 1, episode 9. Podcast, MP3 audio, 17:47. https://www.elizabethgilbert.com/magic-lessons/.

Giuletti, Corrado. 2014. "The Welfare Magnet Hypothesis and the Welfare Take-Up of Migrants." *IZA World of Labor* 37 (June). http://wol.iza.org/articles/welfare-magnet-hypothesis-and-welfare-take-up-of-migrants.

Glassner, Barry. 1999. *The Culture of Fear: Why Americans Are Afraid of the Wrong Things*. New York: Basic Books.

Good Morning America. 2020. "Couple Speaks Out after Wife Pulls Gun on Family in Parking Lot." Reported by Alex Presha, aired July 11, 2020, on ABC. YouTube video, 2:39. https://www.youtube.com/watch?v=6h36cu_96CY.

Grossman, Paul, Ludger Niemann, Stefan Schmidt, and Harald Walach. 2004. "Mindfulness-Based Stress Reduction and Health Benefits: A Meta-analysis." *Journal of Psychosomatic Research* 57 (1): 35–43.

Guenther, Lisa. 2013. *Solitary Confinement: Social Death and Its Afterlives*. Minneapolis: University of Minnesota Press.

Gusterson, Hugh, and Catherine Besteman. 2010. *The Insecure American: How We Got Here and What We Should Do about It*. Berkeley: University of California Press.

Hale, Chris. 1993. *Fear of Crime: A Review of the Literature*. Report to the Metropolitan Police Service Working Party on the Fear of Crime.

Haraway, Donna. 2016. *Staying with the Trouble: Making Kin in the Chthulucene*. Durham, NC: Duke University Press.

Harbin, Ami. 2014. "Mentorship in Method: Philosophy and Experienced Agency." *Hypatia: A Journal of Feminist Philosophy* 29 (2): 476–92.

Harbin, Ami. 2016. *Disorientation and Moral Life*. New York: Oxford University Press.

Harbin, Ami. 2022. "The Relational Calibration of Fear." *Synthese* 200: 256.

Hartley, Catherine A., and Elizabeth A. Phelps. 2012. "Anxiety and Decision-Making." *Biological Psychiatry* 72 (2): 113–18.

Hebert, M. A., D. C. Blanchard, and R. J. Blanchard. 1999. "Intravenous Cocaine Precipitates Panic-Like Flight Responses and Lasting Hyperdefensiveness in Laboratory Rats." *Pharmacology Biochemistry and Behavior* 63 (3): 349–60.

Hettema, John M., Peter Annas, Michael C. Neale, Kenneth S. Kendler, and Mats Fredrikson. 2003. "A Twin Study of the Genetics of Fear Conditioning." *Archives of General Psychiatry* 60 (7): 702–8.

Hillcoat, John, director. 2009. *The Road*. 2929 Productions.

Hochschild, Arlie Russell. 2016. *Strangers in Their Own Land: Anger and Mourning on the American Right*. New York: New Press.

Hoffman, Caroline J., Steven J. Ersser, Jane B. Hopkinson, Peter G. Nicholls, Julia E. Harrington, and Peter W. Thomas. 2012. "Effectiveness of Mindfulness-Based Stress Reduction in Mood, Breast- and Endocrine-Related Quality of Life, and Well-Being in Stage 0 to III Breast Cancer: A Randomized Controlled Trial." *Journal of Clinical Oncology* 30 (12): 1335–42.

Hölzel, Britta K., James Carmody, Mark Vangel, Christina Congleton, Sita M. Yerramsetti, Tim Gard, and Sara Lazar. 2011. "Mindfulness Practice Leads to Increases in Regional Brain Gray Matter Density." *Psychiatry Research: Neuroimaging* 191 (1): 36–43.

Hunsinger, Matthew. 2010. "Threat on the Mind: The Impact of Incidental Fear on Race Bias in Rapid Decision-Making." PhD diss., University of Massachusetts Amherst. Scholarworks@UMassAmherst: Doctoral Dissertations. https://doi.org/10.7275/5671793.

Izard, Carroll. 1984. "The Facets and Interfaces of Emotions." In *Interfaces in Psychology*, edited by R. Bell, J. L. Greene, and J. H. Harvey, 57–85. Lubbock: Texas Tech Press.

IZA World of Labor. 2017. "Five Common Fears about Immigration." IZA World of Labor website, December 4, 2017. Video, 1:58. https://wol.iza.org/videos/five-common-fears-about-immigration.

James, William. 1884. "What Is an Emotion?" *Mind* 9 (34): 188–205.

John, E. 1941. "A Study of the Effects of Evacuation and Air-raids on Children of Pre-school Age." *British Journal of Educational Psychology* 11: 173–79.

Johnson, Eric J., and Amos Tversky. 1983. "Affect, Generalization, and the Perception of Risk." *Journal of Personality and Social Psychology* 45 (1): 20–31.

Johnston, Elizabeth, and Leah Olson. 2015. *The Feeling Brain: The Biology and Psychology of Emotion*. New York: W.W. Norton.

Joseph, Janice. 1997. "Fear of Crime among Black Elderly." *Journal of Black Studies* 27 (5): 698–717.

Kabat-Zinn, Jon. 2013. *Full Catastrophe Living: Using the Wisdom of Your Body and Mind to Face Stress, Pain, and Illness*, 2nd ed. New York: Bantam.

Kaiser, Erika M., Craig S. Gillette, and Joseph Spinazzola. 2010. "A Controlled Pilot-Outcome Study of Sensory Integration (SI) in the Treatment of Complex Adaptation to Traumatic Stress." *Journal of Aggression, Maltreatment and Trauma* 19 (7): 699–720.

Kasperson, Roger E., Ortwin Renn, Paul Slovic, Halina S. Brown, Jacque Emel, Robert Goble, Jeanne X. Kasperson, and Samuel Ratick. 1988. "The Social Amplification of Risk: A Conceptual Framework." *Risk Analysis* 8 (2): 177–87.

Kellner, Robert. 1982. "Psychotherapeutic Strategies in Hypochondriasis: A Clinical Study." *American Journal of Psychotherapy* 36 (2): 146–57.

Kenny, Anthony. 1963. *Action, Emotion and Will*. London: Routledge and Kegan Paul.

Klein, Melanie. 1984. *Love, Guilt, and Reparation and Other Works 1921–1945*. New York: Free Press.

Klein, Naomi. 2007. *The Shock Doctrine: The Rise of Disaster Capitalism*. Toronto: Alfred A. Knopf Canada.

Kosslyn, Stephen M., Lisa M. Shin, William L. Thompson, Richard J. McNally, Scott L. Rauch, Roger K. Pitman, and Nathaniel M. Alpert. 1996. "Neural Effects of Visualizing and Perceiving Aversive Stimuli: A PET Investigation." *NeuroReport* 7 (10): 1569–76.

Kwong, Peter. 2010. "Walling Out Immigrants." In *The Insecure American: How We Got Here and What We Should Do about It*, edited by Hugh Gusterson and Catherine Besteman, 255–69. Berkeley: University of California Press.

Lancaster, Roger. 2010. "Republic of Fear: The Rise of Punitive Governance in America." In *The Insecure American: How We Got Here and What We Should Do about It*, edited by Hugh Gusterson and Catherine Besteman, 63–76. Berkeley: University of California Press.

Lear, Jonathan. 2005. *Freud*. Routledge Philosophers series. New York: Routledge.

LeDoux, Joseph. 1996. *The Emotional Brain: The Mysterious Underpinnings of Emotional Life*. New York: Simon and Schuster.

LeDoux, Joseph. 2002. *The Synaptic Self: How Our Brains Become Who We Are*. New York: Viking.

LeDoux, Joseph. 2015. *Anxious: Using the Brain to Understand and Treat Fear and Anxiety*. New York: Viking.

LeDoux, Joseph. 2020. "Thoughtful Feelings." *Current Biology* 30: R617–R634.

LeDoux, Joseph E., and Stefan G. Hofmann. 2018. "The Subjective Experience of Emotion: A Fearful View." *Current Opinion in Behavioral Sciences* 19 (February): 67–72.

Lerner, Jennifer S., and Dacher Keltner. 2001. "Fear, Anger, and Risk." *Journal of Personality and Social Psychology* 81 (1): 146–59.

Lilley, Sasha. 2012a. "The Apocalyptic Politics of Collapse and Rebirth." In Sasha Lilley, David McNally, Eddie Yuen, and James Davis, *Catastrophism: The Apocalyptic Politics of Collapse and Rebirth*. Oakland, CA: PM Press, 1–14.

Lilley, Sasha. 2012b. "Great Chaos under Heaven: Catastrophism and the Left." In Sasha Lilley, David McNally, Eddie Yuen, and James Davis,

Catastrophism: The Apocalyptic Politics of Collapse and Rebirth. Oakland, CA: PM Press, 44–76.

Lilley, Sasha, David McNally, Eddie Yuen, and James Davis. 2012. *Catastrophism: The Apocalyptic Politics of Collapse and Rebirth.* Oakland, CA: PM Press.

Low, Setha. 2003. *Behind the Gates: Life, Security, and the Pursuit of Happiness in Fortress America.* New York: Routledge.

Low, Setha. 2010. "A Nation of Gated Communities." In *The Insecure American: How We Got Here and What We Should Do about It,* edited by Hugh Gusterson and Catherine Besteman, 27–44. Berkeley: University of California Press.

Maina, Ng'ethe, and Staci K. Haines. 2008. "The Transformative Power of Practice." GenerativeSomatics.org. 1–4. https://generativesomatics.org/wp-content/uploads/2019/10/Transformative-Power-of-Practice.pdf.

Marcus, George E., W. Russell Neuman, and Michael MacKuen. 2000. *Affective Intelligence and Political Judgment.* Chicago: University of Chicago Press.

Mele, Alfred R. 1987. *Irrationality: An Essay on Akrasia, Self-Deception, and Self-Control.* New York: Oxford University Press.

Miller, George, director. 2015. *Mad Max: Fury Road.* Warner Bros. Pictures.

National Center for Victims of Crime. 2017. "Crime and Victimization Fact Sheets: Homicide." US Department of Justice, Office of Justice Programs, Office for Victims of Crime. https://www.ncjrs.gov/ovc_archives/ncvrw/2017/images/en_artwork/Fact_Sheets/2017NCVRW_Homicide_508.pdf.

Nguyen, C. Thi. 2020. "Echo Chambers and Epistemic Bubbles." *Episteme* 17 (2): 141–61.

Öhman, Arne, and Susan Mineka. 2001. "Fears, Phobias, and Preparedness: Toward an Evolved Module of Fear and Fear Learning." *Psychological Review* 108 (3): 483–522.

Paris, Bernard J. 1996. *Karen Horney: A Psychoanalyst's Search for Self-Understanding.* New Haven, CT: Yale University Press.

Parker, Michael T., and Linda M. Isbell. 2010. "How I Vote Depends on How I Feel: The Differential Impact of Anger and Fear on Political Information Processing." *Psychological Science* 21 (4): 548–50.

Peele, Jordan, director. 2017. *Get Out.* Universal Pictures.

Phelps, Elizabeth A., Sam Ling, and Marisa Carrasco. 2006. "Emotion Facilitates Perception and Potentiates the Perceptual Benefits of Attention." *Psychological Science* 17 (4): 292–99.

Poushter, Jacob, and Christine Huang. 2019. "Climate Change Still Seen as the Top Global Threat, but Cyberattacks a Risking Concern." Pew Research Center, February 10, 2019. 1–36. https://www.pewresearch.org/global/2019/02/10/climate-change-still-seen-as-the-top-global-threat-but-cyber attacks-a-rising-concern/.

Poushter, Jacob, and Moira Fagan. 2020. "Americans See Spread of Disease as Top International Threat, Along with Terrorism, Nuclear Weapons,

Cyberattacks." Pew Research Center, April 13, 2020. 1–22. https://www.pewresearch.org/global/2020/04/13/americans-see-spread-of-disease-as-top-international-threat-along-with-terrorism-nuclear-weapons-cyber attacks/.

Rachman, Stanley. 1972. "Clinical Applications of Observational Learning, Imitation and Modelling." *Behavior Therapy* 3: 319–91.

Rachman, Stanley. 1976. "The Passing of the Two-stage Theory of Fear and Avoidance: Fresh Possibilities." *Behavioural Research and Therapy* 14: 125–34.

Rachman, Stanley. 1977. "The Conditioning Theory of Fear Acquisition: A Critical Examination." *Behaviour Research and Therapy* 15: 375–87.

Radway, Noleca. 2019. "The Wonder of the Unknown." *Raising Rebels*, December 12, 2019. Podcast, MP3 audio, 54:37. https://raisingrebelspod.com/episodes.

Ray, Susan L., and Meredith Vanstone. 2009. "The Impact of PTSD on Veterans' Family Relationships: An Interpretive Phenomenological Inquiry." *International Journal of Nursing Studies* 46 (6): 838–47.

Robin, Corey. 2004. *Fear: The History of a Political Idea*. New York: Oxford University Press.

Ropeik, David. 2010. *How Risky Is It, Really? Why Our Fears Don't Always Match the Facts*. New York: McGraw Hill.

Rorty, Amélie Oksenberg. 1980. "Explaining Emotions." In *Explaining Emotions*, edited by Amélie O. Rorty, 103–26. Berkeley: University of California Press.

Roseman, Ira J., Cynthia Wiest, and Tamara S. Swartz. 1994. "Phenomenology, Behaviors, and Goals Differentiate Discrete Emotions." *Journal of Personality and Social Psychology* 67 (2): 206–21.

Scarantino, Andrea, and Ronald de Sousa. 2018. "Emotion." In *The Stanford Encyclopedia of Philosophy*, edited by Edward N. Zalta. Article published September 25, 2018; last modified April 7, 2021. https://plato.stanford.edu/entries/emotion/.

Scheman, Naomi. 1980. "Anger and the Politics of Naming." In *Women and Language in Literature and Society*, edited by Sally McConnell-Ginet, Ruth Borker, and Nelly Furman, 22–35. New York: Praeger.

Scheman, Naomi. 1996. "Feeling Our Way toward Moral Objectivity." In *Minds and Morals: Essays on Cognitive Science and Ethics*, edited by Larry May, Marilyn Friedman, and Andy Clark, 221–36. Cambridge, MA: MIT Press.

Sears, David O. 1988. "Symbolic Racism." In *Eliminating Racism: Profiles in Controversy*, edited by Phyllis A. Katz and Dalmas A. Taylor, 53–84. New York: Plenum.

Seligman, Martin E. P., and Joanne Hager (Eds.). 1972. *Biological Boundaries of Learning*. New York: Appleton-Century-Crofts.

Sherif, Muzafer, O. J. Harvey, B. Jack White, William Hood, and Carolyn Sherif. 1961. *Intergroup Conflict and Cooperation: The Robbers Cave Experiment*. Norman, OK: University Book Exchange.

Shrader-Frechette, Kristin S. 1990. "Perceived Risks versus Actual Risks: Managing Hazards through Negotiation." *RISK: Health, Safety & Environment* (formerly *RISK: Issues in Health & Safety*) 1 (4): 341–63.

Sjöberg, Lennart. 2000. "Factors in Risk Perception." *Risk Analysis* 20 (1): 1–12.

Skenazy, Lenore. 2009. *Free-Range Kids: How to Raise Safe, Self-Reliant Children (without Going Nuts with Worry)*. San Francisco: Jossey-Bass.

Skitka, Linda J., Christopher W. Bauman, Nicholas P. Aramovich, and G. Scott Morgan. 2006. "Confrontational and Preventative Policy Responses to Terrorism: Anger Wants a Fight and Fear Wants 'Them' to Go Away." *Basic and Applied Social Psychology* 28 (4): 375–84.

Slovic, Paul, Baruch Fischhoff, and Sarah Lichtenstein. 1982. "Why Study Risk Perception?" *Risk Analysis*. 2 (2): 83–93.

Smith, Craig A., and Phoebe C. Ellsworth. 1985. "Patterns of Cognitive Appraisal in Emotion." *Journal of Personality and Social Psychology* 48 (4): 813–38.

Soderbergh, Steven, director. 2011. *Contagion*. Warner Bros. Pictures.

Solomon, Robert C. 1973. "Emotions and Choice." *Review of Metaphysics* 27 (1): 20–41.

Spade, Dean. 2015. *Normal Life: Administrative Violence, Critical Trans Politics and The Limits of Law*. Durham, NC: Duke University Press.

Spelman, Elizabeth V. 1989. "Anger and Insubordination." In *Women, Knowledge, and Reality: Explorations in Feminist Philosophy*, edited by Ann Garry and Marilyn Pearsall, 263–74. Boston: Unwin Hyman.

Stafford, Mark C., and Omer R. Galle. 1984. "Victimization Rates, Exposure to Risk, and Fear of Crime." *Criminology* 22 (2): 173–85.

Thunberg, Greta, Svante Thunberg, Malena Ernman, and Beata Ernman. 2020. *Our House Is on Fire: Scenes of a Family and a Planet in Crisis*. New York: Penguin Books.

Tiedens, Larissa Z., and Susan Linton. 2001. "Judgment under Emotional Certainty and Uncertainty: The Effects of Specific Emotions on Information Processing." *Journal of Personality and Social Psychology* 81 (6): 973–88.

Timrots, Anita D., and Michael R. Rand. 1987. "Violent Crime by Strangers and Nonstrangers" US Department of Justice, Bureau of Justice Statistics Special Report, NCJ-103702. https://www.bjs.gov/content/pub/pdf/vcsn.pdf.

Tomasello, Michael. 1995. "Joint Attention as Social Cognition." In *Joint Attention: Its Origins and Role in Development*, edited by Chris Moore and Philip J. Dunham, 103–30. Hillsdale, NJ: Lawrence Erlbaum Associates.

Tversky, Amos, and Daniel Kahneman. 1974. "Judgment under Uncertainty: Heuristics and Biases." *Science* 185 (4157): 1124–31.

Tyson, Sarah. 2014. "Experiments in Responsibility: Pocket Parks, Radical Anti-violence Work, and the Social Ontology of Safety." *Radical Philosophy Review* 17 (2): 421–34.

Valentine, Gill. 1989. "The Geography of Women's Fear." *Area* 21 (4): 385–90.

van der Kolk, Bessel A. 2015. *The Body Keeps the Score: Brain, Mind, and Body in the Healing of Trauma*. New York: Penguin.
Waites, Elizabeth A. 1996. *Memory Quest: Trauma and the Search for Personal History*. New York: W. W. Norton.
Walton, Kendell. 1978. "Fearing Fictions." *Journal of Philosophy* 75: 5–27.
Warr, Mark. 1984. "Fear of Victimization: Why Are Women and the Elderly More Afraid?" *Social Science Quarterly* 65 (3): 681–702.
Warr, Mark. 1987. "Fear of Victimization and Sensitivity to Risk." *Journal of Quantitative Criminology* 3 (1): 29–46.
Warr, Mark, and Mark Stafford. 1983. "Fear of Victimization: A Look at the Proximate Causes." *Social Forces* 61 (4): 1033–43.
Westkott, Marcia. 1986. *The Feminist Legacy of Karen Horney*. New Haven, CT: Yale University Press.
Winnicott, Donald Woods. 2005. *Playing and Reality*. New York: Routledge.
WXYZ-TV Detroit Channel 7. 2020. "Wife, Husband Charged with Felonious Assault after Pulling a Gun on a Woman with Her Children." Cell phone video recorded by Makayla Green on July 1, 2020, in Orion Township, Michigan. Posted online July 2, 2020. YouTube video, 3:08. https://www.youtube.com/watch?v=skGh_5tVJZg.
Yamada, David C. 2019. "On Anger, Shock, Fear, and Trauma: Therapeutic Jurisprudence as a Response to Dignity Denials in Public Policy." *International Journal of Law and Psychiatry* 63 (March–April): 35–44.
Young, Iris Marion. 1980. "Throwing Like a Girl: A Phenomenology of Feminine Body Comportment Motility and Spatiality." *Human Studies* 3 (2): 137–56.
Young, Iris Marion. 2011. *Justice and the Politics of Difference*. Princeton, NJ: Princeton University Press.
Zahn-Waxler, Carolyn, Grazyna Kochanska, Janice Krupnick, and Donald McKnew. 1990. "Patterns of Guilt in Children of Depressed and Well Mothers." *Child Development* 50: 319–30.
Zakin, Emily. 2011. "Psychoanalytic Feminism." In *The Stanford Encyclopedia of Philosophy*, edited by Edward N. Zalta. Published May 16, 2011. https://plato.stanford.edu/archives/sum2011/entries/feminism-psychoanalysis/.
Zanoveli, Janaina Menezes, Cristina Ferreira Netto, Francisco Silveira Guimarães, and Hélio Zangrossi Jr. 2004. "Systematic and Intra-dorsal Periaqueductal Gray Injections of Cholecystokinin Sulfated Octapeptide (CCK-8s) Induce a Panic-like Response in Rats Submitted to the Elevated T-maze." *Peptides* 25 (11): 1935–41.

Index

For the benefit of digital users, indexed terms that span two pages (e.g., 52–53) may, on occasion, appear on only one of those pages.

Tables are indicated by *t* following the page number

9/11, 46, 157

acceptance, 96, 121, 123, 125
acquisition of fear, 13–21, 30–31
　tripartite theory of, 28–29
　vicarious, 28–29, 168n.12
aggression, 76–77
Ahmed, Sara, 78
alarm, 67
Alexander, Michelle, 94–95
alexithymia, 127
alief, 11–12, 39, 73–74, 164n.6
amygdala, 5, 42–43, 171n.10, 172n.14
anger, 44–45, 46–48, 49–50, 125
anxiety, 11, 36–37, 63–64, 75–77, 108, 126, 159
　as distinct from fear, 45–46, 171–72n.13
assimilation, 92, 102–4, 109, 110–12
attachment, 28, 175–76n.12
attention, 28, 81–82, 84, 123, 124, 132
authoritarianism, 2, 67, 72–73
authority, 15, 20, 58–59
avoidance, 3, 11–12, 44, 76–77, 78, 114, 122–23, 124, 132, 136, 142, 144, 147–48, 158–59
awareness, 62, 68, 73–74, 80–81, 94–95, 121–33

background cognitive set, 39–40, 73–74
Baier, Annette, 28
Baldwin, James, 119
bearable, 8–9, 12, 128, 137–38, 158–59
belief, 10–11, 34, 39–40, 78–79, 118, 119, 147, 149–50

Berlin Wall, 93
bicycle, 1, 12, 13–15, 17, 18
Biss, Eula, 98–99, 119
Black Lives Matter, 33
blame, 18–19, 131, 136
borders, 72
　border wall, 65–66, 93, 94–95
breathing, 36–37, 42, 123, 124, 134–35, 161
Brexit, 65–66
Brooks, Kim, 63–65, 86–87
Butler, Judith, 114–15

Calhoun, Cheshire, 37, 39–40, 73–74
calibration, 160–61
Campbell, Sue, 5–6, 9, 48–59
Camus, Albert, 152
cancer, 22–23, 96
Cannon, Walter, 37, 171n.11
capacity, 9, 11, 28, 50, 133, 134, 142
capital punishment, 7–8, 100, 101
caregiving, 159. *See also* parenting
catastrophism, 71, 72
cause of emotion, 34–41, 58, 61
　immediate, 38–39
　significant, 38–39
Chapman University Survey of American Fears, 16–17, 20, 27, 120
chemical, 99–100, 110
Child, Brenda, 103
children, 2–3, 22–23, 28–29, 63–67, 77–78, 86–87, 94, 95–96, 98–99, 103–4, 105–6, 119, 134–38
citizenship, 65–66, 89, 93, 103, 108–9

clarity, 96
classic emotions, 49–50, 52–53
climate, 1–2, 142–43, 152, 158, 165n.1, 165n.2
coercion, 103–4
co-fearer, 9, 85–86
cognitive, 4–5, 23–24, 28, 43–44, 126–27
cognitive theory of emotions, 34–42, 47
colonialism, 95–96, 104
combat, 97, 100, 130
compel, 7, 62, 85–90, 91, 110, 118–19, 120, 133, 134, 144–45, 147, 150, 153–57
conditioning, 28–29, 42
contamination, 98, 99
conversion therapy, 7–8, 103
coping, 4, 11–12, 54–55, 75, 81, 129, 156–57
COVID-19, 121, 152–57, 158–61
crime, 2–3, 16, 26, 30, 66–67, 97
criminal justice, 57, 94–95, 100
crisis, 70–71, 72–73, 152–61
culture of fear, 6, 22–23, 62, 68, 72–73, 83, 91
curiosity, 137–38

D'Arms, Justin, 40
Davidson, Donald, 50
Davis, Angela, 94–95
decision-making, 44, 45
depression, 159
destruction, 99–102, 109, 110–11, 118
developmental psychology, 28–29
Dewey, John, 37
disability, 108–9, 151
disaster, 71, 78
dismissal, 51–52, 53, 55–56, 136, 138–39, 149–50, 160–61
displacement, 62, 74–81, 82–83, 85–86, 88, 89
dissociate, 122

echo chamber, 141, 147, 180n.7
election, 65–66, 150–51
eliminative strategy, 94
embodiment, 41–48, 133, 134–35

employment, 66, 69–70, 86–87, 108–9, 116, 145, 150–51,
escape, 97–99, 110–11
eviction, 92–93, 94
evolution, 17–18, 20, 43–44
expression, 48–59, 85, 90, 129–30
expressive resources, 5–6, 49–50, 51–52, 53–54
eye movement desensitization and reprocessing (EMDR), 127, 162

failure, 12, 24–25, 30–31, 75, 143, 152, 153, 161
fallibility, 5, 41
family, 54–55, 81–82, 84, 115–16, 129–30, 145, 152
fear for one's life, 57, 58–59
fight or flight, 42
first-person, 2, 21, 28
fittingness, 40
food aversion, 28–29
formal objects, 37–38, 39–40
freestyle feelings, 50, 58
Freud, Sigmund, 74–81, 82–84

gaslighting, 20
gated community, 97–98, 110–11, 117–18
gender, 2–3, 26, 30, 77, 83, 105–6, 110–11
Gendler, Tamar, 10–12, 39, 73–74
Generative Somatics, 131–33
genetic, 20, 46
genocide, 100
germs, 64. *See also* illness
Glassner, Barry, 22–24, 68–70, 72–73, 81–82, 86–87
Grand Canyon, 10–11, 39
great threats, 3, 7, 30–31, 62, 73–74, 78–79, 85–86, 113–17, 143, 152, 153–57
grief, 30–31, 152, 153–57
Guenther, Lisa, 99–102
gun, 14–15, 22–23, 33–34, 145–46

habit, 116–17, 121–33
Haines, Staci, 131, 132, 133
Halloween candy, 22–23, 63, 73–74, 91
Hans case (Freud), 76–80, 82
Haraway, Donna, 119

INDEX

harm, 3, 24–25, 59–60, 81, 86–87, 94, 104, 111–17, 134, 143–52, 153–57
harm reduction, 4
healing, 131, 133, 148–49, 151
health, 120, 124
   and healthcare, 153
   insurance, 97–99, 105–9, 140, 150–51
   outcomes, 55–56
heteronormativity, 57, 64, 103
Hochschild, Arlie, 148
homeless, 110–11, 112–13, 140–41
hostile architecture, 7–8, 92–96, 112–13
Hurricane Katrina, 71
hypervigilance, 29, 35, 43–44

illness, 16, 95–96, 153–57
immunity, 98, 110–11
incarceration. See prison
Indigenous, 104, 109
   residential schools, 7–8, 95–96, 103
individualism, 5–6, 9, 31, 48, 52, 131, 151
individuate, 37, 47–59
information processing, 44, 46
insecurity, 12, 87–88, 110–11
institutionalization, 7–8, 95–96
interpreters, 48–59, 85, 90, 129–30, 136–39, 141–43, 144–52, 160–61

Jacobson, Daniel, 40
James-Lange theory, 36–37
James, William, 36–37, 47–48
joint attention, 28
judgment, 37–38, 47–48

Kabat-Zinn, Jon, 123–26
Kahneman, Daniel, 23–24
Kenny, Anthony, 39–40
kidnapping, 63, 82–83, 104
killing, 99–102
Klein, Naomi, 68, 70–71, 72–74
know better, fear less, 6, 67–74, 81, 91
Kwong, Peter, 65–66

law, 57, 58–59, 150–51
learning, 45, 120, 132
legitimacy of fear, 55–56, 58, 73, 86–87
LeDoux, Joseph, 42–44, 45, 47–48, 52

LGBTQ. See queerr
Lilley, Sasha, 67–74, 83, 86–87
loss. See grief
luck, 30–31, 153, 161

Maina, Ng'ethe, 131–33
manipulation, 6, 19, 68, 69, 72–73, 74
media, 16–17, 26, 68, 72–73, 81–82, 120, 148
meditation, 123–26
memory, 42, 133
mental illness, 69, 95–96, 156, 159
methodology, 28, 47
Mexico, 72, 93
Middle East, 70
migrants, 63–67, 73, 80–81, 85–90, 145
mindfulness, 123–26, 158–61
   mindfulness-based stress reduction (MBSR), 123
moral, 4, 8, 12, 55–57, 113–17, 144–52
moral failure, 24–25, 111–13, 148
mortality, 56–57, 144
motivation, 56, 126
multiple realizability, 82–83

nationalism, 65–66
National Rifle Association, 69
neglect, 2–3, 101
neurological, 5, 34, 41–48, 59–60, 129
neurologize, 69–70
nonconscious, 42
nonthreats, 10, 26–27, 45, 63–74, 96, 112, 113–18, 139–40, 146–47

objects of fear, 34–41, 49–50, 52–53, 55–56, 59–60, 82–84, 109–18
oppression, 131, 148
overpowering, 105–9, 155

pain, 12, 28–29, 122, 123, 126, 129–30
parenting, 28–29, 63–67, 76–77, 81–82, 119, 134–36, 151, 157. See also caregiving
perceived threat, 21–27, 42, 74, 78–79, 88–89, 91, 109–18
pesticide, 102, 118
phallocentrism, 77
phobia, 18, 19, 75–77

pipeline, 114, 116
pocket park, 7–8, 94–95, 114, 115
police, 7–8, 33, 63–64, 69, 94–95, 100, 142–43
politician, 16–17, 20, 54–55, 70, 81–82, 105
poverty, 66–67, 69–70, 104
powerlessness, 72, 92, 119
presumption of identity, 14–15, 17
prison, 67, 94–95, 96, 119
  solitary confinement, 100–1
protection, 63, 97, 99, 150–51
protest, 58, 106, 154–55
proxy threat, 79–90, 110, 114, 154
  acquiring fears of, 82–84
  experiencing fears of, 84
  expressing fears of, 85
psychoanalysis, 75–76
PTSD, 97. *See also* trauma
purity, 98

queer, 103, 150–51

Rachman, Stanley, 28–29
racism, 1–2, 22–23, 33, 58, 63, 95, 138–39
reactivity, 125
relational
  practices of fearing well, 129, 134–52, 158–61, 162
  theory, 9
  understanding of fearing, 3–4, 28–31, 48–59, 81–90
relief, 78, 79–80, 86–87, 118, 121, 160
removal, 92–96, 116
reproductive justice, 8, 106
resistance, 56, 120–21, 127, 133, 160–61
responsibility, 4, 12, 18–19, 56–57, 62, 148. *See also* moral
right-wing, 71–73, 150, 154–55
risk perception, 23–27, 41–42, 44
Robin, Corey, 70, 72–73, 83
Roosevelt, Franklin D., 22–23
Ropeik, David, 22–23
Rorty, Amélie, 37, 38–40

safety, 2–3, 63, 117–18, 135, 155, 160
Sartre, Jean Paul, 119

schools, 1–2, 95, 105–6, 154
second person, 28
self-deception, 86–87
self-defence, 30, 57, 116
self-harm, 101
sensation, 50, 124, 125–26, 132, 161t
sensitivity to risk, 4–5, 24, 26
settler, 95–96, 104
sexism, 62
sex offender, 7–8, 80–81, 94, 110–11, 150
shame, 21, 130, 133, 136, 144–45, 150
Skenazy, Lenore, 65
snake, 5, 35–36, 38, 52–53, 57, 61–62
Solomon, Robert, 37–40
somatic
  politicized somatics, 131–33, 161t
  regulation, 126–31, 161t
spirituality, 64, 71, 95–96, 104
staying with fearers, 134–52, 161t
stimulus, 28–29, 42, 43–44, 50
storm, 97, 99
strangers, 16, 22–23, 54–55, 83, 86–87
substance use, 68–69
suggestibility, 83–84
survival, 98, 133

temperament, 45
terrorism, 16–17
The Shock Doctrine, 70–71, 72–73
therapy, 89–90, 122–23, 126–31, 136–37, 161t
threat
  actual, 13–27, 80–81, 91, 109–18
  nonstatistical, 63–81, 146 (*see also* nonthreats)
trauma, 71, 126–33, 146, 152.
  See also PTSD
treaty, 95–96, 104
triangulation, 50–51
Trump, Donald, 65–66, 106–7
trust, 15–16, 20, 44–45, 78–79, 86–87, 120, 121, 139–41, 150
Tversky, Amos, 23–24, 25–26
Tyson, Sarah, 94

unemployment, 156
unpredictability, 3, 7, 12, 30–32, 46, 62, 110, 114, 150–51

unreasonable, 2
uptake, 48–59, 85, 89–90

vaccine, 79–80, 99, 110, 158
   refusal, 2–3, 85
van der Kolk, Bessel, 126–31, 134–35
video games, 22–23, 63, 69, 86–87
vigilance, 45, 98
violence, 1–2, 82–83, 105–6, 114–15
   domestic, 22–23
   police, 142–43, 153
   school, 1–2
   workplace, 69–70

virus, 16, 153–57, 158–61
vulnerability, 12, 30, 114–15, 119, 158

water, 87–88, 100
welfare, 65–67, 69, 86–87
well-being, 30–31, 63, 86–87, 95–96, 98, 120–21, 135–36, 151, 160
withdrawal, 11, 44–45
Wuestenberg, Jillian, 33, 57–58

Young, Iris Marion, 83, 112

Zakin, Emily, 77